Race and Class
in Colonial Oaxaca

Race and Class
in Colonial Oaxaca

JOHN K. CHANCE

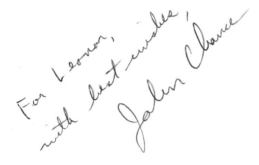

STANFORD UNIVERSITY PRESS

Stanford, California

1978

Stanford University Press
Stanford, California
© 1978 by the Board of Trustees of the
Leland Stanford Junior University
Printed in the United States of America
ISBN 0-8047-0937-8
LC 76-48011

Published with the assistance of
the Andrew W. Mellon Foundation

For my parents, my wife, and my children

Preface

Race relations and the nature of racial and ethnic identity have long been topics of considerable interest for those concerned with the genesis and structure of post-conquest societies in the New World. Anthropologists, sociologists, and historians, among others, have shown the importance of "social race," as Charles Wagley calls it, in the history of intergroup relations both north and south of the Rio Grande. Though ethnic relations in much of mainland Latin America are not normally phrased today in racial terms, the fact remains that racism has been a major element in the history of most Latin American nations, and there is still a strong correlation between phenotype and socioeconomic status. Thus the study of race and ethnic relations in Latin America becomes at once a historical and sociological problem that must be treated from a multidisciplinary perspective.

This book presents a case study of the changing system of social stratification, and the role of racial and ethnic factors within it, in the city of Antequera (now called Oaxaca) in southern Mexico during the colonial period. As such, it constitutes a social history of a small, provincial urban center from the time of its founding by the Spanish in 1521 until 1812, two years after the outbreak of the Mexican war of independence, I selected Antequera for study for a number of reasons. First, and most important, it was typical of colonial Spanish towns in highland Mesoamerica in that it had significant numbers of Spaniards, Indians, and *castas* (people of mixed racial ancestry), surrounded by a dense and highly developed rural Indian population. Second, on a more practical note, it was small enough to enable a single investigator to examine all the relevant documentation pertaining to all segments of the urban population during the entire colonial period. This would not have been possible for larger cities like Mexico City or Puebla, where much larger populations and greater quantities of colonial records necessarily impose strict limits on research. Third, the Spanish colonial cities, in addition to their intrinsic interest to those concerned with comparative urbanism, constitute perhaps the best point of departure for the study of intergroup relations, for it was within their confines that virtually all segments of society came together: Spaniards, Indians, blacks, castas, the rich and the poor, the slaves and the free.

The central concern of this study is the analysis of the development and functioning of the *sistema de castas*—a cognitive and legal system of ranked socioracial statuses created by Spanish law and the colonial elite in response to the growth of the racially mixed population in the colonies. The discussion is not limited solely to the mestizos, mulattoes, and other castas, however; I also give detailed coverage of the Spaniards and the city's large urban Indian population in an effort to provide as well-rounded an account as possible of one colonial urban society in its totality. Attention is also directed to the course and rate of social change in Antequera, for the colonial social structure was far from static during its three centuries of existence. To be a mestizo in 1550, for example, was quite a different matter than it was in 1700, and even further removed from the state of affairs in 1800. Though much of the racial and ethnic vocabulary employed in Antequera remained static over time, the referents of the various terms and the composition of the society did not, and periodization necessarily becomes an important part of the analysis of change.

The sources on which this book is based are drawn from a number

of archives, principally the Archivo General de la Nación in Mexico
City, the Archivo General de Indias in Seville, and local parish archives in Oaxaca. Data of the type necessary for rigorous sociological analysis are not evenly distributed throughout the colonial
period, and like any book that deals with a large and complex social
system over a long period of time, this one has its gaps. Treatment
of the significant divisions in the society and their interrelations
must necessarily remain largely inferential for the sixteenth century, though the early sources for the urban Indian population are
quite rich. The analysis is strongest for the latter halves of the seventeenth and eighteenth centuries, for which detailed census data
and parish registers are available. Nonetheless, the extant information does permit the continuous study of a changing urban social
system over the course of three centuries.

Considering the promise of the colonial Spanish cities as important foci for the analysis of race and ethnic relations, it is surprising
that they remain so little known. Studies of urban architecture and
town planning abound, but works dealing with questions of social
structure are more difficult to come by. In New Spain only Mexico
City and Puebla had received serious attention until the recent
studies by D. A. Brading on Guanajuato and P. J. Bakewell on
Zacatecas. More important as sources of inspiration for the present
book are Gonzalo Aguirre Beltrán's classic *La población negra de
México* and Magnus Mörner's more recent *Race Mixture in the History of Latin America*. Yet as important as these studies are, they
remain general and synthetic in their orientation, as does most of
the literature on race and class in colonial Latin America. Local and
regional studies that deal with social life in particular communities
are badly needed. The findings for Antequera presented here will
be seen to differ in several respects from the generalized portraits of
the sistema de castas and colonial social structure, particularly with
reference to the presumed rigidity and racial basis of the stratification system. Future studies carried out in different types of cities in
other regions of Latin America will allow us to judge to what extent
Antequera was typical of the provincial highland towns.

Financial support for the archival research was provided by a Foreign Area Fellowship, a Dissertation Research Grant from the National Science Foundation, and a grant from Lawrence University. Preliminary work in Mexican archives and the libraries of the University of Illinois and the University of Michigan was supported by a National Defense Foreign Language Title VI Fellowship and supplementary funds from the Department of Anthropology, University of Illinois, Urbana.

This book and the research on which it is based owe much to the patience, friendship, and goodwill of many people. Special thanks are due to the staff of the Archivo General de la Nación and its director, Jorge Ignacio Rubio Mañé. Miguel Saldaña aided my work there considerably, and Licenciado Eduardo Báez Macías and Javier Carreño Avendaño were also helpful in alerting my attention to several important sources. I also wish to thank the staff of the Archivo General de Indias in Seville.

In Oaxaca, I am especially indebted to Licenciado Luis Castañeda Guzmán, who graciously gave me access to his personal collection of colonial records. The Most Reverend Ernesto Corripio Ahumada, Archbishop of Oaxaca, and Fathers David Elías Mendoza, José Miguel Pérez, Fernando Vázquez N., and Francisco Cruz Camacho kindly granted me permission to study in local parish archives. The late don Fausto Mejía and Sara Matadamas helped acquaint me with the Archivo del Estado de Oaxaca, and don Fausto García Pujol, Secretario del Ayuntamiento de Oaxaca de Juárez, made the contents of Oaxaca's municipal archive available to me. I also thank Cecil R. Welte for permission to use his extensive library of Oaxaca materials, as well as for much useful information.

From the very beginning Ronald Spores has given much advice and encouragement, and took the trouble to introduce me to the complexities of archival research and paleography. Charles Gibson gave very freely of his time; he helped guide me through the literature on colonial Mexico and provided me with much insightful criticism and encouragement. I am deeply indebted to Douglas Butterworth for introducing me to Mexico and to Oaxaca in particular, as well as for continued advice and support during the course of my work. Joseph B. Casagrande, David C. Grove, and Joseph L. Love read an earlier version of the manuscript, and each offered many constructive comments. I have also benefited from discussions with John Paddock, Norman E. Whitten, Jr., and R. T. Zuidema.

I am particularly grateful to William B. Taylor for much invaluable criticism and commentary. He graciously accepted my collaboration in the analysis of the census material presented in Chapter 6 and granted me permission to include the results of our study in this book. Intellectually, I owe a special debt to Ruben E. Reina, my undergraduate teacher, who stimulated my interest in Latin America and impressed on me the value of the historical perspective in anthropology. Finally, my wife, Julia Hernández de Chance, was instrumental in seeing the project through to its completion. Her many patient hours in the archives of Oaxaca and Seville and her constant support over the years are deeply appreciated.

Map 3 and the materials on the urban Indian population in Chapters 4–6 have appeared in slightly different form in "The Urban Indian in Colonial Oaxaca," *American Ethnologist*, 3, 4 (1976): 603–32. Similar versions of Tables 10 and 19, along with the discussion of seventeenth-century marriage records and parts of Chapter 7, have appeared in "The Colonial Latin American City: Preindustrial or Capitalist?," *Urban Anthropology*, 4, 3 (1975): 211–28. The bulk of the analysis of race and class in the late eighteenth century in Chapter 6 and also parts of Chapter 7 have been published in similar form in John K. Chance and William B. Taylor, "Estate and Class in a Colonial City: Oaxaca in 1792," *Comparative Studies in Society and History*, 19, 4 (Oct. 1977): 454–87, Cambridge University Press, publishers. I am grateful to all three journals for permitting me to use these materials in this work.

J.K.C.

Contents

Tables and Maps

Tables

Maps

Race and Class
in Colonial Oaxaca

CHAPTER ONE

Introduction

One of the principal features of the Spanish conquest of America was its urban character. Indian populations were subjugated and other areas colonized by the founding of Spanish cities and garrisons from which the countryside was pacified and brought under control. The isolated homesteads established in Brazil by the Portuguese had no counterparts in early colonial Spanish America, nor were there any European communities of peasant farmers. In the early years of the conquest, when control by the Crown was weak, the founding of towns for Spaniards was a spontaneous occurrence on the part of the conquistadores, a practice conditioned by the centuries-long struggle against the Moors in Spain, which had only recently come to a close.

The most striking aspect of colonial Spanish cities in the New World was their architectural uniformity. With the aid of Spanish friars and Italian architects, the grid concept of town planning was faithfully transmitted to the Americas, and hundreds of cities and towns were laid out with straight streets crossing at right angles and with at least one central plaza flanked by government offices and usually a church. Traces of the grid plan can be seen in Santo Domingo, the first Spanish city in America, established on Hispaniola in 1496. Though royal orders for the laying out of new cities were not promulgated until 1573, under Philip II, Ferdinand gave instructions to Pedrarías Dávila in 1514 for the founding of Panama City.[1] Essentially the same plan was repeated in cities all over Spanish America, including Mexico City, Puebla, Morelia, Guadalajara, Antequera, Bogotá, Santiago de Chile, and La Paz, as it was in the rebuilding and founding of towns for Indians, 273 of which were built in New Spain alone before 1580.[2]

These new Spanish cities were founded for a variety of reasons: as ports (Veracruz, Panama City, Cartagena); as garrisons for defense against warring nomadic bands of Indians (Celaya, León); as centers of mining operations (Potosí, Zacatecas, Guanajuato); as administrative capitals (Mexico City, Cuzco, Lima); and simply as places of residence for the colonists (Puebla). Of special interest for the present study are the highland cities founded in areas of high civilization with dense Indian populations. In many ways these cities constituted the heart of colonial Spanish America, and the presence of large, sedentary Indian populations gave them a very special character.

In their conquest of Mesoamerica and the Andes, the Spaniards were immediately attracted by the Indian cities and densely settled areas of the highlands, where the climate and geography were closest to those with which they were familiar. The first Spanish cities were erected on the ruins of the Indian capitals of Tenochtitlán and Cuzco; and other Indian cities, such as Cholula, Texcoco, and Xochimilco in Mesoamerica, also attracted white settlers. Most centers of Spanish population, however, were founded at new sites, many of them chosen for strategic reasons. In New Spain about thirty cities and towns for Europeans were founded before 1574, with populations ranging from a few families to 500 or more, according to the royal cosmographer-chronicler López de Velasco.[3]

Town settlement was often very uncertain in the early period; sites were frequently abandoned and whole towns transplanted to more favorable locations.[4] A case in point is the Villa de Segura de la Frontera in New Spain. Originally founded by Fernando Cortés in 1520 in or near the Indian town of Tepeaca, the villa was reestablished a year later in the Valley of Oaxaca at the Aztec garrison of

Huaxyacac. However, Cortés soon discovered that this new site was on fertile ground (he in fact later claimed the land for his Marquesado),* and in 1522 he ordered the men to move once more, this time to the Mixtec kingdom of Tututepec on the southern coast of Oaxaca. But the tropical climate and hostile Indians proved too much for many of the settlers; later the same year they returned to the Valley of Oaxaca and resettled the villa against Cortés's wishes. Some years thereafter the name was changed to Antequera (and later, Oaxaca).

A common procedure was followed in the founding of most Spanish towns that served to accentuate their political nature from the very beginning. As Charles Gibson has observed, town governments were often organized before the settlements themselves were established. Municipal governments took the responsibility of planning the settlement, assigning lots, establishing markets, and overseeing urban affairs in general.[5] Most cities were founded with the labor of Indian workers, who simultaneously established separate settlements (barrios or *arrabales*) adjacent to the Spanish towns. Villa Alta was founded in the northern mountains of Oaxaca by thirty Spanish settlers and a group of Aztec and Tlaxcalan Indians.[6] Likewise, the town of Ciudad Real (now San Cristóbal las Casas) was laid out in 1528 with separate barrios for the Mexicans and Tlaxcalans.[7] The situation in Antequera was similar, as we shall see later, in Chapter 3.

Very early in the sixteenth century, cities founded in the Indian areas came to exhibit a common settlement pattern. The *traza*, or grid plan, formed the central portion and was the center of Spanish residence and all administrative and commercial activity. The traza was normally reserved for the use of Europeans, though this rule frequently proved impossible to enforce. At the heart of the city lay the *plaza mayor*, flanked by the *casas de cabildo* (town hall) and other administrative offices, stores, the homes of the most prestigious families, and frequently the church. As the population grew, the city came to be divided into barrios or parishes, each with its

---

*This and other important Spanish terms are defined in the Glossary, Appendix A.

own chapel. Following the practice of rigid separation of European and Indian, the Indian barrios were always located on the fringe of the city. Often they constituted separate parishes in themselves. These settlements were not as well planned as the European sectors, though they were occasionally provided with trazas of their own, as in the case of Jalatlaco near Antequera. This was not the case in Mexico City, however, where the barrios were so congested in 1541 that passage through them was difficult even on foot.[8]

In the first few decades following the conquest, the towns were mostly composed of small nuclei of Spaniards supported by Indian labor and tribute. The *cabildo* (municipal council) had the power to distribute land and house lots to the colonists, and once communal and town lands had been set aside, this was one of its first functions. Every so-called *vecino* was entitled to a lot and some land. In broad terms, a vecino was a European household head, but what precisely qualified a person for that characterization (if there was a precise definition) is not clear. Drawing on sources from all parts of Spanish America, Constantino Bayle claims that only *encomenderos* (possessors of grants of Indians, mainly as tribute payers) could be vecinos in the early years, other Spaniards with fixed urban residence being designated as *habitantes* or *moradores*.[9] In Peru, merchants were distinguished from vecinos for a time, but a royal *cédula* of 1554 declared that any Spaniard with a *casa poblada* (fixed residence) was to have the status of vecino.[10]

Spanish municipalities were legally classified as *ciudades* (cities), *villas* (towns), or *lugares* (places), the status being originally determined in most cases by the founder. Ciudades were of two types, metropolan and diocesan or suffragan, but the distinction was only honorific. Villas could be elevated to the rank of ciudad merely through an act of service to the Crown, such as the donation of money.[11] A variant of the Roman concept of *civitas* was also applied in the New World, not only in Spanish towns, but also in Indian communities where, in Mesoamerica, it coincided with the pre-conquest community of a head town plus its satellites. In sixteenth-century Tlaxcala, Gibson notes, the term ciudad often referred to a central urban site and the surrounding rural areas. The phrase Ciudad de Tlaxcala was frequently used by the early colonists to refer to the entire province of Tlaxcala.[12]

As to the general functions of the city in Spanish American society, Richard Morse has distinguished two broad stages in the post-conquest history of Latin American urbanism. The first phase began in a centrifugal manner, stemming from the nature of Spanish colonialism: the political structure preceded the economic base, and the hinterland had to adjust to meet the needs of the city. The second, or centripetal phase, began in the nineteenth century with the loosening of latifundiary ties and the beginning of heavy cityward migration.[13]

It is above all the administrative and exploitative nature of the colonial cities that clearly distinguishes them from their Old World counterparts. Though trade certainly began to acquire some importance in Spanish America as early as the second half of the sixteenth century, it was not responsible for the initial location and founding of urban centers. Indeed, the economic development of the colonies before 1750 was frequently blocked by the mercantilist commercial policies of the Crown. Especially in the early years, the colonial economy was in fact not a single economy, but several distinct regional or local economies, each relatively self-sufficient and each centering around a Spanish city.

Though the principal economic activities of the colonial period were based on the mines and haciendas (large landed estates), this should not lead us to underestimate the importance of the cities. The urban centers remained throughout the colonial period, as they are today, the effective seats of power. The Spanish conquest and colonization in effect established a polyethnic society characterized by a high degree of social segmentation and economic interdependence in which an urban elite successfully dominated a largely rural peasantry. To be sure, the sustenance of the city never came from within but always from without, from Indian tribute, mines, and haciendas; but all wealth was funneled into the dominant urban centers, and all power was concentrated there. The development of the

hacienda in the seventeenth century has led some to believe that colonial urbanism was often "ephemeral" in nature, and that power increasingly shifted to the rural estates.[14] But this ignores the important fact that the *hacendados*, like the encomenderos before them,
were essentially urban-based. Though they lavished large sums of
money on their *casas grandes* in the hinterland, the large landowners usually formed the mainstay of the urban upper class and dominated the cities politically.

The role of the highland cities in the life of the Indian population
must not be overlooked, and here it becomes evident that the
analysis of urban centers along a centripetal–centrifugal axis depends on one's point of view. Despite their exploitative nature as
outposts of empire, the cities soon attracted large numbers of Indians. Epidemics, harsh labor practices in the countryside, and a
number of other factors made urban residence attractive to many
Indian peasants. In the Valley of Oaxaca, for example, Indians were
often drawn to Antequera in the hope that labor on public works
projects would free them from the burden of paying tribute. As we
shall see in Chapter 3, the Indians became established in Antequera
at a very early date, and to say that rural to urban migration was of
little significance before the nineteenth century would be to ignore
much evidence to the contrary. Furthermore, many Spanish towns
soon became the most important marketing centers for the indigenous population, usurping the role of pre-conquest trading centers.
A symbiotic relationship was thus established between the urban
center and its hinterland: the city prospered only insofar as it was
able to subjugate the Indians, but the Indians came to depend heavily on the city for many of their basic needs. From this point of
view, the overall functions of the city and its relationship with the
hinterland were much the same in colonial times as they are today.

In many ways, the Valley of Oaxaca with its mild climate, large
sedentary Indian population, and abundant water supply was an
ideal location for a Spanish settlement. Originally, Antequera was
little more than a vehicle for the conquest and subjugation of Zapotec and Mixtec Indians. But the city soon became a permanent fea-

ture of the landscape—the only major Spanish settlement in the Valley itself and the only town of any importance between Puebla and the territory of Guatemala.

After a brief look at Indian society in the Valley of Oaxaca as the Spaniards encountered it in 1521, this book will trace the history of Antequera and its diverse inhabitants throughout the three centuries of Spanish colonial rule. My aim, however, is not merely to provide a detailed study of local history. The principal goal of the book is rather to analyze through time the city's social structure, in particular the web of interethnic relations and the related system of social stratification. To this end, special attention is given to the behavior of the residents themselves—particularly their marriages and occupations—and to the significance of the *sistema de castas* and the role of racial factors in the context of daily social interaction. As I hope to show, the social hierarchy was also based on other factors, especially economic ones, which were not as well defined in the cognitive outlook of the white elite as was the racial classification embodied in the sistema de castas. What interests me most, then, is not the delineation of distinct strata, but rather the principles or determinants of stratification at work and how they changed during the course of the colonial period. The determinants of social rank in Antequera were multiple and complex, and it is not always wise to subsume some under others or to postulate a single fundamental pattern for the entire period, as Gonzalo Aguirre Beltrán, Magnus Mörner, and others have done.[15] For this and other reasons discussed at length in the conclusion, the European-derived estate model of stratification, which emphasizes legally defined social segments, is rejected in favor of the more flexible scheme of Max Weber, which distinguishes among class, status, and power hierarchies.[16] Racial and ethnic divisions will be assessed alongside political powerholders and a hierarchy of economic classes, all in the context of a developing system of commercial capitalism that emerged in New Spain during the latter half of the sixteenth century. This was the setting that gave rise to a multiracial society inhabited not only by Spaniards and a distinctive group of urbanized Indians, but also by Negro slaves and the products of miscegenation—the mestizos, mulattoes, and other castas.

Though there is much in the social history of Antequera that was repeated many times in other parts of Mesoamerica and the Andes, there are also important regional differences that must be taken into account, especially when Oaxaca is compared with the mining areas on the northern border of New Spain. The Valley of Oaxaca's dense indigenous population, its lack of rich gold and silver deposits, and its relative remoteness and inaccessibility in the vast expanse of territory between Puebla and Guatemala City all combined to create significant differences in social structure between the heavily Indian south and the mining centers to the north.

CHAPTER TWO

The Pre-Hispanic Setting

Geography and Prehistory

The State of Oaxaca in southern Mexico is one of the most linguistically and ethnically diverse regions of Mesoamerica. Its modern indigenous population can be divided into fifteen major linguistic groups (see Map 1), and these in turn are marked by countless dialectical variations. One of the principal reasons for this diversity is the extremely mountainous, broken terrain that characterizes most of the state. The eastern and western cordilleras of the Mexican plateau come together in Oaxaca, forming a seemingly endless series of ridges dotted with a few high valleys. Three of the largest of these valleys unite in the central portion of the state to form the Valley of Oaxaca, a wide alluvial plain occupying about 700 square kilometers (see Map 2). This fertile basin of the Atoyac River has the general form of a T and stands approximately 1,500 meters above sea level. The average width of the Valley is from six to eight kilometers. At the hub of the three component valleys lies the city of Oaxaca, from which the Valley of Etla extends twenty kilometers to the northwest, the Valley of Tlacolula some thirty kilometers to the southeast, and the Valley of Zimatlán about forty kilometers to the south. The area has a characteristic tropical highland climate—temperate, warm, and fairly dry—though each of its three arms exhibits some climatic variation. Temperatures do not vary much from

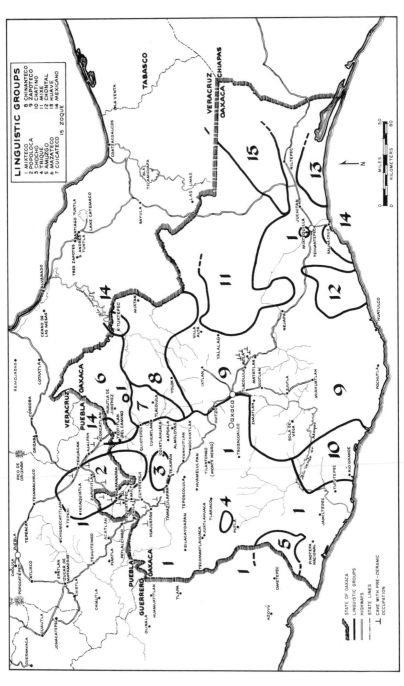

Map 1. The State of Oaxaca and Its Major Linguistic Divisions. *Source:* p. 86. *Note:* All text references to the speakers of Náhuatl refer to the

season to season, but the year is marked by a wet spell (May to September) and a dry one (October to April). The southeastern region of the Valley of Zimatlán is consistently the driest area, followed by the Valley of Tlacolula; more rainfall and extensive irrigation made the Valley of Etla the most productive region during the colonial period, some towns in it harvesting two or three crops annually. Taken as a whole, the Valley in colonial times was much like it is today in climate and physiography, and its fertility made it one of the few areas within the Bishopric of Oaxaca able to sustain a large colonial population.[1]

The Valley of Oaxaca has a long history as a major power center in the southern highlands of Mexico. Angel Palerm and Eric Wolf count it as one of the five key areas of Mesoamerica that were instrumental in stimulating cultural evolution over wide geographic regions from the Archaic period up to the time of the Spanish conquest.[2] Continuously inhabited from as early as 8000 B.C., the Valley had a higher agricultural potential than most of the surrounding areas, due to water-control practices and its ability to assimilate new agricultural techniques through time.[3]

The predominant settlement pattern of large, nucleated villages and towns that was in effect at the time of the Spanish conquest (and continues today) dates to as early as 1500 B.C. Recent excavations at San José Mogote, in the Etla arm of the Valley, suggest that status differentiation, together with long-distance trade and formal relations with other Indian groups of Mesoamerica, became increasingly important between 1200 and 900 B.C.[4] By this time there were more than thirty ceremonial mound groups in the Valley, the most impressive of which was the mountaintop city of Monte Albán, just outside the modern city of Oaxaca. During this period the Valley began to extend its stylistic and economic influence into surrounding areas, including within its domain a vast expanse of territory from the Pacific Coast to the Tehuacán Valley.[5]

By the beginning of the Christian Era the Valley of Oaxaca constituted the dominant political entity in the southern highlands of Mexico; archeological evidence attests to a decidedly urban society with full-fledged state organization. From this time until its aban-

1. Antequera
2. Villa de Oaxaca
3. San Pedro Ixtlahuaca
4. Cuilapan
5. San Andrés Huayapan
6. San Sebastián Tutla
7. Santo Domingo Tomaltepec
8. San Agustín de las Juntas
9. San Bartolo Coyotepec
10. Zaachila (Teozapotlan)
11. San Lucas Tlanechico
12. Santa Catarina Quiane
13. San Lorenzo Zimatlán
14. Santa Ana Zegache
15. San Pablo Huistepec
16. San Juan Chilateca
17. Santo Domingo Ocotlán
18. Santa Catarina Minas
19. San Pedro Apostol
20. Santa Ana Tlapacoya
21. Santa Cruz Mixtepec
22. Magdalena Mixtepec
23. San Felipe del Agua
24. San Miguel Tlalixtac
25. Santa María del Tule
26. San Gerónimo Tlacochahuaya
and San Sebastián Abasolo
(San Sebastián Tlacochahuaya)

27. San Sebastián Teitipac
28. San Juan Teitipac
29. Santo Domingo Jalieza
30. Santa Cecilia Jalieza
31. San Juan Guelavia
32. Macuilxóchitl
33. Teotitlán del Valle
34. Santa Ana del Valle
35. Tlacolula
36. Mitla
37. Santiago Matatlán
38. Santa María Azompa
39. San Jacinto Amilpas
40. San Felipe Tejalapan
41. San Pablo Etla
42. San Sebastián Etla
43. Guadalupe Etla
44. Soledad Etla
45. San Andrés Zautla
46. Villa de Etla
47. Reyes Etla
48. Magdalena Apasco
49. San Juan del Estado
(San Juan del Rey)
50. Huitzo (Guaxolotitlán)

Principal Colonial Towns

- ○ Zapotec
- ● Mixtec
- ◉ Zapotec and Mixtec
- △ Aztec
- ◆ Congregation Spanish

VALLEY OF ETLA

VALLEY OF ZIMATLÁN

VALLEY OF TLACOLULA

Atoyac River

Salado River

Atoyac River

MILES

0   5   10   15

0   5   10   15   20

KILOMETERS

N

Map 2. The Valley of Oaxaca. *Source*: William B. Taylor, *Landlord and Peasant in Colonial Oaxaca* (Stanford University Press, 1972), p. 25.

donment around the year 1000, the city of Monte Albán dominated the Valley and surrounding regions, and the presence of monumental architecture, bas-relief carving, a stela-altar complex, calendrics, and hieroglyphic writing leave little doubt about its importance.[6] The city prospered for a thousand years, reaching its peak sometime after A.D. 400, when it occupied "not only the top of a large mountain, but the tops and sides of a whole range of high hills adjoining, a total of some fifteen square miles of urban construction."[7]

The rise of this urban center around 100 B.C. marked the flowering of Valley Zapotec culture, which Kent Flannery has identified at San José Mogote as early as 1400 B.C.[8] From at least that time until the Spanish conquest, the Zapotec cultural tradition predominated in the Valley of Oaxaca. As John Paddock notes:

Neither the abandonment of Monte Albán, nor the Mixtec conquest and occupation (some three centuries of it), nor, finally, the relatively trifling Aztec invasion caused any sharp break in Valley Zapotec ways. Except for the abandonment of Monte Albán and the later capture of a number of towns by the Mixtecs, change in the Valley of Oaxaca from the time of Christ until the Spanish conquest tended to be both very gradual and the work of the Valley's own Zapotec inhabitants.[9]

By A.D. 400 all of the best land in the Valley was being utilized, and at some point during the next few centuries the Valley's population reached the limits of its sustaining capacity, given the technology of the period. Continuing building activity and other evidence of a steady population increase during the 350 years between 400 and 750 suggest that the Valley Zapotecs may have tried to bring surrounding areas under political control. But the uniformity of ceramic remains in the Valley does not extend beyond its geographical limits, and it seems doubtful that any outside communities ever became integrated into the Valley's way of life.[10]

Thus it is clear that for hundreds of years before the arrival of the Europeans the Valley of Oaxaca constituted a distinct ecological and cultural unit. The Zapotecs of Monte Albán had forged a powerful state society based on intensive farming methods, social stratification, and occupational specialization. They developed a distinctive art style, a method of hieroglyphic writing, and a complex calendric system, and to this day the Valley remains linguistically and culturally distinct from surrounding areas.

Why Monte Albán and other classic cities and ceremonial centers in Mesoamerica should all have been abandoned about A.D. 1000 is not completely clear. By all evidence, Monte Albán began to decline some 250 years earlier, in about 750, and the absence of any signs of conquest or destruction indicates that the decline came from within Zapotec society itself. One of the causes may have been the increasing rigidity and traditionalism of the ruling class. Paddock points out that at the height of the city's power, in the period A.D. 300–900, there was a slow falling off in the quality of its art, and concludes that "the ruling class was becoming more and more exclusive, less and less open to talent of all kinds from below."[11] In any case, the demise of Monte Albán marked the beginning of a new era in the Valley in which no one site was an obvious dominant center. The situation came to resemble the Mixtec pattern, with many small city- or town-states united on the basis of shifting and frequently unstable alliances. Most likely it was a period of sporadic warfare, both among the various Zapotec groups of the Valley and between them and neighboring ethnic groups like the Mixes.

It is in these centuries—from the time of the abandonment of Monte Albán to the time of the Spanish conquest—that ethnic considerations become increasingly important in the history of the Valley. The two major ethnic and linguistic groups in the state are the Zapotecs and Mixtecs; they have been the central and most powerful figures in Oaxaca's history, and are by far the best known archeologically, historically, ethnographically, and linguistically. The central Valley, as we have seen, was the focal point for Zapotec culture and appears to have been ethnically homogeneous throughout most of its history. In the neighboring Mixteca Alta, a distinct Mixtec cultural tradition was developing well before the time of Christ.[12] As far as the other minority peoples of Oaxaca are concerned, recent studies indicate that they became linguistically distinct at times ranging from roughly 1000 B.C. to A.D. 1000.[13]

At the time of the Spanish conquest Zapotec speakers occupied the mountains north of the Valley of Oaxaca and most of the territory to the southeast as far as Tehuantepec, as well as the Valley itself. The northern mountainous area also contained speakers of Mixe, Chinantec, Cuicatec, Mazatec, and Náhuatl; the Southern Zapotecs east of Miahuatlán had Huave, Chontal, Mixe, and Náhuatl speakers as their neighbors. Farther east was a block of Zoque speakers of the Maya language family. Mixtec speakers occupied the highlands (the Mixteca Alta) to the west and northwest of the Valley, down to the coastal region to the southwest, where the kingdom of Tututepec was located. These broad linguistic divisions, however, were not in a one-to-one correspondence with cultural and ethnic groupings.* Thus the Zapotec speakers were divided into three cultural groups: the Valley Zapotecs, the Southern Zapotecs, and the Mountain Zapotecs. Likewise, we can distinguish three groups of Mixtec speakers: those of the Mixteca Alta, the Mixteca Baja, and the Mixteca de la Costa. Though population figures for most of these groups are lacking, Ronald Spores estimates that in 1519 all of Oaxaca had a population of 1,500,000 to 1,760,000. William Taylor puts the population of the Valley in that same year at 350,000,[14] suggesting that the Valley may well have contained as much as one-fifth of Oaxaca's total population at the time of the conquest; it was certainly the most densely inhabited part of the entire region.

The Mixtec and Aztec Penetrations

After the abandonment of Monte Albán, no one site in the Valley was dominant until the emergence of Zaachila, later called Teozapotlan by the Aztecs and known by this name throughout most of the colonial period. However, at the time the Spanish arrived there was a large Mixtec population in the Valley engaged in hostilities with the Zapotecs, and the ruler of Teozapotlan had been

---

*The concept of ethnicity used throughout this book is that of Fredrik Barth, who argues that a distinction must be drawn between ethnic groups and culture-bearing units. Ethnic groups are defined as categories of ascription and identification used by the people themselves. Thus, for example, ethnic identities such as Zapotec or Mixtec may persist intact through time even though the cultural differences between the groups may be drastically reduced (as they were in the Valley during the colonial period). See Barth, *Ethnic Groups and Boundaries*, p. 14.

forced to flee to Tehuantepec. Cuilapan had emerged as the largest Mixtec town in the Valley, the entire central portion of which was heavily inhabited by Mixtec speakers. This included the area where the city of Antequera later came to be founded, bounded on the northeast by San Andrés Huayapan, on the northwest by Santa María Azompa, and to the south by Teozapotlan.*

From their base at Cuilapan, the Mixtecs founded new towns, established themselves in Zapotec towns (including a Mixtec quarter within Teozapotlan itself), and subjected Zapotec towns to tribute.[15] The Valley of Oaxaca and many parts of the Mixteca continued to be linked by intermarriage among the native nobility during the entire colonial period. Various *caciques* (native rulers) of Cuilapan were related through marriage with the Mixtec dynasties of Tututepec, Jamiltepec, Jaltepec, Tejupan, and other towns at different times during the seventeenth and eighteenth centuries.[16] The caciques of Etla also had marriage ties with the Mixteca in the eighteenth century.[17]

By 1521 the Mixtecs appear to have been politically influential in the central part of the Valley. Early colonial documentation is replete with references to the caciques of Cuilapan, but little is said about those of Teozapotlan. Indeed, the *cacicazgo* (estate or institution of cacique rule) of Cuilapan was one of the largest in the Valley during the colonial period, whereas Teozapotlan suffered from a chronic shortage of land because Cuilapan lands surrounded it on all sides.[18] A document of 1520 refers to Cuilapan as the *cabecera* (head town) of the Province of Oaxaca, and in 1529 the *juez visitador* Cristóbal de Barrios referred to the *cacica* of Cuilapan, doña Isabel, as "señora of the Valley of Oaxaca."[19] Indicative of her power is the fact that in the same year Antequera's first *alcalde*

---

*The precise nature of Mixtec influence, and whether or not there were Mixtec speakers in the Valley during the thirteenth and fourteenth centuries, is currently being debated. John Paddock ("Mixtec Ethnohistory") and Ignacio Bernal ("The Mixtecs") speak of large-scale migrations and invasions of Mixtecs during these centuries. But several scholars remain skeptical and assert that there is no conclusive proof of a widespread Mixtec occupation at such an early date. See, for example, H. B. Nicholson, "The Use of the Term 'Mixtec'"; Joseph Whitecotton, *The Zapotecs*; and Ronald Spores, "Review of *El Tesoro*."

mayor, Juan Peláez de Berrio, tried to enlist doña Isabel's help in extorting gold from the caciques of towns in the Mixteca Alta and Baja, as well as the Valley towns of Etla and the Villa de Oaxaca.[20]

By 1521 Mixtecs clearly predominated over Zapotecs in the vicinity where the city of Antequera was founded. According to the seventeenth-century account of Francisco de Burgoa, when the Spanish arrived they found "all the flat lands that are occupied by the city of Oaxaca [Antequera], and the surrounding area, occupied by Mixtec hamlets."[21] Among the definably Mixtec communities were Santa Cruz Xoxocotlán, San Raimundo Jalpan, San Juan Chapultepec, Santa María Azompa, San Pedro Ixtlahuaca, San Andrés Ixtlahuaca, and perhaps San Andrés Huayapan.[22] The Mixtec population in the Valley at this time was well above 20,000 and may have been as high as 70,000.[23] As late as 1565 the Mixtec population of Antequera and its vicinity contained 232 adults; the number of Zapotecs, in contrast, was only 159.

In addition to the Valley Zapotecs and Mixtecs, the Spaniards on their arrival in the region encountered a small but important group of Aztecs. The precise date of Aztec penetration into the Valley of Oaxaca is open to debate, but the most reliable estimate places it at the beginning of the reign of Ahuitzotl in 1486.[24] The Aztecs hoped to subject the inhabitants of the Valley to tribute and thus bring them nominally into the area of Aztec dominion; but perhaps the most important reason for their incursion was their desire to ensure the safety of their growing trade with Soconusco.[25] Indeed, it was the Zapotecs' hostility toward Aztec traders (who at the same time functioned as spies) that provoked Ahuitzotl's invasion.[26] Aztec forces managed to overcome the Valley Zapotecs and Mixtecs and within the year established a garrison called Huaxyacac on the site later to be occupied by the city of Antequera.[27] After the conquest the name of this settlement was corrupted to Oaxaca by the Spaniards and applied thereafter to the entire province.

According to Fray Diego Durán, Huaxyacac was originally populated with 600 married men with their wives and children recruited from different provinces of the Aztec domain. The settlement was reportedly laid out in accordance with precise instructions from the

Aztec ruler Ahuitzotl, who "commanded that the city be ordered in such a way that the *mexicanos* be settled in one place, the *texcocanos* in another, the *tepanecas* in another, the *xochimilcas* in another, and all the groups separately in their barrios." Ahuitzotl further instructed the governor of the garrison to look to the safety of the settlers, "since they were going to a region surrounded by barbaric and wicked people."[28]

When the conquistador Francisco de Orozco arrived in the Valley in 1521, he thus found "a very large garrison of Mexican Indians with their houses, wives, and children."[29] According to the Aztec Matrícula de Tributos, Huaxyacac was governed by a *tlacatectli* (or *tlacatecutl*) and a *tlacochtectli*.* An Indian witness in a 1563 lawsuit refers only to a *tlacatecutl*. But whatever the man's title, our witness tells us that this governor's residence stood on one side of a plaza (today occupied by the city market, only one block from the central plaza) that was flanked on its other sides by a temple, a jail, and a complex of rooms where government officials and nobles met. Another witness claimed that a *tianguis* (market) was regularly held in the plaza, which also contained a *tzompantli*, a rack to display the skulls of sacrificial victims.[30] Other than Durán's, we have no population estimates for Huaxyacac, but it could not have had any more than 4,000 or 5,000 inhabitants at the time of the conquest. Founded on land controlled by Cuilapan, Huaxyacac occupied an area half a league (about two kilometers) in length and something less in width.[31] Within or bordering on this tract were the "lands of Huitzilopochtli," used to support the Aztec priesthood,[32] and the "lands of Moctezuma," farmland acquired by the Aztecs through conquest.[33]

About the social organization of Huaxyacac we know very little beyond what has already been stated. Ethnic subdivisions among the Náhuatl-speaking population were retained, with the different groups living in separate barrios, a practice that continued well into the sixteenth century.

---

*Robert Barlow, *The Extent of the Empire of the Culhua Mexica*, p. 120. The holders of these offices were military commanders and members of the Aztec ruler's war council. See Pedro Carrasco, "Social Organization of Ancient Mexico," p. 357.

The Aztecs, as was their custom in other provinces, left the Valley Zapotecs and Mixtecs free to govern themselves through their own institutions and nobilities. They did not interfere in any way with localized warfare between the two groups. During the approximately thirty-five years of Huaxyacac's existence as an Aztec settlement, it functioned primarily as a center of tribute collection for the Valley and a way station for traders bound for Tabasco and Soconusco. Valley towns formed part of the tribute province of Coyolapan, which took its name from the large Mixtec town. The Matrícula de Tributos lists six major identifiable towns in the Valley that paid tribute to Huaxyacac, along with six others in the category of subject towns.[34] That at least eight of these twelve towns did in fact pay tribute is confirmed by the Crown's sixteenth-century surveys, the *Relaciones geográficas*. Tribute varied from town to town, depending on local resources, and included such items as gold, cotton mantles, staple foodstuffs, slaves, feathers, and military service.[35]

Compared with what other regions were forced to give to the Aztecs, however, the tribute paid by Valley towns was quite small and reflected the Aztecs' weak foothold in the area.[36] Their greatest cultural influence in the area was linguistic: at the time of the conquest many of the Valley's caciques and *principales* were fluent in Náhuatl.[37] Burgoa remarks that the Valley Indians in 1521 "knew it [Náhuatl] very well, and it was generally used in those towns that were dependents of, or communicated with, the ministers of the Emperor Montezuma."[38]

The *Relación de Guaxolotitlán* (now Huitzo) tells us that intermarriage was one tool the Aztecs used to incorporate Zapotec leaders into their political and social hierarchy, and Taylor believes that "the Zapotec nobility in particular seems to have adopted elements of Aztec culture and to have mixed with the Aztec nobility."[39] Yet there is no supplementary evidence to support this view, and archeologists have yet to unearth any material signs of Aztec influence or occupation in the Valley. The available documentation indicates that with the exception of language, Aztec culture was strictly limited to the Náhuatl-speaking population of Huaxyacac. The same holds true for the colonial period, when the entire Nahua population of the Valley lived in or around the city of Antequera.

Thus on the eve of the conquest the Valley was inhabited by three distinct ethnic groups speaking three different languages. Of this population of about 350,000, 78 percent or more was Zapotec, 10 to 20 percent Mixtec, and 1 to 2 percent Nahua. In the more distant corners of the Valley, Guaxolotitlán, bordering on the Mixteca Alta, had a mixed population of Zapotecs and Mixtecs, and Santa Ana Zegache, in the southern part of the Valley of Zimatlán, was divided into Zapotec and Mixtec settlements.

The Nahuas held themselves aloof from the other two groups, confining themselves to the pursuit of their economic interests. The Mixtecs and Zapotecs, however, appear to have been at war over political control of the Valley, and the indications are that the Mixtecs had gained the upper hand and were generally regarded as socially superior to the Zapotecs. As late as 1580 the Valley Mixtecs were said to be of a different "lineage" than the Zapotecs, and the *Relación de Cuilapan* leaves little doubt that the two groups were ethnically quite distinct:

This town, called Cuyolapan in Mexican, is populated by Mixtec Indians. They call it Ynchaca in their language. . . .

The people of this town do not have their origins here and were not even born in this community. They are immigrants and are considered to be foreigners.

The Indians of the Zapotec region (where this town is) are very different from the Mixtecs. One reason for the difference is that the Mixtecs are newcomers. Another reason is that they are more lordly in their behavior and dress, as well as in the way they treat their women, because even though the Zapotec lady may be of the nobility, she does her grinding in the same manner as the *macehuales* [commoners].[40]

Zapotec Society at Spanish Contact

Our ethnographic knowledge of the Valley of Oaxaca at the time of the Spanish conquest is limited almost entirely to Zapotec society. There is thus no guarantee that such data as we possess can be applied to the Mixtec-speaking central portion of the Valley, where the city of Antequera was established. However, the indications are that the differences between the aboriginal Zapotec and Mixtec societies were not great, and so the lack of specific information on Valley Mixtec social structure is not an insuperable handicap.

The Valley's chief crops consisted of the items that have always been the mainstay of the Mesoamerican diet—corn, beans, squash, and chile peppers. The maguey cactus was cultivated both for pulque and for its many nondietetic uses. Cacao was important and was used to make a kind of chocolate drink; cacao beans also served as currency. A variety of plants (some of them domesticated) were eaten, including prickly pears of the nopal cactus, roots, nuts, avocados, and several fruits. Beekeeping was common, but apart from this, animal husbandry was confined to the dog and the turkey; all three were used primarily for ritual feasting, sacrifice to the gods, and payment of tribute.[41]

Not all parts of the Valley were equally productive. Etla and Guaxolotitlán were particularly noted for their agricultural productivity, for example, whereas Tlacolula and Mitla, located in a drier part of the Valley, could not even meet their own needs in corn. Nor did all parts produce the same crops, a diversity that is reflected in the tribute paid to Teozapotlan by various towns: there was little overlap in the items given. These differences stimulated trade and commerce, and by the time the Spaniards arrived there was a well-developed system of regional markets, each held every five days. Large markets were located at Etla, Santa Ana (probably Tlapacoya), and Chichicapan, and also in Aztec Huaxyacac.[42] In addition, we have evidence from the colonial period of four other markets in the Valley that may date from pre-Hispanic times. These were at Tlacolula (noted in 1579), San Andrés Huayapan (1653), San Juan Chilateca (1743), and Ocotlán (1764).[43]

Many commodities and raw materials were imported from outside the Valley, such as cotton from Tehuantepec, Jalapa, and Nejapa and salt from Tehuantepec. It is likely that metals, precious stones, feathers, fish, and animal skins also came from the outside. Transport was always by human carriers using the tumpline or headstrap; there were no draft animals, and the wheel was used only for toys in Mesoamerica.[44]

We know very little about trade and craft specialization in the Valley. The Tlacolula arm, one of the drier regions and the principal center of maguey cultivation, was noted for its merchants and traders, especially those from Teotitlán del Valle, Tlacolula, Mitla, and Tlalixtac.[45] It is likely that the village craft specialization of the colonial period (and continuing today) had its roots in the pre-conquest era. The people of Teotitlán del Valle, for example, gave cotton mantles to Teozapotlan as part of their tribute—evidence of the strong weaving tradition in the town that has persisted to this day. Another example is formerly Mixtec Azompa, a town that was noted for its pottery production in the seventeenth century, and that is still the source of much of the utilitarian pottery sold in the Oaxaca market.[46]

It is clear that the Valley of Oaxaca was far less technologically developed than, for example, the Valley of Mexico. Practical metalworking never evolved among the Zapotecs, and local craftsmen were unable to compete with the more advanced Nahuas who came to the Valley with the Spaniards. In a census of Antequera's adjoining Indian barrios in 1565, the vast majority of the Zapotecs (and Mixtecs) were agricultural laborers on small Spanish farms, whereas a great percentage of the Nahuas practiced skilled trades and crafts.[47]

The pre-conquest settlement pattern in the Valley consisted of nucleated settlements with farmlands spread out around the residence center. Joseph Whitecotton estimates that the size of the cabeceras ranged from 2,000 to 11,000 persons, and whole communities from 5,000 to 13,000.[48] Each community or town-state had a hereditary aristocracy, but the one real ruler was the cacique, a member of a separate royal lineage. Succession to this position was by direct lineal descent and appears to have been very similar to the pattern in the Mixteca Alta, studied in detail by Spores.[49] The sources indicate that within their respective communities the caciques had virtually absolute power; it is doubtful that there existed any sort of town council with offices comparable to those of *alcalde* (judge) or *regidor* (councilman) implanted by the Spanish. The cacique had the right to exact tribute and personal service from his subjects, and his functions included the administration of justice, the supervision of labor, the governance and maintenance of the community, and the waging of war. He was aided by a number of appointed officials (*tequitlatos* in Náhuatl), who were placed in the wards and hamlets to collect tribute, take notice of crimes, and settle disputes.[50]

The caciques were large landholders, and the cacicazgo estates may have been the only form of private landownership in pre-Hispanic times. Though cacicazgo holdings may have been reduced somewhat under Spanish rule, many of them were nevertheless still of considerable size. The two largest in the Valley were those of Cuilapan and Etla. During the seventeenth and eighteenth centuries, "nearly every land site between Zaachila to the south and Azompa to the north was bordered on at least one side by lands of the cacique [of Cuilapan]."[51] The caciques of Oaxaca may have had more power in pre-Hispanic times than their counterparts in most other areas. Taylor points out that a distinguishing feature of colonial society in the Valley was the retention of large landholdings and high social status by the native nobility after 1550, when the fortunes of the caciques in other areas were generally on the decline.[52]

Above the community level, political integration in the Valley was weak. Loose, unstable federations were formed with one "lordship" as the head unit and its cacique as supreme lord. The primary means of political integration was the payment of tribute to the supreme lord by the subject populations. The precise nature of political control is not known, but Spores argues that the Teozapotlan federation was an involuntary alliance.[53]

Warfare was a constant feature of Valley life during late pre-Hispanic times. Aside from the wars with the Mixtecs, there was a constant struggle for power among the Zapotec lordships. Most warfare was of a local nature, though such towns as Macuilxóchitl and Teitipac are known to have gone to war under orders from Teozapotlan. "Long-distance" warfare was not uncommon. Mitla fought the Mixtecs from the coastal kingdom of Tututepec, Tlacolula had conflicts with the Mixes, and Teozapotlan did battle with the Mixtecs of Tututepec and Tlaxiaco. War was waged for the privilege of exacting tribute and to obtain captives for slaves or for human sacrifice; victory seldom involved any territorial gain. Indicative of the instability of political alliances is the fact that the vanquishing of a supreme lord of a confederation did not necessarily imply dominion over his allies. Thus the people of Ixtepeji in the Sierra Zapotec region were subject to the Zapotecs of Tehuantepec and the coastal Mixtecs of Tututepec at the same time.[54]

Of all the aspects of Zapotec society and culture, social organization is the most difficult to reconstruct. The broad outlines of social stratification are clear enough, but detailed information on status differences, occupational groups, and the kinship system is lacking.

Zapotec society was stratified into four rigid divisions: nobles, commoners, serfs, and slaves. Membership in the first two strata, and possibly the third, was perpetuated by heredity, unwritten sumptuary laws, and probably endogamy. The most clear-cut division was between the nobility and the rest of the society, which were set apart by dress, diet, and certain linguistic habits. The nobles wore brightly woven cotton mantles and adorned themselves with lip plugs, earrings, feathers, and gold and stone beads; the rest of the population wore clothing made of maguey fiber devoid of ornamentation. The consumption of meat and chocolate was restricted to the elite, and commoners were required to use a special set of pronouns and a "reverential" verb when addressing nobles.[55]

The nobility itself was divided into two groups, the caciques (ruling families and their spouses and children) and the principales (lesser nobles who served as tequitlatos, administrative officials, and priests). The ruling families of the various town-states formed a kind of endogamous stratum, since caciques were proscribed from marrying into the less prestigious group of principales. Though this restriction was sometimes relaxed where junior wives were concerned—and polygyny was the rule among the caciques— aspiring rulers were forced to choose their first and most important mates from outside the community. This choice was often crucial for the continuance of the dynasty, for succession was traced through the senior spouse as well as the cacique himself.[56]

The commoners, or macehuales, formed the bulk of the population and were primarily farmers. Other occupational groups fell in this category, but we know little about them. The Spanish-Zapotec dictionary compiled by Fr. Juan de Córdova in the mid-sixteenth century lists several non-farming occupations that may have been held by macehuales: weaver, dancer, music instructor, curer, witch, diviner, merchant, peddler, sculptor, painter, interpreter, scribe, writer.[57] All commoners were required to pay tribute to their cacique and to give services to the other nobles. Marriage among the macehuales was probably mostly monogamous, though polygyny was permitted. Judging from twentieth-century marriage patterns in the Valley and the Mixteca Alta, Spores hypothesizes that communities were endogamous apart from the exogamous marriages of the ruling families.[58]

Below the commoners were the serfs, or *mayeques*, who were permanently bound to the caciques' lands (and possibly those of lesser nobles as well) and formed a part of the cacicazgo estates. The goods and services rendered to one *principal* of Cuilapan in 1558 hint at the privileges exercised by the pre-Hispanic caciques and the abject status of the mayeques. Don Félix de Zúñiga had as part of his inheritance more than 300 household heads from whom he received the following: (1) they collectively worked three plots of corn measuring all together about 6.5 acres, as well as three other plots of unspecified size sown with beans and cotton; (2) each household head gave don Félix 120 cotton mantles per year; (3) for the fiesta of Santiago (Saint James), Cuilapan's patron saint, each household head contributed thirteen pesos, fifteen turkeys, and 3,000 cacao beans, and for Easter festivities each gave two pesos and an unspecified number of turkeys; and (4) don Félix received for his personal service on a weekly basis four women and seven men.[59]

Cuilapan was a Mixtec town, but we have confirmation of the existence of *terrasguerros* (the Spanish colonial term for mayeques) in Nahua and Zapotec communities as well, including the Villa de Oaxaca, Etla, Tlacochahuaya, Tlalixtac, and Guaxolotitlán.[60] A petition sent to the Audiencia by Bishop Albuquerque in 1564 leaves little doubt that mayeques were common in all parts of the Valley in pre-Hispanic times, and emphasizes their role in supporting the caciques and principales. The bishop complained of the inequities of recent reforms in the tribute system, pointing out that many "patrimonial Indians" who had previously paid tribute only to their masters (caciques and principales) were now required to pay tribute to the Crown instead. Consequently, the Indian nobility was stripped of a large part of its resources and base of support. As the bishop put it, "To change such an ancient custom is almost the same as changing a whole way of life." [61]

At the bottom of the pre-Hispanic social hierarchy were the slaves. They were obtained through warfare and could be bought and sold in markets. Slaves were used as personal and household servants and also as sacrificial victims. The largest slave market in the area was at Miahuatlán, south of the Valley of Oaxaca, where slaves were brought from Tenochtitlán, Tlaxcala, Tepeaca, and the Mixteca. [62] Unlike the mayeques, Indian slaves did not survive long into the colonial period. There is barely any mention of them after the early 1530's; they simply disappeared into the ranks of household servants for the Spanish population or into the terrasguerro and macehual strata in the villages.

The preceding ethnographic summary provides a background for the study of colonial society in the Valley of Oaxaca and the place of the Indian within it. [63] The variety of aboriginal societies discovered by the Europeans in the Americas forced them to adjust their activities accordingly from region to region. Their policies and institutions in a given area can be seen as responses, especially in the early years, to a particular set of problems arising from the aboriginal level of sociocultural development. The Valley of Oaxaca was an important part of one of the most culturally advanced regions the Spaniards encountered, a fact that gave the colonizers certain advantages in their effort to control and exploit the Indians, but that created a number of problems as well.

In 1521 the people of the Valley were living in a series of internally stratified town-states in which political positions were quite distinct from the kinship system. As in other societies at a similar level of development, the basic principles of organization were "hierarchy, differential degrees of access to basic resources, obedience to officials, and defense of the area."[64] This organization differed only in degree, not in kind, from that of sixteenth-century Spain, and the culture contact that began in the Valley in 1521 was essentially a confrontation between state societies.

Owing to the conquistadores' previous successes in central Mexico—particularly the conquest of Tenochtitlán—and their technological superiority, the Spanish were able to bring the Valley under control with relative ease. Once the initial power struggle was resolved, the colonizers resorted to a common tactic used in many parts of Mesoamerica and the Andes to maintain their rule, allowing the caciques and principales to retain their positions as rulers and nobles among the Indians and bolstering their status by granting them some of the privileges of the Spanish nobility. The Córdova dictionary helps explain why this policy worked so well in the Valley of Oaxaca: the top levels of pre-Hispanic Zapotec society observed much the same kind of status distinctions as Spanish society, with a comparable division between the *grandes* (titled nobility), and the lower-ranked *hidalgos*.[65]

But the level of sociocultural development of the native population, helpful as it was to the Spanish in their objectives, was also a hindrance. The virtual mountains of petitions, complaints, and lawsuits initiated by the Indians of Oaxaca in colonial times make it clear that they were not a passive element in the society. This was largely thanks to the strength of the Oaxaca caciques under Spanish rule, and to their success in retaining considerable chunks of their lands. Very few Valley communities became dependent on lands they did not own, and only three or four towns became satellites of Spanish haciendas.[66] Though the Indian in Oaxaca was never able to escape the subservient role forced on him by the nature of the colonial situation, neither did he admit defeat. A document from 1552 shows that he quickly understood the Spanish social system implanted in the colony and tried, often successfully, to manipulate it to his own benefit. The Spanish masons, tailors, and potters who served as *corregidores* (local political administrators) in the Valley prior to 1552 were unable to win respect and cooperation from the

Indians because they were not of hidalgo rank or men of letters, but worked with their hands.[67] The Indians' well-developed sense of property ownership, their appreciation of the importance of formal wills, and their quick grasp and utilization of the options open to them in the Spanish legal system helped preserve indigenous traditions—and property—throughout the long period of forced acculturation.

CHAPTER THREE

Economy and Society in the Early Sixteenth Century

The Spanish Conquest and the Founding of Antequera

Spanish soldiers under orders from Fernando Cortés first penetrated the Valley of Oaxaca in November 1521, only four months after the final surrender of the Aztec capital of Tenochtitlán. Cortés had received reports of the riches to be had in the south and realized that control of the Valley of Oaxaca was essential to the further exploration of the Pacific coast.[1] At Tepeaca he placed Francisco de Orozco in charge of an army of 30 horsemen, 80 foot soldiers, and as many as 4,000 Náhuatl-speaking allies and sent them to the conquest of the Provincia de Guaxaca.[2] The peoples of the Valley had been forewarned of the Spaniards' plans, and on arriving at Huaxyacac, Orozco found the resident Aztecs and a large number of Cuilapan Mixtecs well fortified and ready to do battle. But Spanish arms and tactics soon defeated the Indians, and the fighting ended in about a week with comparatively little bloodshed.[3] The Zapotecs took no part in the hostilities, since the lord of Tehuantepec had already abdicated his throne and allied himself with Cortés prior to Orozco's arrival.[4] Transition to colonial rule was relatively smooth and easy compared with the shock and dislocation that accompanied the conquest in other areas, notably in the Valley of Mexico. This was not the first time the Valley of Oaxaca had been invaded by outsiders, and its history of localized warfare, the presence of the indigenous tribute system, and endemic political instability beyond the community level permitted the Spaniards to bring the Valley under control in a short time with a minimum of violence.

Orozco had orders to found a Spanish settlement at Huaxyacac, to be called Segura de la Frontera after the name of the settlement that he and his men had abandoned to pursue the conquest in Oaxaca. But Cortés was quick to perceive the fertility and strategic importance of the Valley and soon ordered the colonizers to move to the vicinity of the Mixtec kingdom of Tututepec on the Pacific coast, with an eye to claiming the entire Valley for the encomienda he was in the process of assembling.[5]

Simultaneously, Cortés sent Pedro de Alvarado with a contingent of 240 men to the conquest of Tututepec; and Segura de la Frontera was reestablished there early in 1522. Without the consent of his superior, Alvarado distributed in encomienda to the soldiers of the villa a large number of Indian communities in the Valley of Oaxaca, the Mixteca Alta and Baja, and the Southern Zapotec areas.[6] The settlement fared badly, however. The men were dissatisfied with the hot, humid climate, to say nothing of the hostile reception they received from the powerful coastal Mixtecs. The Valley of Oaxaca was clearly the best location in the entire region for a Spanish town, and during Alvarado's temporary absence a small band of men fled Tututepec and returned to the Valley. There they settled on land adjoining the garrison of Huaxyacac, naming their village Tepeaca.[7]

Little is known of the numbers and activities of the Spaniards between 1522 and 1529 in this fledgling settlement, but the settlers were undoubtedly attracted by the large supply of Indian labor and the opportunities for gold placer mining in the Etla region. Cortés tried several times to oust them from the Valley, and though he was ultimately unsuccessful, the pressure he brought to bear was sufficient to forestall the town's development for many years. In 1524, during Cortés's sojourn in Honduras, his enemies Peralmíndez Chirinos and Gonzalo de Salazar in Mexico City "re-founded" the town once again; by 1526 it had a population of some 50 families and was officially designated a villa by the Crown.[8] The town met with surprisingly little Indian resistance in these early years, though the Europeans' quest for gold and Indian slaves led to hostilities with the neighboring Mixes and Mountain Zapotecs.[9]

The numerous Aztecs and Tlaxcalans of the Orozco expedition established themselves in Huaxyacac (henceforth to be known as the Villa de Oaxaca) and the two adjoining towns of San Martín Mexicapan and Santo Tomás Xochimilco. San Martín, founded on land ceded by the Mixtec cacique of neighboring San Juan Chapultepec, grew to be quite large in the 1520's; indeed, as early as 1523 it consisted of seven barrios.[10] A document of the period suggests that by this early date the Spaniards had already introduced their concept of local government into these Indian towns: each had a cabildo ostensibly based on the Spanish model with the local cacique as the alcalde and with two regidores. There seems to have been a measure of ethnic solidarity among the three towns, as suggested by the fact that their caciques formed a "confederation" and agreed to appoint one *alguacil mayor* (constable) to serve in all three communities.[11]

After a number of false starts, the Spanish community in the Valley was given a stronger foothold in 1529, the year of its last "founding." Fernando Cortés sailed for Spain in 1527 to seek help from the Crown in strengthening his eroding power base in the colony. His absence allowed the First Audiencia, headed by his bitter enemy Nuño de Guzmán, to reduce his influence still further and to redistribute a large number of goods, jobs, and encomiendas. The Audiencia quickly realized that the Valley of Oaxaca was one of Cortés's most vulnerable fronts, and was determined to support a Spanish town there that would serve as a bridge between Mexico City and the territory of Guatemala. On June 7, 1529, Juan Peláez de Berrio, brother of the Audiencia judge (*oidor*) Diego Delgadillo, was appointed alcalde mayor of the Province of Oaxaca, with instructions to lay out and enlarge the Valley's Spanish community, henceforth to be known as Antequera.

To stimulate interest in Antequera and ensure its growth, the Audiencia announced in Mexico City that all encomenderos with holdings in the Province of Oaxaca were to take up residence in Antequera or lose their encomiendas.[12] Many of the encomiendas had been newly carved out of Cortés's holdings by the Audiencia, which stripped him of virtually all of the important Indian towns in the Valley and allotted them to the settlers.* But the city's sovereignty was meant to reach far beyond the confines of the Valley, for some 70 additional cabeceras fell within Antequera's jurisdiction as decreed by the Audiencia in October 1529.[13] For the first time the Province of Oaxaca was clearly defined, and the territory it encompassed was vast indeed. It stretched from Teotitlán del Camino in the north (which today marks the northern boundary of the state of Oaxaca) to the Pacific coast in the south; Nejapa was its eastern limit, and virtually the entire Mixteca Alta was included to the northwest. In actual practice, however, Antequera's influence was largely restricted to those areas with well-developed indigenous societies that offered the best opportunities for colonial exploitation: the Valley proper, the Mixteca Alta, and parts of the Southern Zapotec and coastal regions. Except for some initial mining activity, Antequera residents had little contact with the Mountain Zapotecs and Mixes (most of this area was placed under the jurisdiction of Villa Alta), and the area surrounding Teotitlán del Camino soon came under the sphere of influence of the city of Puebla.

Peláez de Berrio hastened to take up his post, arriving in the Valley in July 1529 accompanied by some 80 settlers and encomenderos.[14] Though Peláez was empowered to take a *residencia* (inquiry held at the end of a term of office) on the villa's previous cabildo members, witnesses stated that they encountered no local government whatsoever.[15] Nor was the community laid out in any organized fashion. The newcomers initially resided in the homes of Nahuas or Cuilapan Mixtecs,[16] and Peláez himself was said to have lived for a short time in a house belonging to doña Isabel, the cacica of Cuilapan.[17]

*Archivo General de la Nación, Hospital de Jesús 239, exp. 140; Archivo General de Indias, Justicia 117; William Taylor, *Landlord and Peasant*, p. 112. The communities involved were Cuilapan, the Villa de Oaxaca, Etla, Tlapacoya, Macuilxóchitl, Teotitlán del Valle, Chichicapan, Ocotlán, Ixtepec (now Santa Cruz Mixtepec), Tepezimatlán, los Peñoles, Tlalixtac, Tlacochahuaya, Mitla, Tlacolula, Teitipac, Teozapotlan (Zaachila), Zimatlán, Coyotepec, and Guaxolotitlán (Huitzo). The first 4 were later regained by Cortés and designated as head towns (the "Cuatro Villas") of his holdings in the Valley, but the other 16 were to remain in the hands of encomenderos and the Crown.

Within a matter of days a cabildo was formed, with Peláez as the alcalde mayor, assisted by an *alcalde ordinario* (judge), three regidores, and an *escribano público* (secretary or scribe).[18] Alonso García Bravo, the architect of the grid-patterned urban plans of Veracruz and Mexico City, was called on to lay out Antequera in a similar fashion in accordance with instructions issued to the alcalde mayor by the Audiencia:

Because between this city [of Mexico] and Guatemala, a distance of 280 leagues, there is no town of Spaniards whatsoever; and because there are many large settlements [of Indians] between the two . . ., in this royal Audiencia it was decided that we should order a *villa* to be established in the Province of Oaxaca. [This province] is 80 leagues from this city [of Mexico] on the said road to Guatemala, and is the richest and most populated region along this route. . . . You, Juan Peláez de Berrio . . ., are ordered to select the best site you see fit for the founding and erection of the Villa de Antequera. It should be near the mines and at an accessible place, with sun, air, a river, woodlands, and pasture. On this site the *traza* of the said *villa* is to be laid out with the streets arranged in an orderly fashion, designating first the lots for the church, hospital, *cabildo*, your own residence, and those of all the other *vecinos* in your company. The *alcaldes, regidores*, and other officials are to be given lots in the most preeminent locations as is the custom in this land, and the others [vecinos] in accordance with the rank of each person.[19]

The resulting urban form came close to meeting the Spanish ideal of the grid-pattern town with a central plaza that was applied so frequently in the American colonies. Maps from the late colonial period illustrate the city's original form, only slightly expanded to accommodate the larger eighteenth-century population (see Map 3, based on a 1790 city plan).

All indications are that the garrison of Huaxyacac was razed and the Villa de Antequera built on approximately the same site. The Nahuas of Huaxyacac, or what the Spanish called the Villa de Oaxaca, were pushed aside and settled on land contiguous to the city to the northwest.[20] What is now the hub of the city's market, the square just one block southeast of the main plaza, was once the ceremonial and administrative center of Huaxyacac. Known variously as the Plaza del Marqués, the Plaza de San Juan de Dios, and

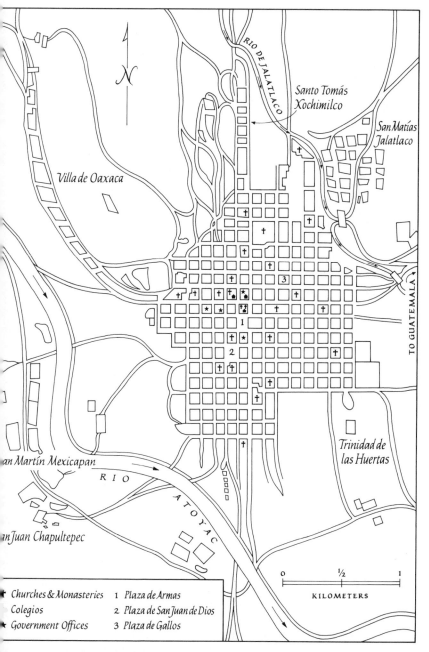

MAP 3. Antequera and Its Indian Satellite Towns in 1790. *Source*: Based on an 1884 copy, drawn by Fernando Arjona Mejía, of an original by F. García Franco. The copy is now in the possession of the Dirección de Obras Públicas del Estado de Oaxaca, Oaxaca, Mexico. *Note*: The Plaza de San Juan de Dios was also known variously as the Plaza del Marqués and the Plaza de Santa Catalina.

the Plaza de Santa Catalina at different times during the colonial period, it was here that Fernando Cortés built a house on the former site of an Aztec temple.[21]

Though the exact circumstances remain unknown, the Indian settlement of Jalatlaco was apparently founded at this time on the site of the original Spanish settlement (Tepeaca) on the eastern bank of the Jalatlaco River.[22] A *sujeto* (subject town) of the Villa de Oaxaca, Jalatlaco was composed almost entirely of Náhuatl speakers; in the latter half of the sixteenth century it became the most urbanized of all the Indian towns, with many of its inhabitants working as skilled artisans and craftsmen.

Thus by the end of 1529 Antequera came to look very much like other Spanish towns founded in the densely inhabited Mexican highlands: a small core of Spaniards occupying a carefully planned grid of streets surrounded by a number of Indian settlements.

The Marquesado del Valle

In the same year that Peláez de Berrio and his men arrived in the Valley to establish Antequera, Fernando Cortés was made the Marqués del Valle de Oaxaca by the Spanish king and was granted in perpetuity twenty-two separate encomiendas located in seven parts of the colony. He was authorized to receive tribute from the Indian population; given the right to their "lands, vassals, income, pastures, and waters"; and granted the privilege of exercising criminal and civil jurisdiction (i.e., appointing magistrates) within his domain.[23] With this patent, the Crown gave Cortés jurisdiction over almost the entire Valley of Oaxaca. But that was back in Spain. Across the ocean, in the meantime, the First Audiencia was stripping Cortés of many of these Valley holdings and redistributing them to other persons in an attempt to encourage the growth of Antequera. This action initiated a long series of court battles, continuing well into the sixteenth century, between the marqués and his descendants on the one hand and the city of Antequera and various encomenderos on the other. The vecinos of Antequera won a partial victory in 1531–32, when the Second Audiencia permanently deprived the marqués of sixteen Indian districts in the southern and eastern regions of the Valley.[24] Moreover, by then the Crown was as committed as the Audiencia to encouraging the growth of a Spanish settlement in the region. A royal cédula of 1533 redefined the terms of the 1529 grant, stating that the marqués was not to have title to lands within the Valley of Oaxaca (or exclusive rights to water and pasture), and that his jurisdiction in the Valley was limited to the "Cuatro Villas" of Oaxaca, Cuilapan, Etla, and Tlapacoya and their sujetos.[25]

By 1534 the Cuatro Villas district had been reduced almost to its final boundaries,[26] though lawsuits involving the Marquesado and Antequera continued well into the colonial period. Each of the Cuatro Villas was assigned a number of dependent cabeceras with their sujetos. The head town of the entire district was the Náhuatl-speaking Villa de Oaxaca, from which an alcalde mayor appointed by the marqués administered the collection of tribute and other enterprises. The Marquesado covered large portions of the southern and eastern arms of the Valley, and in 1743 included forty-one populated places.[27] On the basis of the tribute figures, William Taylor has estimated that about 26,000 Indians lived in the jurisdictions of Etla, the Villa de Oaxaca, and Cuilapan in 1568, which is to say, 17.3 percent of the Valley's estimated Indian population of 150,000 for that year.[28] With Tlapacoya included, the Marquesado had jurisdiction over at least one-fifth of the Valley Indians.

Though Cortés lost control over the majority of the Valley towns he had been granted in 1529, he was able to retain some of the most important ones, notably Cuilapan and Etla. Furthermore, soon after the conquest he had rounded up all the Valley Mixtecs and resettled them at Cuilapan (and its sujetos), thus bringing the entire Valley Mixtec population within his jurisdiction.[29] Since we have no reliable population figures on the Mixtecs who lived outside of the central portion of the Valley, it is impossible to say how great or small were the numbers of Mixtecs who were uprooted and relocated in this move. It is certain, however, that Cuilapan was the largest town in the Valley in late pre-Hispanic times and continued to be during most of the colonial period.

The Marquesado also retained jurisdiction over the settlements of Nahuas surrounding the city of Antequera. Santo Tomás Xochi-milco, San Martín Mexicapan, and Jalatlaco (until the 1560's) were all sujetos of the Villa de Oaxaca, and it appears that Cortés had the Nahuas crowd the city as much as possible to discourage further Spanish settlement there in the early sixteenth century.

Cortés and his heirs limited their interest in the Valley primarily to the collection of tribute; their agent, the alcalde mayor of the Cuatro Villas, in turn relied on a local Indian cacique or *principal* to make the actual collections.[30] In the early period the tribute was col-lected by the cacique of Cuilapan.[31] The tribute paid by the Mar-quesado Indians differed little from what was required generally of towns in encomienda, though in the 1520's and early 1530's Cortés apparently demanded a larger number of Indian slaves for work in the mines. Before the towns of Tlalixtac, Tlacochahuaya, Mitla, Tlacolula, Teitipac, Teozapotlan, and Zimatlán were taken from Cortés in 1529, they paid their tribute to him in gold, corn, beans, chile, turkeys, clothing, and slaves.[32]

During the sixteenth century the Marquesado purchased a group of five *estancias de ganado mayor* and *de ganado menor* (cattle and horse ranches; sheep and goat ranches) in the southern end of the Valley, as well as tracts of arable land and a wheat mill in the Etla area. The cattle estancias supplied Antequera with meat in the 1540's and 1550's, and the Etla lands were an important source of the city's wheat supply. A large stand of mulberry trees was planted on the Etla estate in an effort to profit from the then burgeoning silk industry, but the attempt apparently failed completely; there is no mention of it after 1550.[33] The Marquesado made virtually no at-tempt to acquire urban property in Antequera; it held only a few va-cant lots, Cortés's house (which he never lived in) on the Plaza de Santa Catalina, and a tannery that was already in ruins by 1577.[34] Interest in the Marquesado's commercial operations in the Valley was highest in the 1540's and 1550's, the period in which Fernando Cortés and his son Martín were the titleholders. By the 1560's profits had fallen off, and interest waned. All five cattle estancias had been leased by 1572, and the mill at Etla was sold in 1591. The prin-cipal Marquesado investments in the Valley in the late 1560's took the form of loans to various vecinos of Antequera, and by 1630 all economic activity except the collection of tribute had ground to a halt.[35]

From all this it is clear that the Marquesado was never in any real sense a threat to Antequera. But it is also clear that it impeded the city's growth in two important ways: it severely restricted the number of towns available for distribution in encomienda to city vecinos, and it limited the amount of land available for municipal commons and pasture.

Civil and Ecclesiastic Jurisdictions

In the 1530's and 1540's the Valley and the surrounding territory within Antequera's jurisdiction was divided up into various political and ecclesiastical units. *Corregimientos* were established in numerous Indian districts by the Second Audiencia between 1531 and 1535 in order to exercise more direct control over the Indian population and facilitate the collection of tribute. Meanwhile, the Church was busily carving out its own spheres of influence, especially the Dominican friars, who took the lead in Oaxaca from the very beginning. The geographical boundaries of these corregimientos, secular church parishes, and Dominican *doctrinas* (head mission towns where the friars lived, plus the hamlets, or *visitas*, under their ministry) changed frequently during the course of the colonial period and formed a complex patchwork of overlapping jurisdictions. This subject has been treated in some detail by Peter Gerhard,[36] and I shall give only a brief outline of the system of colonial administration in the Valley here, with special emphasis on the role played by the city and its vecinos.

Before the creation of the corregimientos in the 1530's, Spanish government in the Valley was chaotic. Though Antequera was declared a villa by the Crown in 1526 and could boast of a cabildo at that time, organized government at the provincial level did not begin until three years later.[37] Peláez de Berrio, on his appointment as the alcalde mayor in 1529, was given judicial powers for civil and criminal jurisdiction covering both first instance and appeals, and owing to his political connections and the remoteness of the settle-

ment, he was able to wield considerable power. In many ways a pro-
totype of the conquistador at his rapacious and greedy worst, Peláez
had already achieved some degree of notoriety for his cruel treatment of the Indians before he reached Oaxaca.[38] Arriving in the Valley with the intent of quickly enriching himself and then returning
to Spain, he immediately sought to establish himself as lord and
master of the entire Province of Oaxaca by forcing a number of
caciques from the Valley, the Mixteca Alta, and the Mixteca de la
Costa to appear before him with gifts of gold and jewelry. He informed them that they were to answer to him alone, that the other
Spaniards in the Valley were all his slaves and "macehuales," and
that he had the right to enslave or make any use of the Indians he
wished. His treatment of other Spaniards was frequently almost as
tyrannical, and created much resentment. Among other abuses, he
jailed people in debt to him until the sums were paid (the jail was in
his own house), required encomenderos to purchase with gold a
special license to leave the villa to visit their encomiendas or other
places, and interfered with public property auctions to his own personal gain.[39] Fortunately for those concerned, his career was short-
lived, for he was thoroughly condemned by a 1531 residencia ordered by the Second Audiencia. His property was sold to repay
various persons he had wronged, and he was promptly thrown into
jail, where he soon died.[40]

The growth and consolidation of the colonial government after
1531 placed firmer limits on the powers of Peláez's successors,
though little is known about the men who occupied the post of alcalde mayor or their activities during the next twenty years, except
that they were always political appointees from outside the Province
of Oaxaca. Furthermore, as more people began to acquire vested
interests in the area, political power came to be distributed somewhat more evenly among a small group of encomenderos, corregidores, and clergy. The cabildo was soon dominated by the encomenderos, who were frequently in conflict with the alcaldes
mayores appointed by the viceroys. At least twice during the first
half of the sixteenth century the cabildo petitioned the Crown (unsuccessfully) to do away with the office of alcalde mayor in the prov-

ince because it conflicted with its own interests.[41] But as for the powers and activities of the cabildo itself during this period, we have only the sketchiest information. We know that it sent an emissary to the king in 1531 who returned the following year with a number of concessions, one of which gave Antequera the official rank of ciudad; and that at this time the number of regidores was expanded to eight, and permission was granted to elect an alguacil mayor.[42] We also know that a local branch of the *mesta* (cattlemen's association) was established in Antequera in 1543, and was closely tied to the cabildo through overlapping membership and interests.[43] The cabildo's struggles to acquire funds for public works, common lands, and pasture rights, and to gain sanctions limiting the power and jurisdiction of the Marquesado will be discussed later.

The civil administration of the Valley Indians was carried out primarily through the local political institution of the corregimiento. Corregidores were appointed to Crown villages (i.e., those that were subject to encomienda and that paid tribute to the Spanish king) by the Second Audiencia between 1531 and 1535, each empowered to act as "administrator of Crown charges, magistrate, tribute collector, and constable."[44] The portion of the Valley outside of the jurisdictions of the Marquesado and private encomiendas was carved up into nine corregimientos, centered in the important towns of Teozapotlan-Ixtepec, Chichicapan, Macuilxóchitl, Teitipac, Zimatlán, Tlalixtac, Mitla-Tlacolula, Ocotlán, and Guaxolotitlán. The corregimiento of Teozapotlan-Ixtepec was administered by the alcalde mayor of Antequera; all the others were placed in the hands of men appointed by the viceroys. Their annual salaries in 1545, paid from local tribute assessments, ranged from 150 *pesos de oro común* in Macuilxóchitl and Teitipac to 300 pesos in the larger towns of Chichicapan, Zimatlán, Guaxolotitlán, and Teozapotlan-Ixtepec. The corregidores of Tlalixtac and Mitla-Tlacolula both received 250 pesos a year, and the man in Ocotlán, 200.[45] As we shall shortly see, these salaries were extremely low compared with the quotas the Audiencia set for Antequera's encomenderos in 1547, but they were on a par with those of corregidores with even larger and richer jurisdictions in New Spain.

The legal status of the corregidor in relation to the alcalde mayor of Antequera changed over time. Before 1552 the two positions implied (at least legally) totally separate jurisdictions, but in that year all of the corregimientos were grouped into the Province of the Valley of Oaxaca and placed under the authority of the alcalde mayor. The latter was to administer justice in those corregimientos that had no resident magistrate and in a number of encomienda villages as well. In 1603 the alcalde mayor technically lost his jurisdiction in all but three of the corregimientos in the province, but occupants of that post appear to have continued to assert their authority in some areas as late as the 1630's.[46]

We also have little concrete information on the activities of the early corregidores in the Valley, but a statement from the bishop of Oaxaca in 1544 makes it clear that they ranked well below the encomenderos in terms of both power and wealth:

There are few who do not spend more in the administration of a *corregimiento* than the salary they receive. It will ultimately be clear what hopeless things these *corregimientos* are; their creation has served to increase the oppression and mistreatment of the natives because of the tribute collection. The *corregidor* must collect the tribute by a certain day in order to deliver it to the officials who must take it to Mexico City. If he does not take it or send it [the Indians] destroy it, and in order to give a good account of himself so that his *corregimiento* will be renewed for another year, the *corregidor* must jail the Indians and give them no respite. Those [Spaniards] who have *encomiendas* do not do this because by waiting and teaching [the Indians] to produce Castilian crops and goods, as well as helping them in times of need, they are able to collect [their tribute] and get enough to eat. A small town [i.e., encomienda] with its resources sustains a *vecino* very well, but the profit from four of Your Highness's [towns in corregimiento] together is inadequate to pay the *corregidor's* salary. This is so because [the corregidor's] only intent is to obtain his salary and make use of the Indians as best he can; he does not try to increase the revenue of Your Highness.[47]

The corregidor's salary, of course, did not accurately reflect his true income, since his position provided abundant possibilities to exploit the Indian population. In the first half of the century the abuses were limited to demands for labor, gold, and foodstuffs; later, and especially toward the end of the century, the corregidores turned to forcing the Indians to purchase goods at highly inflated prices.[48] Economic considerations aside, it appears that at least during the early period the post of corregidor was not especially prestigious, despite the opportunities it presented for personal enrichment. The city's cabildo protested to the Crown in 1551 that some corregimientos had been given to manual workers—masons, tailors, and potters—who, because of their low social status, were unable to deal effectively with the Indians.[49]

Most of the corregidores in the Bishopric of Oaxaca were vecinos of Mexico City who had no desire to establish permanent ties in Antequera, a fact that contributed in no small way to the city's halting development. From its very founding, Antequera suffered from the political patronage practiced by the viceroys and Audiencias in the capital. Apart from the cabildo posts, political offices were almost always given to Spaniards from Mexico City who had the requisite political connections, the vecinos of Antequera losing out more often than not. Antequera residents complained in 1539 and again in 1544 that most corregidores in the Bishopric of Oaxaca were vecinos of Mexico City, and that these offices should be given to local Spaniards.[50] Their protests were ignored, however, and the trend continued throughout the colonial period. By 1624, only three of the thirty-two corregimientos in the bishopric were held by vecinos of Antequera; all the rest were in the hands of residents of the capital.[51]

The Church played an influential role in both urban and rural Oaxaca from the very beginning of Spanish conquest and settlement. The early exploratory expeditions regularly included members of the clergy, starting with those of Orozco and Alvarado in Oaxaca in 1521 and 1522.[52] The institutionalization of religious authority began in 1529, when the Dominicans Gonzalo Lucero and Bernardino de Minaya arrived in Antequera with the other settlers sent by the First Audiencia. Fray Lucero immediately set about founding a monastery, and one of the first official acts of the cabildo of Antequera was to donate twelve lots (about three city blocks) for this purpose in July 1529.[53] The Dominicans lost no time in consolidating their position in Antequera and in numerous Indian districts in the Bishopric of Oaxaca. Owing to a lack of manpower, expansion was slow at the start, and the Dominicans established only one other monastery in the next fifteen years—in Yanhuitlán in the Mixteca Alta.[54] But by 1570 there were twenty-two Dominican establishments outside of Antequera, scattered over the Mixtec- and Zapotec-speaking regions of the bishopric. The two other principal mendicant orders, the Augustinians and Franciscans, were never influential in Oaxaca and took no part in the conversion of the Indians to Catholicism, thereby giving the Dominicans nearly an absolute monopoly in this sphere.[55] (The Jesuits and other orders arrived in Antequera later in the century and will be discussed subsequently.)

The Dominicans began their missionary work among the Indians in earnest at mid-century, founding doctrinas at Etla, Cuilapan, and the Villa de Oaxaca in 1550, Guaxolotitlán in 1554, and Ocotlán in 1562. By the end of the sixteenth century they had extended their reach to Teozapotlan, Santa Ana Zegache, Ixtepec, Santa Catarina Minas, Chichicapan, Tlalixtac, Tlacochahuaya, Teitipac, Teotitlán del Valle, and Tlacolula.[56] The urban Indians of Antequera and Jalatlaco soon came under their influence as well, a topic that will be taken up in Chapter 4.

The secular church established its hold in Oaxaca more slowly than the Dominicans. The province was under the jurisdiction of the Archbishopric of Mexico until the Bishopric of Oaxaca was created in 1535, with Antequera as its center and Juan López de Zárate as the first bishop (1535–55). During much of the century the secular clergy was outnumbered and outmanuevered by the Dominicans; Bishop López de Zárate was forced to appeal for more Dominicans in the early years because of a lack of secular priests.[57] Parochial duties were shared between the secular clergy and the Dominicans, though the latter controlled more than two-thirds of the bishopric's Indians by 1550 and were by far the most important churchmen in the Valley. Not surprisingly, this unequal balance of power led to tension and conflict between the Dominicans and the secular church, which first surfaced in 1551 and continued periodically throughout the colonial period.[58] The Dominicans nevertheless remained in charge of most of the Valley Indian parishes until the mid-eighteenth century, when they gave way to the secular clergy in Etla, Zimatlán, Tlalixtac, Teozapotlan, Cuilapan, and the Villa de Oaxaca.[59]

The Dominicans also found themselves in conflict with the city's cabildo on numerous occasions. By the late 1540's they had already acquired enough power and wealth to inspire envy among many of Antequera's vecinos, and the cabildo informed the Crown that the number of monasteries in the area should be limited, lest the clergymen enrich themselves at the expense of the rest of the Spanish population.[60]

The Encomienda

As in other Spanish towns in New Spain surrounded by large sedentary Indian populations, the encomienda was an important element in the economy of Antequera during the first half of the sixteenth century. The available documentation indicates that the encomienda in Oaxaca developed and declined at about the same time and in the same fashion as it did in other regions of New Spain, a historical process that significantly affected the economic position of Antequera and its vecinos. There were, however, two sets of circumstances that uniquely affected the distribution of encomiendas to Antequera residents, and that seriously retarded urban growth in the Valley for several decades. The first and most important was the fact that Fernando Cortés and his heirs controlled a large number of the Valley's Indians throughout the colonial period. The Marquesado's jurisdiction included many of the Valley's largest Indian communities, and though this did not totally preclude the exploitation of some Marquesado Indians as a source of labor for the city's vecinos, it did mean that the number of Valley towns available for distribution in encomienda was greatly reduced. Consequently, most of the encomiendas held by vecinos of Antequera were located outside of the Valley, scattered over a wide area within the Bishopric of Oaxaca. Secondly, only a fraction of the encomenderos with holdings in the bishopric actually lived in Antequera. Here again political patronage came into play, and many Oaxaca encomiendas were assigned to vecinos of Mexico City (and to a lesser extent, Puebla). Despite repeated protests from the vecinos and city fathers of Antequera, and occasional decrees from the Audiencia urging the province's encomenderos to take up residence in Antequera, the number of absentee landholders in the Bishopric of Oaxaca remained high throughout the sixteenth century.[61]

The encomienda in Oaxaca can best be discussed in terms of three periods: early development and peak before the 1550's; stabilization and decline in the second half of the sixteenth century; and decadence in the seventeenth century.

Encomiendas were assigned in Oaxaca as early as 1522 by Pedro de Alvarado from Tututepec, but the institution did not relate to urban development in the Valley until the 1529 settlement of Antequera. The conflict of interest between Antequera residents and the Marqués del Valle over encomienda rights in the Valley led to a stalemate, with neither side winning a clear-cut victory. By the early 1530's Cortés had been deprived of encomienda rights to many Valley towns, but so had the vecinos of Antequera. Most of the Valley encomiendas granted to them by the First Audiencia in 1529 were revoked by the Second Audiencia in 1531–34 and reverted to the Crown. Another, Tlalixtac, was assigned to the bishop of Oaxaca about 1537 but reverted to the Crown in 1544.[62] Only four encomiendas survived in the Valley after 1544—Coyotepec, Tenexpa, Ocotlán, and Tlacochahuaya.[63]

The large majority of Antequera's encomenderos possessed holdings outside of the Valley at some distance from the city, though all were within the confines of the Bishopric of Oaxaca. The Mixteca Alta was a major locus of encomiendas, especially the area around the populous towns of Teposcolula and Yanhuitlán. Both of these towns, together with Nochixtlán, Chachoapan, Iztactepec, Chicaguastepec, Tonaltepec, and Soyaltepec, were held in encomienda by city vecinos in the 1520's and 1530's.[64] Information is better for the year 1560, when at least nineteen of the city's vecinos held encomiendas in the Mixteca Alta, the Southern Zapotec and Chontal regions, and the Mountain Zapotec area.[65]

In return for the right to the tribute and labor of the Indians, the encomendero was legally required to protect them should the need arise and to see to it that they were indoctrinated in the Catholic faith. In practice, however, few encomenderos took these obligations seriously, and the institution operated basically as a disguised form of slavery during the first half of the sixteenth century. Three quotas (*tasaciones*) of goods and services to be rendered to Antequera encomenderos by the Indians of Tonaltepec, Soyaltepec (both in the Mixteca Alta), and Ixtepeji (a Mountain Zapotec community) in the 1530's and 1540's are illuminating. The first two communities, both held by Bartolomé de Astorga in 1536, had adult male populations of 70 and 100, respectively. Assuming that Tonaltepec (as well as the other communities I refer to here) met its quotas, it provided Astorga with twelve workers daily (ten men and two women); five turkeys and a jar of honey every twenty days; and ten pesos of gold and fifteen pieces of cloth every 60 days. In addition, the community worked certain plots of corn and wheat jointly with Soyaltepec. The larger of the two towns, Soyaltepec, furnished thirty-four workers daily; ten were assigned tasks in Antequera where the encomendero resided, and the others probably worked at mining placer gold. The town gave Astorga ten turkeys every twenty days and a number of other items every 60 days, including twenty pesos of gold, twenty pieces of cloth, 2,000 cacao beans, one *fardo* (bundle) of chile, one *carga* (half a *fanega*, thus about three-fourths of a bushel) of salt, one carga of pine logs, and two jars of honey. Its contribution to the plots worked jointly with Tonaltepec consisted of twenty cargas of seed for corn and five for wheat, roughly enough to plant forty-three acres.[66]

In 1543 the important Mountain Zapotec community of Ixtepeji (which had 374 houses in its cabecera around 1548),[67] provided its encomendero, Juan de Aragón, with these goods and services. It sent ten persons to the Valley each day to work as servants in the encomendero's household in Antequera; and each day he received one chicken as well. Every ten days the community gave Aragón 800 cacao beans, and every 70 days he got twenty-five pesos' worth of gold dust, twenty turkeys, two jars of honey, two loaves of bread, and two baskets of chile. Beyond all this, the encomendero provided the Indians with wool with which they wove thirty *mantas* (blankets or shawls) every 70 days. The community was required to deliver annually to Aragón in Antequera 500 fanegas of corn (about 750 bushels) and twenty cargas of beans (about fifteen bushels). Finally, it cultivated two plots of land sown with corn and wheat that the encomendero possessed in the Valley.[68]

Quotas for other Antequera encomiendas recorded around 1548 in the *Suma de Visitas* show that the amount of tribute the encomenderos were authorized to extract had been adjusted downward, though it is not known to what extent these legal quotas were observed. Nevertheless, the items given in tribute remained the same and clearly illustrate that the encomenderos were largely dependent on them for their subsistence. The fifteen Antequera encomiendas listed in the *Suma* for which there are adequate data regularly provided their holders with clothing (no doubt for resale), chickens, turkeys, salt, honey, chile, beans, corn, wheat, wax, and cacao. On the average each encomendero further received 254 pesos in gold dust annually. Each also had at his disposal a specified number of laborers on a daily basis; the actual number varied from six to sixty-two, but the average was ten to fifteen.[69]

The encomenderos' freedom to exploit the Indian population came under attack in mid-century, when the Crown tried to limit the growth of the institution. In 1549 a law was enacted that deprived encomenderos of access to Indian labor, and after the 1550's tribute quotas were fixed by royal officers.[70] Before long, most encomenderos found their power diminished and were left with a reduced income consisting of a yearly head tax. This is one instance where the force of law did have a considerable effect in determining the general shape of the colonial economy and social system. As Taylor points out, there is good evidence to believe that the 1549 law was enforced in the Valley of Oaxaca, for several landowning encomenderos were receiving drafts of corvée labor in the 1590's.[71] In 1560 twenty Antequera encomenderos were receiving the equivalent of 569 pesos in tribute annually, paid more often than not only in specie, grain, and chickens.[72] It is difficult to judge the remunerative value of the encomienda in 1560 as compared with

1548, but the continued decline of the Indian population, the rise in prices during the sixteenth century, and new restrictions on the use of Indian labor indicate that by this time encomiendas had become less profitable.

The encomienda in Oaxaca decreased in importance during the second half of the sixteenth century as it lost its once easy access to the labor supply and came to be redefined as essentially a privilege of collecting a head tax from a dwindling population. The majority of encomiendas held by Antequera vecinos in 1560 were still in effect by the end of the century,[73] but by then they were no longer a guarantee of power and prestige. Though encomenderos still tended to dominate Antequera's cabildo as late as the 1570's, by the 1590's most regidores and alcaldes ordinarios were non-encomenderos.[74]

In the seventeenth century the Valley encomiendas withered away. The Tlacochahuaya encomienda ended in 1639 with the death of Diego de Cepeda. The latest reference to the Ocotlán encomienda dates from 1628, when the encomendero petitioned for the right to demand all his tribute in specie rather than corn. Coyotepec survived as an encomienda as late as 1682, when it was in its fourth life and still in the hands of the descendants of its original holder, Bartolomé Sánchez. but by 1688 all encomiendas in the Valley and the surrounding territory were said to be defunct.[75]

Though the encomienda was an important factor in Antequera's settlement and a major source of power and wealth during much of the sixteenth century, its significance must not be overestimated. The proportion of resident encomenderos in Antequera was small, never numbering more than twenty to twenty-five during the course of the century.[76] Moreover, in the years when the encomienda flourished most as a mechanism of economic exploitation, Antequera's failure to grow in terms of both population and economic development was due largely to the stifling influence of the Marquesado. A tiny community of only about thirty households in 1526, the city did not increase significantly in size until after 1550, when the encomienda began its decline. As late as 1560 of the 59 encomiendas within the Bishopric of Oaxaca only twenty, or about a third, were held by vecinos of Antequera.[77] The remaining two-thirds were in the hands of absentee encomenderos living primarily in Mexico City and Puebla.

To sum up, an encomendero elite can be clearly discerned in Antequera up to the 1560's. It controlled by far the greatest amount of wealth and exercised political control through the cabildo. The encomenderos were also the chief entrepreneurs in Antequera during this period, and their ventures in mining and silk production will be discussed below. But during the last third of the century their prominent position was increasingly undermined by the drop in the Indian population and the efforts of the Crown to limit their powers. At the same time, the urban economy was on the upswing, the Spanish population was growing, and landownership was becoming increasingly important as a source of wealth, power, and prestige. A full-blown landowning elite did not emerge until the seventeenth century, but the process of land acquisition had begun.

Early Mining and Indian Slavery

As in other parts of Mesoamerica with well-developed state societies, the Spaniards in the Valley of Oaxaca were able to exploit for their own benefit existing labor institutions within native society. Slavery, community work service (*tequio*), rotating personal service for ranking nobles, the payment of tribute to local caciques, and a landlord-serf pattern within the cacicazgos were long-established institutions in the Valley that facilitated Spanish control over Indian labor.

Spanish economic interests in the Valley and adjacent areas in the 1520's and 1530's were largely confined to gold mines worked with Indian and Negro slaves. Placer gold was mined in the Etla arm of the Valley until the mid-1540's, but most mining activity took place outside of the Valley, particularly in the district of Las Zapotecas, the mountainous Zapotec- and Mixe-speaking region northeast of the Valley where the small Spanish settlement of San Ildefonso de Villa Alta had been established.[78] Gold was by far the most sought-after metal, though the available supply in Oaxaca was quite small compared with other parts of New Spain.

The principal miners in these years were the encomenderos. The procurement of Indian labor was the key to success, and those without encomiendas were at a disadvantage. Mining was frequently carried out by one man, though partnerships in which labor and tools were pooled were not uncommon.[79] Far from being a guarantee of instant riches, mining in Oaxaca was at best a risky enterprise, and only a handful of men managed to do much more than break even. Part of the problem was that the ore had to be taken to Mexico City for smelting, an arduous and costly journey that took several weeks. Not until 1538 did the Crown authorize the smelting of gold once a year in Antequera.[80] Mining appears to have fallen off considerably by 1544, when the placer deposits in the Valley had been exhausted. Activity did not pick up again until the discovery of mines in the Chichicapan area toward the end of the sixteenth century.

Indian slaves formed the bulk of the labor force in the mines. African Negroes were present in the Valley as early as 1529 and were considered physically superior to the Indians, but they formed only a small fraction of the total number of slaves.[81] Legally, a Spaniard could acquire Indian slaves only by means of a special license from the Audiencia, which stipulated the number allowed, specified that all slaves were to be branded by the alcalde mayor, and enjoined the slaveholder from removing them from his encomienda or selling them. Six such licenses issued to vecinos of Antequera in 1529 and 1530 have been located, each authorizing the "purchase" of thirty to forty slaves.[82] But the legal restrictions were for the most part ignored, and the available documentation indicates that slavery and encomienda were synonymous for Spaniards in the Valley during these years. Most miners obtained slaves from their own encomiendas either directly or indirectly. For example, Diego de Porras claimed to have purchased 120 slaves from his encomienda of Yanhuitlán, and the alcalde mayor Peláez de Berrio was said to have branded 200 slaves from Teposcolula, a town that he himself held in encomienda.[83] Spaniards commonly obtained slaves for a small fee from the caciques or principales of their encomiendas. Nuflo de Benavides, for example, paid 50 cargas of corn to the cacique of his encomienda, Chachopan, who in turn obtained twenty-five slaves from nearby Nochixtlán and Yanhuitlán. A few men managed to obtain large numbers of slaves to carry out their mining enterprises. In 1531 Peláez de Berrio was reported to have had some 400 slaves working in mines in Las Zapotecas.[84] Prior to the resettlement of Antequera in 1529, Fernando Cortés had more than 500 slaves from the Valley towns of Cuilapan, Etla, Guaxolotitlán, and the Villa de Oaxaca mining gold in the mountains.[85]

Slave trading was prevalent in the Valley in the 1520's and early 1530's. During the years 1529–31, when Peláez de Berrio was the most powerful man in Oaxaca, his brother the oidor Diego Delgadillo controlled a slave-trading network between Tepeaca and Guatemala. Antequera was a vital link in the chain, and Peláez traded wine, olive oil, and other goods for slaves in Chiapas and Guatemala.[86] It is likely, too, that the slave market at Miahuatlán south of the Valley continued to operate after the Spanish arrived, though no mention of it has been found.

Indian slavery in the technical sense was short-lived in the Valley of Oaxaca, as it was elsewhere in New Spain. As Charles Gibson has observed for the Valley of Mexico, slavery died out in good part because the encomienda proved to be more effective in harnessing the native institutions of mass labor.[87] There was only one reference to Indian slaves in the Valley after 1531 in the documentation I surveyed. This was in a 1550 inventory of the Marquesado cattle estates in the Valley, which mentions thirty-one Indian slaves and one Negro; twelve of the Indians were natives of other regions.[88] Legal restrictions also had a certain effect, to be sure. There was some discontent among Antequera vecinos in 1531 because slaves acquired through purchase or as captives of war had been ordered freed.[89] The so-called New Laws, promulgated in 1543, specifically forbade Indian slavery, and thereafter forced Indian labor came to be subsumed under the encomienda and the corvée labor system (*repartimiento*). But it would be a mistake to take these legal and administrative changes totally at face value, for the end result from the Indian point of view was not all that different.

The importation of Negro slaves increased in the Valley after the

1540's, though the total black population was never very large. Few Negroes worked on labor gangs in the mines; in the sixteenth century they more commonly served as "cowpunchers, laborers in sugar mills, and household servants for the Spanish in Antequera and for a few Indian caciques."[90] The overwhelming majority of Negro slaves lived in Antequera and were rapidly incorporated into Spanish urban society. The city was said to have 150 slaves (and 350 Spanish vecinos) in 1569,[91] and seventeenth- and eighteenth-century census data show that Negroes and mulattoes continued to be primarily urban dwellers during the entire colonial period.

Interregional Communications and Trade

Though quite small and beset by a number of political and economic problems in the sixteenth century, Antequera was the only Spanish town of any significance in the vast territory bounded by the city of Puebla to the north and Guatemala to the south. Located at a distance of some 80 leagues from Mexico City and 200 from Guatemala, the town was a convenient way station for traders and travelers coming and going from Peru via the port of Huatulco. There were three other Spanish settlements within the Bishopric of Oaxaca—Villa Alta, Nejapa, and Espíritu Santo—but by 1568 each was populated by no more than thirty Spanish families, and none of them ever became an important town.[92]

In the 1520's and early 1530's trade and communication between Antequera and the major sources of supplies—Veracruz and Mexico City—was extremely difficult because of the scarcity of pack animals and lack of roads. With draft animals unknown in pre-Hispanic Mesoamerica, trade routes were frequently little more than narrow footpaths. In the early decades of the century Spaniards commonly used Indian carriers (*tamemes*) as beasts of burden. This practice was frowned on by the Crown, but for all that, the vecinos of Antequera were authorized to use tamemes by the First Audiencia in May 1529, and Spanish goods and supplies reached Oaxaca from Mexico City and Veracruz largely in this manner in 1529 and 1530.[93] Permission was revoked by the Second Audiencia in 1531, only to be granted again by the Crown a year later in response to a plea from Antequera's cabildo to the effect that existing roads were often impassable with draft animals, and the colonists were consequently not receiving necessary supplies.[94] With one exception I have found no mention of the use of tamemes in the Valley after 1531, and it appears that pack trains (*recuas*) rapidly replaced the Indians as the chief means of transport.[95]

Road building began soon after 1529, and by the mid-sixteenth century Antequera had become a necessary stopover on the main route from Mexico City and Puebla to points south—Tehuantepec, Chiapas, Guatemala, and the port of Huatulco. Work began as early as 1531 on a road to connect Antequera with Veracruz; it followed the path of the modern railroad from Oaxaca to Puebla, passing through the Cañada de Cuicatlán, then on to Tehuacán. The portion between Antequera and Tehuacán was completed before 1544 and financed by the city itself.[96] From Tehuacán a road extended north to Mexico City, passing through Tecamachalco, Tepeaca, Puebla, Huejotzingo, and Texmelucan.[97] Another, less frequently used route to the capital in the mid-sixteenth century wound through the Mixteca Alta and Baja, passing through Nochixtlán, Yanhuitlán, Teposcolula, Tamazulapan, Huajuapan, and Acatlán. At Izúcar the road forked, the northern route passing through Atlixco to join the Puebla–Mexico City road, the southern route leading to Cuautla and into the Valley of Cuernavaca.[98] The present highways linking Mexico City and Oaxaca follow essentially the same routes.

Three other roads leading out of Antequera were completed during the first half century. A road to the south led to Huatulco, passing through the Valley towns of Zimatlán, Ejutla, and Miahuatlán, then through the mountains to San José del Pacífico, Río Hondo, and the coast. Travelers bound for Tehuantepec and Guatemala turned southeast at Antequera and followed much the same course as the Pan-American Highway takes today, passing through Tlacochahuaya, Tlacolula, Totolapa, Nejapa, Jalapa del Marqués, and Tehuantepec.[99] Another road, though only of local significance, ran northeast from Antequera to the small mountain town of Villa Alta in Las Zapotecas.[100]

Sources on the role of trade in sixteenth-century Antequera are few, but it is clear that nothing approaching a merchant class existed before 1550. During much of the early colonial period the city served more as a rest and replenishment center for traveling merchants and peddlers than as a locus of interregional trading activity. Bishop López de Zárate remarked in 1544 that "[religious] services should be maintained in [Antequera] because it receives many travelers bound for Guatemala, León, Peru, ports on the Mar del Sur, and other places."[101] The viceroy Antonio de Mendoza (1535–51) noted that the Antequera–Mexico City route was well traveled in this period because of the cacao trade,[102] and the wills of three Spanish traders who died in Antequera in the late 1530's and 1540's tend to bear him out. They mention cacao and goats as items of trade, and the men themselves had their principal contacts and base of operations in Guatemala, Soconusco, or Mexico City.[103]

The considerable traffic out of Huatulco, where shipping operations flourished from about 1537 to 1575, do not seem to have stimulated Antequera's economy to any great extent. Most of the merchants of New Spain who had regular dealings with Peru via that port were residents of Mexico City; Antequera was merely a funnel through which all goods had to pass. Woodrow Borah offers some useful observations concerning the Mexico-Peru trade in the mid-sixteenth century:

The manner in which the trade was carried on can only be guessed at. For the most part it was handled by merchants who traveled in person to invest their funds. If from Peru, they came north to select an assortment of merchandise and returned with specie or mercury. In only rare instances was the trade set up on a fairly permanent basis by appointing a factor. . . . The earlier merchants were essentially peddlers. . . . The ventures of the Marquesado were probably the largest in terms of capital involved during the 1550's and 1560's.[104]

The only known trader in Antequera during the first half of the century was the alcalde mayor Peláez de Berrio. His contacts appear to have been extensive; in 1529 and 1530 he obtained wine, olive oil, tools, clothing, and other goods from Veracruz and sold them to the local vecinos or traded them in Chiapas and Guatemala for gold and slaves.[105] If there were any other men so engaged in this period, all record of them has been lost.

In general, what little capitalistic and mercantile activity as there was in Antequera in these early decades was carried out by the encomenderos. A cleavage between urban entrepreneurs and those who depended more directly on the exploitation of Indian labor for their livelihood did not develop until much later. When mining became increasingly unproductive in the 1540's, many of Antequera's encomenderos turned to sericulture. By the end of the decade the silk industry had become firmly established in New Spain, with the Valley of Oaxaca and above all the Mixteca Alta emerging as the main centers of silkworm cultivation. Within the Valley itself sericulture was most prominent in the Villa de Oaxaca, Zimatlán, Etla, and Guaxolotitlán; in Antequera at least seven encomenderos had their Indians—most of them in the Mixteca Alta—cultivating silkworms by 1548.[106] Indeed, so many worms were raised in Oaxaca that in 1542 the viceroy was concerned about the Indians' being overworked and asked the bishop to determine how much silk each town could "comfortably" produce.[107]

It is impossible to determine with precision how the wealth gained from this activity was distributed among the vecinos of Antequera, but it appears that most of the profits went to the encomenderos during the first part of the century. Silk was not processed to any extent in Antequera at this time. Mexico City was given a total monopoly on silk dyeing and weaving in New Spain in 1543, and Antequera did not begin to participate in that industry until permission was granted by the Crown in 1552.[108] The only other product for export that the Bishopric of Oaxaca could claim in the sixteenth century was the cochineal dyestuff, but trade in this commodity does not appear to have been important before the second half of the century.[109]

Spanish Land and Livestock

As in other parts of New Spain, Spanish interest in landholding was minimal in Oaxaca during the first half of the sixteenth century.[110] The exploitation of the Indian population through the mechanisms of tribute and labor formed the basis of the regional economic system in the early years. Though Spanish landholding was certainly not unknown during this period, it did not become important until the mid-century, when the decline of mining, the decimation by disease of the Indian population, and the restrictions placed on the encomienda made land acquisition considerably more attractive to the colonists. Not until the 1550's did the city's land-holdings and economy significantly expand, and with them its population.[111]

It is important to distinguish between common lands and private holdings. From the earliest times all municipalities—both Spanish and Indian—were by law supposed to be endowed with communal lands for the use of all permanent residents. They generally consisted of woodlands (*ejidos*) and pasturelands (*dehesas*) for cattle grazing. As a rule, part of this land was held in common for all to use, part was distributed as arable fields to particular vecinos, and part—the *propios del consejo*—was rented out, thereby becoming a source of income for the municipality.[112]

With a large Indian population occupying most of the surrounding land and broad expanses of the outlying territory under the Marquesado's jurisdiction, Antequera had a difficult time in securing common lands. The first acreage designated by Peláez de Berrio in 1529 was a wedge of land stretching south of the city to San Agustín de las Juntas, where the Atoyac and Jalatlaco rivers join.[113] In February of the following year the Audiencia authorized the distribution of further plots to Antequera's vecinos, to be drawn in part from the "lands of Moctezuma" held by Huaxyacac before the conquest, with the stipulation that if any of the land belonged to the Indians they were to be paid for it. Only part of these lands were in fact parceled out because of vociferous Indian protests, and the grant was revoked four months later, though a witness in 1531 stated that some of the plots (*huertas*) nearer the city were still under cultivation.[114]

In 1532 the Crown favored Antequera with a grant of common lands extending to a one-league circumference of the city.[115] But given the realities of the Marquesado and the large Indian population, this concession was virtually meaningless. The following year the Audiencia once again granted the vecinos plots in the "lands of Moctezuma," plus others in the "lands of Huitzilopochtli" (the former preserve of the Aztec priests of Huaxyacac).[116] But again the city found itself in conflict with the Indian landholders, with the result that the lands of Moctezuma were soon redistributed to local Indian communities and set aside for the payment of royal tribute.[117]

Clearly, despite the efforts of the Crown and the Audiencia to provide the city with lands of some kind, the Indians were winning the battle. The cabildo informed the king in the late 1530's, that the vecinos "do not have tools or lands in which to sow and plant or do other types of work," and that they feared the city would be abandoned if the situation were not remedied. Antequera continued to depend in a parasitic manner on Indian land and labor into the 1550's, the Indians winning most of the contests until their dwindling numbers left much nearby land vacant and readily available for Spanish usurpation.[118] In 1544 the colonists were still largely landless and had turned to growing grapes and figs in the patios of their homes for lack of anywhere else to plant them.[119] Indeed, as late as 1550 the cabildo was ready to admit defeat and petitioned the viceroy (unsuccessfully) for permission to move the settlement to a more favorable location.[120] Antequera was apparently able to retain only the original ejidos marked out in 1529; records from the late seventeenth century indicate that at that late date the city was still virtually without grazing lands.[121]

In these circumstances, the city's vecinos inevitably began to encroach on nearby Indian holdings. Few Spaniards were interested in agriculture during the early years, and land was needed most for cattle grazing. Ganado mayor and menor were introduced by the Spaniards in large numbers during the first half century, and the need for pasture radically altered the Indian pattern of land use. At least five vecinos received grants of cattle estancias in the Valley from the cabildo in the early sixteenth century, but these were later canceled by the viceroy. Of the known viceregal estancia grants to

Spaniards in the Valley, only two occurred before the 1560's, the first in 1549 and the other in 1555. Spanish ranching in the sixteenth century was concentrated in the southern section of the Zimatlán arm of the Valley and portions of the Tlacolula arm, and damage to Indian crops in these areas was extensive. By 1549 the situation had become so serious that Viceroy Mendoza issued an order prohibiting cattle ranching in the Valley and requiring sheep ranchers to erect guards.[122]

The Urban Economy and Population

Though the early colonists of Antequera continually sought to acquire land for pasture, they were singularly uninterested in engaging in agriculture to sustain themselves, being content to rely almost totally on the Indians for food.[123] But the Indians were less than willing to cooperate, and the city suffered from periodic shortages of foodstuffs well into the seventeenth century. This became a problem as early as 1531, when the cabildo petitioned the Crown for lands on the grounds that the Indians could not be depended on for urban labor or a steady supply of foodstuffs, especially wheat.[124] Grain was still in short supply in 1538, when the cabildo again complained to the king, blaming the shortage on the fact that most Indian towns in the vicinity of Antequera were in corregimiento and therefore could not legally be compelled to sow wheat (or anything else).[125] And in the same year Bishop López de Zárate noted that the supply of corn was also inadequate, the result, he said, of the Valley Indians' not cultivating all the land available to them.[126] Compounding the problem was the fact that the Marquesado had a measure of control over the production of these items. The Etla region within its jurisdiction contained some of the most fertile land in the Valley, and early in the colonial period came to be the chief source of wheat, corn, and vegetables for Antequera.[127] In 1551 the marqués was said to hold a virtual monopoly on wheat production in the Valley, and the city urged the viceroy to order all Valley towns to plant a specified amount of corn and wheat each year so that the needs of the city could be met.[128] In the 1540's and 1550's the city was dependent on the Marquesado for its supply of meat as well, the marqués holding the monopoly for the town during these years.[129]

Food was not the only thing that was in chronically short supply in Antequera. The town was consistently pinched for municipal revenues as well. Far from being unique, this situation was the general rule throughout colonial Spanish America.[130] In most towns municipal funds were obtained from renting out portions of common lands or any property held by the municipality (*propios*). Antequera was extremely disadvantaged in this regard, having no land or property at all that could be used as a source of income. Town propios could be defined in many ways. In 1529 the alcalde mayor claimed the entire Villa de Oaxaca and its inhabitants as propios of Antequera, but this arrangement did not last long. Within a matter of months the Villa was returned to the jurisdiction of the Marquesado.[131] A few years later, in 1531, the city's emissary in Spain attempted to persuade the Crown to authorize the cabildo to distribute annually to the vecinos 100 *castellanos de oro de minas* to make up for the lack of propios. The king was reluctant to approve a cash payment of this magnitude, though he did authorize the distribution of "a quantity of *maravedises*." * Occasionally, the Crown allowed towns to use local judicial fines (*penas de cámara*) or a specific portion thereof for the financing of public works. In Antequera's case, this right was apparently granted only once in the first half of the century, for the three-year period 1532–34. In return, the cabildo was required to keep records of the amount spent and the purpose for which it was used.[132] In later years the city was given taxation rights (the *sisa*) on wine as a further supplement to municipal revenues, but neither this nor the income derived from the penas de cámara amounted to very much in a town as small as Antequera. In short, the only substantial source of "revenue" available to Antequera in the sixteenth century was forced Indian labor and, for a time, tribute revenues from the Indian community of Jalatlaco. This topic will be treated in detail in Chapter 4.

Antequera residents in the sixteenth century were also plagued

---

*Archivo General de Indias, Audiencia de México, 1088, lib. 2: 65r–65v. Three hundred maravedís commonly equaled 1 *peso de oro commún*.

by periodic Indian rebellions. Though little is known about them, it appears that most of the uprisings occurred outside of the Valley in areas on the fringe of Spanish control, primarily among the Mountain and Southern Zapotecs, the Mixes, and the Chontals. Few if any of the uprisings appear to have reached the vicinity of Antequera itself, but the colonists were clearly concerned about their safety and requested permission to build a fortress at least twice before 1550 (in the end, though, no fortress was ever built).[133]

One of the earliest disturbances occurred in 1530 at Ozolotepec in the Southern Zapotec region. One Spaniard was killed, and the Indians were said to be threatening any European who passed by the town. Ozolotepec was a major trouble spot for the colonists in the early years, prompting the alcalde mayor to call its inhabitants the "worst Indians of the land."[134] The only other rebellion in the sixteenth century that cost a Spanish life took place in 1547, when the Indians of Titiquipa (now Río Hondo) attacked and burned Miahuatlán, killing several Indians from Cuilapan and one Spanish tribute collector. The leaders of the uprising were determined to break the hegemony of the Spaniards and restore the pre-conquest situation, with the balance of power divided among the Aztecs, Zapotecs (at Tehuantepec), and Mixtecs.[135] Other rebellions were concentrated in the Mountain Zapotec, Mixe, and Chontal areas; one source states that there were ten uprisings in these areas prior to 1563.[136]

It is difficult to judge the true nature and significance of these events, for the only available sources are the inflated statements of Spaniards who hoped, with tales of personal valor or reports of the community's hardships, to procure special favors from the Crown. It appears that most of the rebellions were local affairs, involving only a few towns, and that they were primarily defensive attempts on the part of the Indians to retain their territorial and cultural integrity. There was no concerted attempt to destroy Antequera or remove the Europeans from the Valley; with few exceptions the uprisings were quelled by a small number of Spaniards and Nahua intermediaries with a minimum of bloodshed.

Given the problems involved in founding and sustaining a colonial settlement in the Valley, it is not surprising that Antequera's population remained quite small through the 1530's and 1540's. Beginning with only about 80 men (Spanish vecinos) in 1529, the city saw little or no growth in its first eight years; the population in 1537 still consisted primarily of the original settlers.[137] By 1544 the number of vecinos was reduced to thirty, and the figure was not to grow substantially until the 1550's. Antequera and other Spanish settlements during this period were subject to laws that forbade the townsmen to leave their place residence and establish homes elsewhere, but those laws were clearly unenforceable.[138]

Yet it would be a mistake to attribute Antequera's erratic development in the early years to purely local circumstances. All over the colony conditions worked to encourage settlers to pull up stakes and move on. By 1530 it was clear to many conquistadores that encomiendas were not so easy to come by, and that gold mining was beginning to yield diminishing returns in all but the richest sites. Discouraged by the lack of opportunity in Mexico, many conquistadores and settlers returned to Spain or the Antilles, or migrated to Peru. Veracruz, Coatzacoalcos, San Luis, Villa Alta, Zacatula, Colima, Puebla, Michoacán, and even Mexico City all experienced a similar population decline in the 1530's and 1540's.[139]

To sum up the social and economic situation of Antequera in the early years, as it was perceived by the colonists themselves, I quote at length from Bishop López de Zárate's report to the king in 1544. His account is somewhat exaggerated, but on the whole fits with the facts as we know them and is the only source of its kind for this early period.

With respect to secular matters in this city of Antequera, all is lost; so much so that things could not be worse short of total abandonment. Because the matter of the estate of the Marqués del Valle has not yet been settled and because he claims Oaxaca (which is the same as Antequera) for himself, the viceroy has not attended to the city or even visited here. The *vecinos* of Antequera are very needy and overworked since few of them possess anything, and if any ever were rich they are now dead. Because nothing is stable in this land, [the vecinos] have lost their wealth and property they had in Mexico City. [Antequera] stands alone, without people, and in great danger because there is no fortress or means of defense of any kind; and the natives have not completely given up their thoughts of rebellion, as is often written, said, and thought over there [in Spain]. Finally, it is impossible to understand, as I have said and written, how Your Majesty's Antequera and the marqués's Oaxaca (which are both the same thing) can belong to two different lords. This is not good for the Spaniards and even worse for the natives, because the Spaniards have no place to plant or harvest their crops except on the natives' land. The city has no woodlands, pasture, or exits of its own; consequently the natives cannot be treated as well as they should be because [the Spaniards] cannot but harm them with their cattle, which have nowhere else to go but onto the natives' land. This is the reason why the city has no wheat except what is bought from the marqués, and no supplies other than those sold by his Indians. Prices in general are so high that few [Spaniards] are able to sustain themselves any longer.

If no remedy is found, this land will no longer be worth inhabiting. The number of Spaniards in the city has declined so much that there are barely thirty *vecinos* left. Even these are trying to leave, and they will go and [the city] will be destitute (that is, without Spaniards) if the situation is not quickly remedied. All those who hold Indians [in encomienda] within this province and bishopric should be ordered to live in the city, and *corregimientos* established within the bishopric should be given to those who reside here. . . . Because the city was placed here maliciously to spite the marqués, adversity now plagues its inhabitants. They have fallen into the trap prepared for them by the original founders. The natives have grown in numbers and have encroached upon the outskirts of the city in such a way that they have not left the Spaniards passageway for their cattle, or pastures or woodlands for their animals, or lands to cultivate.[140]

As the bishop's words make plain, Antequera was barely able to hold its own during its first thirty years. After the 1550's its survival was no longer in doubt, but even then, trade and commerce were slow to develop. Until the mid-eighteenth century the city functioned primarily as an administrative center and hub of a regional market system. Economic and social ties to other areas of the colony were always present, to be sure, but they were of minimal importance, and it would be misleading to speak of economic integration or interdependence with other cities or regions.

Surrounded by substantial Valley Indian communities, which retained their demographic stability at least until the epidemic of *cocoliztli* (measles?) in the late 1540's, the city led a parasitic existence, depending on Indian labor and agriculture for its survival through its first several decades. Most aspects of the Indian society and culture probably survived more or less intact until at least the 1560's, when the position of the nobility was seriously threatened by the reorganization of the colonial tribute system.[141] These two circumstances—the persistence of much of the traditional way of life at the community level and the fact that the Indians were the chief producers for a small number of Europeans in a subsistence-oriented economy—gave the Indian population a considerable degree of independence from Spanish colonial society. To quote once again from Bishop López de Zárate:

> The Indians are so favored that they have the temerity to mistreat the Spaniards. They give them no food except for money, and then only if they are well paid and only when they want to, not when the Spaniards ask for it. Among them are constables who dare to arrest a Spaniard, and they tie him up and bring him to me or to other officials. For every little thing they know enough to come and complain. . . . The natives are in control of their resources and many of them are rich. . . . All the wealth of the land is in their hands, because they control all the provisions and sell them at high prices.[142]

Spaniards, Indians, and Blacks

Until the middle of the sixteenth century social differentiation in Antequera closely resembled the classic colonial situation, with a handful of whites ranked above a steadily increasing urban Indian population and a small group of black slaves. Social strata were defined in ethnic terms, and the cleavages separating the three categories were clear-cut and virtually absolute.

The Spanish community at this time was certainly marked by differences in economic and social status, but they were not nearly as sharp as they would become in later periods. Essentially, there were but two social groupings: in one were the twenty or so encomenderos and the clergy, who commanded the most prestige and influence; in the other those Spaniards who worked as artisans or at other manual occupations.[143] As the number of vecinos dwindled during the early 1540's, the encomenderos were able to consolidate their power in the community and effectively controlled the cabildo during these years. A list of eighteen conquerors-vecinos who sought special favors from the Crown in 1532 shows that almost all were encomenderos.[144] The less fortunate colonists who did not receive encomiendas were more apt to leave Antequera to seek their fortunes elsewhere.

The documentation for the period down to 1550 contains barely a word about Spanish women. Most of the original married settlers had left their wives behind in Spain or the Antilles, and it does not appear that women were present in any numbers before the mid-century. But the supply of Indian women was abundant, and if the Spaniards were often reluctant to marry them, they did not hesitate to take them as concubines. Indeed, when the alcalde mayor Peláez de Berrio came to the Valley in 1529, he brought along two daughters of Indian principales whom he had "kidnapped" from a convent in Texcoco. One of them died soon thereafter, but he lived openly with the other and expressed his affection for her in public on many occasions.[145] Many other early settlers in Antequera made similar arrangements with Indian women. Wills from the 1530's and 1540's show that though many Spaniards did not recognize their Indian concubines as wives (if they had married in Spain, this would have laid them open to charges of bigamy from the Inquisition), the children of these unions were usually acknowledged by their fathers and received part of the inheritance.[146]

That the illegitimate offspring of Spaniards and Indian women were to create considerable social and economic problems for the colonial regime was evident as early as 1533, when the Audiencia informed the Crown of a number of children of mixed parentage "who are lost among the Indians, and many of them die and are sacrificed."[147] As early as 1531 such *vagamundos* (literally, vagabonds) were accused of robbing Indian villages in the Valley.[148] On the whole, however, the number of such socially disenfranchised persons was quite small in the early part of the century. Rather, the children of Spaniards and Indian women in early Antequera came to belong to one group or the other, depending on the circumstances of birth. If a child's parents lived together in an open conjugal relationship, the child was likely to be identified as a Spaniard. The child born of a clandestine union or casual relationship had less chance of being acknowledged by the father and was apt to assume an Indian identity.

Negro slaves formed a third, though small, social entity. Those who married outside the group took Indian spouses. It is doubtful that any Spaniard of this period would have entertained the idea of marrying a black slave or recognizing as his own an illegitimate mulatto child. Negroes were regarded by the Spanish as being even more inferior and degraded than the Indians, and in this early period most offspring of white-Negro and Negro-Indian unions remained within the slave or Indian categories.

In sum, though the inexorable process of race mixture had begun, it was not yet of sufficient scale to require definitions of new categories of people or new ethnic identities. The few mixed offspring who had appeared were easily accommodated within one of the three ethnic categories, and the basis of Spanish power and white hegemony was not as yet threatened by any intrusive miscegenated sector. This situation proved to be short-lived, however, and before the sixteenth century drew to a close, the white vecinos of Antequera found themselves confronted with a number of ethnic and racial problems that few of them could have anticipated.

CHAPTER FOUR

The Crystallization of Colonial Society, 1550-1630

Changing Economic and Political Conditions

Economic and political conditions in the Valley changed markedly in the decades after 1550, and Antequera began a period of growth that continued into the 1580's. The city's jurisdictional struggles with the Marquesado del Valle eased during these years, and the development of Spanish landholding, coupled with the increasing cochineal trade and silk production, stimulated the local economy. Antequera's population began to increase steadily in the 1550's, and the danger that the town would depopulate altogether or be engulfed by the Marquesado soon disappeared.

A major impetus to urban development occurred in 1552, when Antequera received a license from the Crown to dye and weave the silk it produced. The city had petitioned for such a license on several occasions in previous years, pointing out the high cost of transportation to Mexico City and the need for more manufacturing to ensure the town's growth. As in Mexico City and Puebla (the only other cities authorized to produce silk goods at the time), guilds for ribbonmakers, embroiderers, and capmakers were undoubtedly organized in Antequera as "the city became a famous center of silk manufactures."[1] The silk boom tapered off in the 1570's, and the industry went into full decline about 1580. It limped along for a time, primarily as an Indian industry centered in the Mixteca Alta, then faded from the scene altogether in the seventeenth century in the face of competition from China. In 1794 there were only five silk looms in Oaxaca, all depending on imported thread for their product.[2]

Though of little importance before 1550, the cochineal trade greatly increased during the second half of the century, and by 1600 *grana* was second only to silver among New Spain's exports.[3] Puebla and Oaxaca were the two main centers of production of the dyestuff, and the prospect of quick fortunes undoubtedly attracted many aspirants to Antequera. The actual cultivation of the cochineal bugs was done by Indians under pressure from encomenderos, alcaldes mayores, and corregidores, but people from all levels of society were involved in the traffic.[4] Antequera's position as a focal point in the trade was bolstered in 1587, when all the grana produced in Oaxaca for export had to pass through the town to be registered by the alcalde mayor before it was shipped to Puebla, Veracruz, and eventually to Spain.[5] Cochineal was also a valuable item in interregional trade, and Antequera itself provided an expanding domestic market for the dyestuff after it became a silk weaving center.[6] The trade continued in Oaxaca throughout the colonial period, reaching its apogee in the mid-eighteenth century.

Increased Spanish interest in land and livestock after the mid-century was also important in ensuring Antequera's growth and permanence. William Taylor has confirmed twenty-five viceregal land grants to Spaniards and creoles in the Valley during the late sixteenth and early seventeenth centuries, most of them clustering in the 1560's and 1590's.[7] But the acquisition of land on a significant scale came only after 1570, when the silk boom ended and the city's population had risen to over 1,000. Before that, says Taylor, few Spaniards showed any real interest in land. The Spanish estates in this period were small and primarily devoted to raising cattle, sheep, and goats; not until 1630 did the hacienda and large-scale agricultural enterprise emerge in the Valley.[8]

Another kind of estate of some importance by the 1560's was the *huerta*, the precursor of the eighteenth-century *labor*.[9] Like the labores, the huertas were small, privately owned and intensely cultivated estates clustered near Antequera. They had the appearance of small family farms but used a system of labor more characteristic of the hacienda.[10] By 1565 there were forty-six huertas in the Valley, most of them owned by prominent Spanish encomenderos and vecinos of Antequera. Together they employed a labor force of 157 Indian families. Most of them were quite small and employed fewer than five families; five estates were in the middle range, using between six and twelve families, and the two largest enterprises employed twenty and thirty families, respectively.[11]

Most of these estates were acquired in the 1550's, when much land near the city was left vacant as its Indian owners fell to disease.[12] Indeed, Spanish landholding increased in an inverse relationship to the Indians' decline, the large hacienda estates emerging about 1630, the period in which the Indian population reached its nadir.[13]

Estimates put the Valley Indian population on the eve of the conquest at about 350,000. By 1568 the figure had dropped to about 150,000, and the slide continued unabated until the 1630's, when the total Indian population had been reduced to a mere 40,000 to 45,000—a decline of roughly 87 percent in a little over 100 years.[14] This demographic catastrophe, primarily the result of epidemic disease, had contradictory effects as far as the growth of Antequera and the local economy were concerned. On the one hand, it made it easier for the Spanish vecinos to acquire land and thus ensured Antequera's position as an agricultural and ranching center. On the other, it sharply curtailed the supply of labor available for urban construction, agricultural work, and mining. This was in part compensated for by the importation of Negro slaves, but as we have seen, there were never enough of them to permit their efficient use in corvée labor gangs.

Silver was discovered in Teitipac in the late 1570's, after the silk industry had begun to decline, and some years later other lodes were found in the vicinity of San Baltazar Chichicapan and Santa Catarina Minas. The deposits in the Valley were quite small in comparison to the much larger ones mined in northern Mexico, but they managed to provide a livelihood for many families until they were exhausted in the mid-seventeenth century. Mining operations took the form of individual capitalist enterprise. No one family or group of families succeeded in amassing great amounts of wealth; rather the pattern was that of a lone proprietor working a relatively small claim with an unstable supply of repartimiento labor. In general, mining in the Valley was hampered by a shortage of labor and lack of capital.

By 1578 operations were well under way at Teitipac, and the miners collectively petitioned the viceroy for a repartimiento of 100 Indians a week, to be distributed among them according to the size of their claims.[15] Most of the mineworkers came from the nearby Valley towns of Mitla, Tlacolula, Teozapotlan, Cuilapan, Macuilxóchitl, Ocotlán, and Chichicapan. Twenty-three years later, at the turn of the century, only four mines were being worked at Teitipac, and their repartimiento had been cut to forty-five men a week.[16] By this time new strikes had been made at Chichicapan and Santa Catarina Minas, and Antequera had begun to lose some of its population as the miners moved out to establish new settlements near each of these Indian towns.[17] Between 1598 and 1601 at least 79 claims were registered at these new sites, most of them averaging from ten to twenty square *varas* (a vara was roughly equivalent to 33 inches). However, many of these soon proved to be unproductive. For example, in 1605 the fairly substantial holdings in the estate of one of the first miners in Chichicapan, Alonso Ruiz de Huelva—over 185 square varas all told—brought only 150 *pesos de oro común* at a public auction.[18] In 1601 there were only about ten miners active in Chichicapan, each receiving a weekly repartimiento of ten or eleven Indians.[19] But soon after 1605 the output and the numbers of people involved in the Chichicapan mines increased rapidly, and by 1611 the miners were receiving a weekly repartimiento of some 400 Indians drawn from twenty-two communities.[20]

From this time until the 1640's silver mining clearly flourished in the Valley, but the lack of documentation for the second half of the seventeenth century suggests that the deposits had been largely exhausted by 1650. Only one document pertaining to colonial mining in the Valley after this date has been found. In it, we learn that

Gregorio Martínez de Otalvaro was mining silver and mercury at Teitipac and Tlalixtac in 1684.[21]

The impact of mining on the urban economy is difficult to assess. It is clear that the industry was controlled by Spaniards and creoles, and that many miners left Antequera in order to be closer to the base of operations. As early as 1579 silver from Teitipac was being used for coinage,[22] and in later years the increased volume of the metal undoubtedly created a need for more silversmiths. But there does not seem to have been any brisk trade in silver in Antequera; a document from 1620 mentions just five merchants who dealt in the metal.[23] The fragmentary data we have indicate that mining in the Valley was never as important to the local economy as agriculture and ranching. Mining involved a greater degree of risk and depended on a steady supply of labor; one of the principal reasons for the industry's failure to expand is that the mines flourished just at the time that the Indian population was reaching its lowest level. There is ample evidence to show that miners could not obtain enough laborers to work their claims effectively, and that the Indians in turn were overexploited and subjected to considerable abuse.[24] By 1643 the practice of buying and selling Indian laborers for work in the mines had become well established, and some persons apparently made a living off this new form of slave trading.[25]

Politically, the decade of the 1560's marked the last serious clash over jurisdiction between Antequera and the Marquesado del Valle. Hard-pressed for land, labor, and foodstuffs, the city in 1562 tried to wrest the towns of Cuilapan, Etla, and the Villa de Oaxaca away from the Marquesado and have them placed under the authority of the alcalde mayor of Antequera. The then-marqués, Martín Cortés, filed suit against the city the following year to regain his privileges and carried the matter one step further, arguing that Antequera's limits were confined wholly to the traza, and that since the land it occupied had belonged to Cuilapan and Huaxyacac in pre-Hispanic times, the city was rightfully his.[26] Given the realities of the situation at the time, the arguments presented by both the city and the marqués bordered on the absurd, and the case soon drew to a close, with the marqués retaining his jurisdiction over the Cuatro Villas and the city's position remaining unchanged. In the following decades, the Cuatro Villas jurisdiction became increasingly unprofitable. Once the port of Huatulco was eclipsed by Acapulco in the late sixteenth century, the Valley of Oaxaca became one of the least important and most neglected portions of the Marquesado holdings. Tribute collection became the prime source of revenue, and friction between Antequera and the Cuatro Villas decreased.

The Spanish City and Its Hinterland

There are unfortunately no detailed population statistics or descriptions of Antequera for the sixteenth and seventeenth centuries, and only a very general approximation can be pieced together from a few scattered sources. Table 1 summarizes the population figures for the city during the colonial period. Several of the figures for the sixteenth and seventeenth centuries are suspect, but they are the only statistics available. Particularly troublesome is the figure for 1579. From what appears to be a fairly accurate estimate of 980 people in 1569, it is difficult to believe that the population had risen to 2,500 in only ten years, an increase of over 150 percent. The source for the 1579 estimate is a *Relación geográfica* written by a local priest and is most probably an exaggeration.[27] What increase did occur during the 1570's can be attributed to the cochineal trade and the increasing availability of land to city vecinos. Population fell off during the period 1579–95, with the decline of the silk industry and the emigration of families to the newly discovered mines. During the seventeenth century the population again began to increase gradually, and the trend continued into the eighteenth.

The principal drawback of the sixteenth- and seventeenth-century estimates is that they exclude Antequera's Indian population. Even though considerable numbers of Indians were living in the city by the mid-sixteenth century, in the eyes of the Spaniards they did not qualify as members of urban society and were therefore overlooked in the population estimates. The 1569 figure of 980, for example, would have to be increased by as much as 50 percent to include the Indian population. (See Table 2 in the section on urban Indians, below).

TABLE 1

The Population of Antequera (Oaxaca), 1529–1970

Year	Households (vecinos)	Census or population estimate	Source
1529	80	320	AGN, Hospital de Jesús 293, *135*: 14v
1541	130	650[a]	RAHM A113: 29v
1544	30	150	CDII, 7: 547
1569	—	980	AGI, Indiferente General, 1529, no. 229: 3v
1579	500	2,500	Barlow, "Descripción," p. 135
1595	—	1,740	Cook and Borah, *Indian Population*, p. 83
1621	400	2,000	AGI, Audiencia de México 358
1628	—	2,000	Gage, p. 120
1643	600	3,000	Díez de la Calle, p. 177
1646	500	2,500	Gay, 2: 221
1660	—[b]	3,000	Portillo, fol. 145
1777	—	18,558	Cook and Borah, *Essays*, 1: 238
1792	—	18,008	AGN, Padrones 13; AGN, Tributos 34, 7: 51r
1797	—	19,062	Portillo, fol. 145
1804	—	18,626	Cook and Borah, *Population of Mixteca Alta*, p. 77
1808	—	17,000	Humboldt, 2: 242
1810	—	17,056	Humboldt, 2: 242
1815	—	15,704	Esteva, "Copias"
1826	—	18,118	Murguía y Galardi, fol. 20v
1970	—	99,509	IX Censo general de población 1971

NOTE: The figures for the sixteenth and seventeenth centuries do not include the Indian population.
[a] Adult men.
[b] Burgoa (*Geográfica descripción*, 1: 30) gives a figure of 2,000 vecinos.

As Table 1 shows, Antequera's population had increased considerably by the mid-eighteenth century. The cochineal boom and thriving textile industry accounted for much of the increase, and the recovery of the Indian population was a further contributing factor. The city's slow rate of growth prior to 1750 can be attributed to a number of things. Most important was Antequera's geographical isolation from the seat of power in Mexico City and the ports of Acapulco and Veracruz. The city of Puebla, midway between the capital and the Gulf coast, was more favorably located, and by the mid-sixteenth century had already eclipsed Antequera in size, trade, and manufacturing. Also of importance was the Valley Indians' success in retaining a considerable amount of land, "certainly

more than enough to meet their basic needs and keep them independent of Spanish landholders."[28] This state of affairs placed
severe limits on the Valley's potential as a center of Spanish agriculture and ranching, and Spanish estates in the region were consequently small and unstable compared with those of northern
Mexico.[29] For all these limitations, however, Antequera emerged
very early in the colonial period as the third-largest city in New
Spain after Mexico City and Puebla.

From the start, the plaza mayor was the heart of city life (much as
it is today)—the focal point of all important social, religious, political, and economic activities. Around it were located the principal
shops and businesses, and the residences of many members of the
elite. The cathedral occupied the same site as the present one (built
in the eighteenth century), standing on the northern side of the
plaza and facing west onto an open space. Lots for the casas de
cabildo were originally designated opposite the cathedral but were
apparently never used for this purpose, and the town council had no
permanent quarters of its own until it was housed on the southern
side of the plaza much later in the colonial period. The plaza mayor
was also the site of the city's weekly market, which began to acquire
some importance in the latter half of the sixteenth century; and on
Saturdays the square was filled with Indians from surrounding
towns selling their produce. As in many other preindustrial cities,
the plaza dominated Antequera both physically and symbolically;
the Spanish and creole elite clustered around it, pushing the poorer
inhabitants out toward the periphery. As Robert Ricard has remarked, "A Spanish American city is a Plaza Mayor surrounded by
streets and houses, more than a group of streets and houses around
a Plaza Mayor."[30]

In the early sixteenth century the area south of the Plaza de Santa
Catalina (the city's present market square and the heart of pre-
Hispanic Huaxyacac) was uninhabitable because of its proximity to
the Atoyac River, which flooded periodically. In 1561 the river was
rechanneled 550 yards to the south in the direction of Monte Albán,
giving the city some room for expansion.[31] The center of Spanish

settlement was to the north, east, and west of the plaza mayor, expanding outward from the center as the population grew.

Construction proceeded slowly in the early sixteenth century, but increased rapidly after 1550 to meet the needs of the growing population. The first structures, including private homes, churches, and public buildings, were almost uniformly built of adobe bricks with thatched roofs. Those who could afford them built houses of stone gathered from nearby quarries. Stone construction increased in the late sixteenth century, though adobe never lost its popularity. The style of Spanish homes generally conformed to the peninsular pattern of rectangular dwellings with a central patio where fruit trees and other plants were often cultivated.[32] By 1569 Antequera was said to have 200 houses.[33]

By far the most ambitious building programs were carried out by the religious establishment. The original contingents of Dominicans and secular priests were joined by a small number of Jesuits sometime before 1577, and a Franciscan monastery (*descalzo*) was in operation by 1569.[34] Before the end of the century the convents of Santa Catalina de Sena and La Concepción were established; and by then there was a small Augustinian monastery as well.[35] At the end of the century the city thus had twelve religious establishments of various sorts: the cathedral, three monasteries, a Jesuit college, two convents, and five churches.[36] Within a decade or two they were joined by two others: the monastery of La Merced and the convent of Santa Clara, both of which were completed by 1630.[37]

The Dominican order was the largest and most powerful in Antequera throughout the colonial period. Its original quarters had become inadequate by the mid-sixteenth century, and in 1558 the order had acquired twenty-four contiguous city lots for the construction of a new church and monastery.[38] Actual work on the church was not begun until 1575 and was still unfinished in 1628,[39] but the immensity and extravagance of the structure can be appreciated in Oaxaca today, where Santo Domingo stands as one of the monumental works of Mexican colonial architecture. The Dominicans also staffed the monastery of San Pablo, which administered the sacraments to the Indians of the parish of the Villa de Oaxaca.[40] The Dominican nunnery of Santa Catalina de Sena, founded in 1571 with the help of Bishop Bernardo de Albuquerque, rapidly became the most wealthy and prestigious of Antequera's convents; many of the daughters of the local elite entered the order in the late sixteenth and early seventeenth centuries.[41]

Antequera was built with Indian labor and continued to rely heavily on the Indians for foodstuffs and supplies during most of the colonial period. As in other Spanish cities in New Spain, "the white townsfolk ate food raised by Indians, clothed themselves in materials produced by Indians, and in most instances worked into cloth by them, lived in houses built by Indians and largely furnished by them, and remitted to Europe specie mined and processed largely by Indians."[42]

In the early sixteenth century Indian labor in Antequera was harnessed primarily through the institutions of slavery and encomienda, or various illegal means of coercion. Even in the early years, however, labor practices began to be regulated by the colonial bureaucracy, and a steady stream of permits began to emanate from Mexico City authorizing the use of Indian labor by particular individuals or institutions. In this manner the repartimiento system was established, whereby Indians were forced to serve on public works projects, in mines, on Spanish estates, and for a time simply as household servants.

The earliest known repartimiento grants for Antequera date from 1539–42, when several vecinos were authorized by the viceroy to use Indians from specific towns to build their houses. Permission was also granted to the secular church and the Dominicans to use Indian labor for the construction of the cathedral and monastery.[43] Such licenses frequently specified that the Indians were to be taken from certain towns or a certain class of towns (i.e., Crown, encomienda, or Marquesado), and that they were to be paid for their work, but seldom placed limits on the number of laborers that could be employed. These viceregal favors were available only to those with solid political connections, however, and many Spaniards resorted to more abusive tactics. In 1550 the Mixtecs of Cuilapan protested that villagers jailed by local Indian authorities were being removed by Antequera vecinos and put to work as laborers. Some years earlier, Viceroy Antonio de Mendoza had granted the city repartimiento rights over an unknown quantity of Indians, but the arrangement was apparently unsatisfactory, for at mid-century Antequera petitioned that its vecinos be permitted to take Indians from towns within a distance of five leagues of the city for house building and public works.[44]

As the city's population grew in the 1550's, the need for labor became more urgent, and by the 1570's large numbers of Indians were imported on a weekly basis from surrounding Valley towns for distribution to the white vecinos and for religious construction. In 1578 the city had official license to import 209 Indians each week, drawn from eleven towns.* The actual number was probably much higher, since evidence from other sources indicates that these quotas were frequently ignored.[45]

In the 1580's the office of *juez repartidor* (labor distributor) was created specifically to handle the increasing volume of workers, till then dealt with by the alcalde mayor. This change led to still worse abuses, for the jueces repartidores were paid according to the number of Indians they handled.[46] At the same time a system was established whereby each white vecino of the city was to receive at least one Indian a week for his personal service. In actual fact the distribution did not meet this ideal: Antequera's *procurador* (city attorney) pointed out in 1591 that since some vecinos received two Indians each week, many of the poorer whites were forced to go without.[47] Nevertheless, the practice continued until 1624, when repartimiento labor for personal service was prohibited by the Crown.[48] When one considers the number of laborers involved in church construction and public works in addition to those engaged in personal service, the figure must have been high indeed. In 1591, for example, a total of 105 workers were employed just in the con-

---

*The towns and their labor obligations were Cuilapan, 50; Teozapotlan, 35; Ocotlán, 25; Chichicapan, 20; Tlalixtac, 16; Teotitlán del Valle, 12; Mitla, 11; Tlacochahuaya, 10; Macuilxóchitl, 10; Tlacolula, 10; Coyotepec, 10 (Archivo General de la Nación, Tierras 2872, exp. 6).

struction of the monastery of Santo Domingo and the convent of Santa Catalina de Sena.[49]

As the sixteenth century drew to a close, the need for labor became more acute. More men were needed to work the expanding Spanish estates; and the mines and the city were pressed for labor as well. But disease had taken its toll, and the number of Indians available for repartimiento labor was steadily decreasing. By the beginning of the seventeenth century the Chichicapan mines were receiving large labor drafts at the expense of the city's quota, and it became clear that the Valley Indian population could no longer meet the labor needs of the Spanish colonial economy.[50] Consequently, the geographical area from which the city's repartimiento was taken was significantly expanded. Though undoubtedly an underrepresentation, a source from 1609 shows that in that year the urban labor force numbered some 300. Indians from the Valley accounted for 75 percent of the total, and the Mixteca Alta supplied another 21 percent; a little over 11 percent came from the Mountain Zapotec region, and the remainder came from two Peñoles Zapotec towns (a region southeast of Antequera, interstitial between the Valley and the Mixteca), three Cuicatec towns, and one Chontal town. The majority of the non-Valley Indians came from Mixtec-speaking towns in the vicinity of Nochixtlán and small Sierra Zapotec-speaking communities centered around Ixtepeji, Teococuilco, and Ixtlán.[51]

On any given day in Antequera there were thus hundreds of Indian peons, drawn from a wide variety of communities but speaking principally Zapotec, Mixtec, and Cuicatec. Many of them had traveled great distances—in some cases more than 50 kilometers—on foot over difficult terrain to reach the city, simply to repeat the tedious trek a week later as they made way for the next contingent. Repartimientos were supposed to last six days, Monday through Saturday, but in practice this rule was frequently violated, and Indians were often forced to work on Sundays as well.[52] Workers were also supposed to be paid for their services, and sometimes were, though it did not adequately reimburse them for the time they lost on the road and in the fields.

Where the repartimiento Indians lived while they were in Ante-quera is a matter of conjecture. Those assigned to personal service (usually no more than one or two) probably lived with slaves or in makeshift quarters in the homes of their masters. Possibly the ones who worked in large groups in church construction or public works projects were housed in labor camps at the work site or on the edge of town. There is no evidence to indicate that the workers brought their families with them to the city; most likely each repartimiento included a small number of women, who prepared meals for the men.

Since repartimiento personnel changed every week, there was no opportunity for permanent relationships of the patron-client or master-slave type to develop between the peons and Antequera's white vecinos. The system brought rural Indians into contact with colonial urban society in only the most fleeting and superficial way. Some, to be sure, became familiar with city life, notably those who chose to take up permanent residence in the city or who lived in nearby towns. But the repartimiento laborer's only meaningful rela-tionships in the city were with his co-workers, who were often from different ethnic groups and spoke different languages or dialects. In sum, the repartimiento system did not contribute significantly to the processes of acculturation, assimilation, or urbanization of the Indian population. It was the chief means by which the city was built, but it had no lasting impact on the urban social structure.

Though temporary agricultural repartimientos persisted in the Valley until the last quarter of the eighteenth century, the institu-tion in its urban manifestation died out by the mid-seventeenth cen-tury. Several factors contributed to its demise. The Crown was al-ways partial toward a free labor system, and the local whites were less than satisfied with the repartimientos, since the number of la-borers was never sufficient. Moreover, they disliked having to de-pend on regular renewals by the government and found it difficult to maximize productivity because workers had to be retrained every week.[53] What replaced the repartimiento system in Antequera after the mid-seventeenth century? Since there is no mention of corvée labor after this time, it appears that the growing urban Indian and mixed population came to assume much of the burden, and that with the city's economic expansion, the occupational structure was growing. In addition, the development of debt peonage side by side with the haciendas during this period made it possible for the hacendados to force their peons to work in the city when needed. The repartimiento system thus failed to bring about any real economic or social integration between Antequera and its hinterland because of its rotating nature and the fact that the Indians had nothing to gain from it and therefore resisted it.

The economic integration of city and country, when it came, resulted primarily from the Valley's developing regional market system. Antequera did not have a well-developed market of its own prior to 1570. In earlier years foodstuffs and other locally produced supplies were acquired by whites (often by force) directly from Indian communities or at the various Indian markets in the Valley. A city official noted in 1551 that Antequera's market remained little developed for precisely this reason, and in an attempt to remedy the situation the viceroy ordered that no one be allowed to buy corn, wheat, or other staples outside of the city, and that all such purchases be made instead at the market in Antequera's plaza mayor.[54] But his remedy did not cure the city market's ills, for it was still in so precarious a condition in 1563 that the alcalde mayor had Indians who attended the tianguis in the Villa de Oaxaca whipped and jailed in order to force them to come to Antequera instead.[55]

Though Antequera continued to suffer chronic shortages of foodstuffs well into the seventeenth century, a new set of circumstances emerged in the second half of the sixteenth century that threatened the heretofore almost complete self-sufficiency of the Indian population and forced city and country into a degree of interdependence. Of primary importance was the incorporation of a growing sector of Indian society into the colonial money economy through the rising trade in silk and cochineal and changes in the system of royal tribute. As discussed in Chapter 3, in the early decades of settlement tribute was paid in a wide variety of products and services, and Indians were ordinarily not required to make payments in specie. This changed significantly about 1557, however, with the imposition of a unitary tribute system, and by 1560 each adult Indian male was required to pay annually either to the Crown or to his encomendero eight silver *reales* and one-half fanega of corn. By 1565 the standard money quota per tributary had been upped to ten reales.[56] This requirement forced the Indians into a limited participation in the Spanish colonial economy.

By 1580 many Indians were offering for sale in Antequera's marketplace goods that in earlier years the colonists often had to obtain by force from Indian communities. The principal items sold were wooden beams and boards, charcoal, corn, wheat, beans, turkeys, and fodder.[57] Indeed, by the final decade of the century the obstacles to Antequera's development as a regional market center were due as much to the monopolistic practices of local corregidores and encomenderos as to the reluctance of the Indians to involve themselves in the cash economy. In many Valley towns corregidores and encomenderos routinely bought up several of the products that the Indians customarily sold in Antequera and then resold them to the city's residents at inflated prices.[58]

The Indians' growing involvement in the market economy was also reflected in the large number of Indian traders (*tratantes*) who were active in the Valley by the 1570's. Most of them seem to have been from towns in the Tlacolula arm of the Valley (including Tlacolula, Mitla, Teotitlán del Valle, Macuilxóchitl, and Teitipac), where farming was most precarious because of the lack of rain. All of these towns contained significant numbers of traders, who transported their goods to other Indian towns and Antequera by means of horses and pack trains.[59]

Thus by 1570 a pattern of economic integration between Antequera and its immediate hinterland can be discerned that was largely absent in previous years. The principles of the market system partially (but never totally) supplanted those of physical coercion in the economic relations between the colonizers and the colonized, and helped create a web of interdependence between Spaniards and Indians. Antequera had begun to create some wealth of its own and to escape its former parasitic dependence on Indian society. Valley Indians, on their side, found it increasingly difficult to ignore the city with its alien inhabitants once they came to understand that it was economically disadvantageous to do so. The large measure of independence they enjoyed from Spanish urban society in the early sixteenth century could no longer be maintained.

The Urban Indians

The Indians of Antequera and its satellite towns occupied a unique position in the colonial social system of the Valley of Oaxaca. From the very beginning of the colonial era the urban Indians were sharply differentiated from the Valley Mixtecs and Zapotecs, not only because of their role in urban society, but also because of ethnic, linguistic, and cultural differences. Indians living in and around Antequera in the sixteenth century were predominantly Náhuatl-speakers, descendants of the pre-conquest inhabitants of Huaxyacac or of the Nahuas from the central plateau who arrived in the Valley with Francisco de Orozco in 1521. Like the garrison of Huaxyacac in pre-Hispanic times, Antequera and its ring of Marquesado towns contained the Valley's entire Nahua population during the colonial period. Despite the eventual blurring of the cultural differences between the Valley Zapotecs, Mixtecs, and Nahuas as a result of prolonged colonial domination, each group succeeded in maintaining its language and ethnic identity well into the eighteenth century. Though there was considerable migration to Antequera from Valley Zapotec and Mixtec towns, the Nahuas effectively dominated the urban Indian sector because of their original status as allies of the conquerors and their superior skill as artisans. Second only to Spanish, Náhuatl quickly became the lingua franca among the Indians of Antequera, the language every Zapotec and Mixtec migrant had to learn in order to adapt to the urban setting.

As described in the preceding chapter, the Nahua towns of Santo Tomás Xochimilco, San Martín Mexicapan, Jalatlaco, and the Villa de Oaxaca were established at the time of the conquest or soon thereafter, and may originally have had as many as 4,000 inhabitants. All were under the jurisdiction of the Marquesado del Valle, with the Villa de Oaxaca as the head town. Jalatlaco, where most of the Nahua artisans lived (the other three towns were primarily agricultural), came under the jurisdiction of city authorities in the mid-sixteenth century. The diverse origins of the Nahua population are reflected in the names of the various barrios within these settlements, most of which were named after important Nahua towns in central Mexico. Xochimilco, directly north of Antequera and the smallest of the four towns, had three barrios: Chiautla, Tula, and Tecutlachicpan.[60] San Martín Mexicapan, a large town from the beginning, had four barrios: Mexicapan, Cuernavaca, Tepoztlán, and Acapixtla.[61] The Villa de Oaxaca had two barrios in the early sixteenth century called Istapalapa and Tlacopan;[62] most likely there were others not mentioned in the documentation. Jalatlaco had by far the largest number of barrios, and they will be treated below in some detail. The barrios of Cuernavaca, Tepoztlán, Acapixtla, and Istapalapa were inhabited by terrasguerros of the caciques of the Villa de Oaxaca, San Martín Mexicapan, and Xochimilco. With the consolidation of the cacicazgo of the Villa de Oaxaca, the towns of San Martín and Xochimilco were relegated to the status of dependencies, and by the eighteenth century these four barrios formed part of the terrasguerro community of San Pedro Ixtlahuaca, itself a part of the Villa's cacicazgo.[63]

Our present concern, however, is not with the terrasguerros, but with the so-called *naborías* of the city of Antequera. This term, of Antillean origin, was applied by the Spaniards to a certain category of Indian workers who, with the demise of Indian slavery in the 1540's, emerged to serve the needs of colonial urban society and were rapidly incorporated into city life. Neither slave nor truly free, the naborías worked as artisans to supply Antequera's material needs, as agricultural laborers on nearby Spanish huertas, as household servants, and as unskilled laborers on various public works projects. They did not, however, constitute a group in the sociological sense, nor did they share a common ethnic identity. On the contrary, Antequera's naborías were from diverse ethnic backgrounds, and the only characteristic they held in common was that they had all, for one reason or another, severed their ties with their native communities and cast their lot with Spanish society. Thus the term naboría had little descriptive meaning but was merely a catch-all word used by those in power to refer to urbanized Indians and those permanently employed in some servile capacity.*

On the basis of a census taken for tribute purposes, I have estimated that the adult urban naboría population—excluding household servants, who appear not to have been counted—numbered about 1,400 in 1565 (see Table 2).[64] Despite the Spanish policy of racial segregation, whereby the Indians were supposed to be confined to outlying settlements, some 450 naborías (32 percent of the total) lived within the traza of Antequera, about a third of them on the city's western fringe next to the Villa de Oaxaca. Roughly 28 percent of the naborías lived in the adjoining town of Jalatlaco, and 39 percent—the largest group of all—on or near forty-six Spanish-owned huertas. The ethnic diversity of the population is evident in the places of origin of the naborías (or their parents) listed in the census. Fully 47 percent were Náhuatl-speakers from large communities in central Mexico, and most notably from the Aztec capital Tenochtitlán, Colhuacán, Tlaxcala, and Tepeaca. About 8 percent were of Guatemalan origin, having been brought to Antequera during the early years of the conquest. The two largest groups after the Náhuatl-speakers were the Zapotecs and Mixtecs, who together accounted for 46 percent of the total. The census does not say from which communities they were drawn, but most were probably from nearby towns in the Valley. The numerical superiority of Mixtecs over Zapotecs, though seemingly anomalous given the predominantly Zapotec composition of the Valley as a whole, is not surprising when we consider that the bulk of the Mixtecs in the Valley were clustered in and around this area in pre-Hispanic times.

Apart from the city proper, the settlement of Jalatlaco was the chief place of residence of Indians who participated directly in city life and the urban occupational structure. Established soon after the conquest by the Spaniards' Nahua allies, Jalatlaco was built on lands

---

* Legally, the naborías were free to live wherever and with whomever they chose, and could not be bought or sold. But in practice they were forced to work against their will for particular Spaniards or for entire Spanish towns. Thus in the late sixteenth century the Indian residents of Jalatlaco were often referred to by the whites as "naborías of the city of Antequera." See Silvio Zavala, *Esclavos indios*, pp. 77–78; and Richard Konetzke, *Colección de documentos*, 1: xviii.

ceded to it by Antequera. As a result it soon came to occupy the status of naboría community to the city, for in return for their land and house lots, the Jalatlaqueños were obligated to serve the city and its Spanish vecinos in various ways. In addition to working as household servants and agricultural laborers, they served as assistants to Antequera's alguacil mayor in policing the city's weekly market (in 1590 there were fourteen such assistants), helped maintain the conduit that provided the city's water supply, served as caretakers of the town hall and jail, and formed part of Antequera's repartimiento labor pool.[65] During much of the sixteenth century Antequera also received tribute from Jalatlaco, which was used to finance public works projects and repair municipal buildings.[66]

In 1563, at the urging of the viceroy, another naboría settlement was established by the city authorities in order to accommodate the growing number of Indians who were settling on the fringe of the traza in a haphazard fashion.[67] The need for more space for the naborías was apparent as early as 1551, when a group of peddlers and artisans (*oficiales*) petitioned the city for a separate quarter of their own.[68] Crowding was greatest on the northwestern side of town adjoining the Villa de Oaxaca, and city officials were at a loss to find some solution to the problem, soliciting advice from the viceroy in 1552 on how to separate the city and the villa so that each would have its own entrances and exits.[69] Three years later the alcalde mayor, Juan Baptista de Avendaño, designated an area on the southeastern fringe of the traza as a settlement site for 220 Indian artisans and their families. A long list of conditions accompanied this grant of land, the most important being that (1) the settlement was to be reserved exclusively for artisans; (2) no Negroes or Spaniards would be permitted to live there; (3) the residents were to have no church of their own but were to patronize those of the city; (4) the settlement was to have no political officials of its own but be dependent on city (Spanish) authorities; (5) all residents were to work in the city on public works projects; (6) house lots were to remain the property of the city and could not be bought or sold by the residents; (7) the settlement was to have no cultivated lands of its own, for it was surrounded by Antequera's ejidos; and (8) no market (tian-

TABLE 2

The Adult Urban Indian Population of Antequera (Excluding Household Servants), 1565

Ethnic group or place of origin	Jalatlaco		City of Antequera								Total		
			Western fringe		Other parts		Huertas		Elsewhere				
	No. trib-utaries	Pop. est.	No. trib-utaries	Pop. est.	No. trib-utaries	Pop. est.	No. trib-utaries	Pop. est.	No. trib-utaries	Pop. est.	No. trib-utaries	Pop. est.	Percent
Nahuas													
Tenochtitlán (Mexicanos)	18	59	13	43	28.5	94	10	33	1	3	70.5	232	16.4%
Tlatelolco	.5	1	2	7	5.5	18	6.5	21	—	—	14.5	47	3.3
Colhuacán	14.5	48	5	17	4.5	15	6	20	—	—	30	100	7.1
Tlaxcala	21.5	71	1	3	5	17	6	20	—	—	33.5	111	7.8
Huejotzingo	2	7	—	—	1.5	5	6	20	1	3	10.5	35	2.5
Cholula	5	17	.5	1	3.5	12	1	3	—	—	10	33	2.3
Tepeaca	8	26	3	10	6	20	15.5	51	.5	1	33	108	7.6
Others													
Guatemala	8.5	28	1	3	14.5	48	6	20	2	7	32	106	7.5
Zapotecs	20	66	8	26	16	53	33.5	111	2	7	79.5	263	18.5
Mixtecs	22	73	11.5	38	7	23	75.5	249	—	—	116	383	27.0
TOTAL	120	396	45	148	92	305	166	548	6.5	21	429.5	1,418	100.0%

SOURCE: Archivo General de la Nación, Hospital de Jesús 285, 98.

guis) was to be held within the settlement.* These conditions show the strong measures taken to ensure that the artisans would remain permanently under the control of city officials; they also show that artisans as a group were sharply distinguished from other naborías.

The actual settling of the barrio of San Juan, as it came to be known, did not occur until 1563, largely because of the opposition of the Spanish vecinos to this use of the city's meager ejido lands. To what extent the original conditions were adhered to is not known, though earlier, in 1559, when other, non-artisan naborías had asked to be permitted to live with the oficiales, the viceroy had ordered the cabildo to locate them separately.[70] In any case, San Juan soon became a sujeto (or barrio) of Jalatlaco, and kept this status until the early eighteenth century, when it became a separate pueblo with the name Trinidad de las Huertas.[71]

With only fragmentary data to work with, we must piece out what we can of the internal social and political organization of Jalatlaco. But one thing at least is clear: the barrio differed considerably in many respects from most Valley Indian communities because of its multi-ethnic and heavily Nahua population, its economic and political subordination to Antequera, and its increasingly nonagricultural occupational structure. Politically, Jalatlaco was regarded as a barrio of Antequera until the mid-seventeenth century, when it became a separate pueblo. Though it possessed its own cabildo, composed of an alcalde, two regidores, and varying numbers of alguaciles, for all practical purposes Jalatlaco was under the jurisdiction of Antequera's alcaldes ordinarios and was effectively controlled by white city authorities.[72] Despite its close ties to the city, however, Jalatlaco did have a local cacique of Nahua descent, for in 1729 an Indian *principal* of Jalatlaco, don Antonio de Velasco y Moctezuma, was in possession of a cédula dating back to the mid-sixteenth century, when his forebear don Juan de Velasco had been given the rights to "the tribute, salt mines, and lands of some towns."[73]

*Archivo General de la Nación, Hospital de Jesús 285, exp. 98: 46r. The original settlement was made up of 40 weavers, 33 stonecutters, 31 shoemakers, 30 tailors, 22 carpenters, 16 gorget-makers, 15 candle-makers, 14 painters, 4 swordsmiths, 4 blacksmiths, 3 butchers, and 3 halter-makers. Five additional artisans worked either as stonecutters or as carpenters.

The ethnic composition of Jalatlaco in the sixteenth century was quite varied, and in 1565 the settlement contained representatives of all of the major ethnic groups that made up Antequera's naboría population (see Table 2). In that year Jalatlaco was divided into ten barrios, each named after the place of origin of its inhabitants. In each barrio, depending on its size, were one or more tequitlatos who were responsible for collecting the royal tribute from all residents of the barrio, as well as those members of the group who lived in Antequera or on Spanish huertas. According to the census figures shown in Table 2, Náhuatl-speakers accounted for 58 percent of Jalatlaco's population. Though the overall proportions of the different groups may be presumed to be fairly accurate, the figures almost certainly do not accurately portray the size of Jalatlaco's total population. The total of 120 tributaries for the entire settlement is undoubtedly too low; a tributary count made only the year before, for example, yielded a total of 257 married couples, 50 widows and widowers, 21 bachelors and unmarried women, and 36 youths still living with their parents.[74] No certain explanation can be given for this discrepancy, but it appears either that those listed in the second census as living on the huertas actually lived in Jalatlaco, or that many of those who were registered for tribute in Jalatlaco lived in Antequera. Furthermore, the 1565 census completely ignores the Indians who worked as household servants in the city, nor does it list any of the inhabitants of Jalatlaco who engaged in agriculture. There is no way of establishing the settlement's true size unless further data are uncovered. In any case, the implications for the maintenance of ethnic identity based on place of origin are clear enough.

During most of the sixteenth century the seven Náhuatl-speaking groups maintained separate identities. The policy of ethnic segregation practiced by the Aztecs in the settling of Huaxyacac in pre-Hispanic times and later by the Spanish colonial administration encouraged ethnic diversity. The role of the tribute system was also important in this respect. The colonial regime relied to a great extent on indigenous forms of organization for tribute collection, and the system was one of the principal determinants of social differentiation in the sixteenth century.[75] Thus tribute was collected separately from each ethnic group in Jalatlaco, and the pre-Hispanic office of tequitlato was maintained for this purpose.

At the same time, however, the possibility of a common Nahua identity and ethnic allegiance cannot be ruled out. As late as 1611 a knowledge of Náhuatl was indispensable for Spanish priests working in the parish of Jalatlaco; parish registers were kept in that language, and the various divisions of the settlement were identified as *tlaxilacalli*, a close Náhuatl equivalent of what is comprehended in the Spanish term barrio.* Moreover, the Aztec goddess Tonantzin (the predecessor of Mexico's patron saint, the Virgin of Guadalupe, who began to supplant her in the early sixteenth century) was worshiped in Jalatlaco, the only known instance of this practice in the Valley of Oaxaca.[76]

The place of Mixtec- and Zapotec-speakers within the complex network of urban Indian ethnic relations is less clear. Records from Jalatlaco dating from the early seventeenth century indicate that relatively large numbers of Zapotecs came from the Etla region, Teozapotlan (Zaachila), and Teotitlán del Valle,[77] and a large number of the Mixtecs were presumably from Cuilapan or its sujetos. In the urban setting, Mixtecs and Zapotecs occupied an inferior position relative to the Nahuas. In 1565 only 12.4 percent of the Mixtec and Zapotec naborías worked as artisans, bakers, or butchers in Antequera and Jalatlaco; the vast majority (75.9 percent) served as agricultural laborers on Spanish huertas. The pattern among the Nahuas was just the reverse: 81.4 percent were employed in urban occupations and only 20.3 percent worked as laborers on the huertas.[78] These figures suggest that of all the naborías, the Nahuas occupied a dominant position in terms of power and prestige, integration into colonial urban society, and

---

*Archivo Parroquial de Jalatlaco, *Libro de Casamientos*, 1611–31. There is still some confusion over the meaning of the term tlaxilacalli. Pedro Carrasco ("Social Organization of Ancient Mexico," p. 364) points out that it has been construed as synonymous with the Aztec *calpulli*, but can also refer to subdivisions or streets within a calpulli. In early colonial Náhuatl texts, however, it generally corresponds to the Spanish term barrio (ward). It was so defined by Fray Alonso de Molina in 1571 (*Vocabulario*, vol. 146r), and the Jalatlaco data seem to fit with this view. There is no evidence to indicate that the barrios of Jalatlaco were structured along kinship lines.

overall skill in the trades and services required by the city. The occupational roles of the Mixtecs and Zapotecs were largely confined to the lower-status jobs of manual laborer, peddler, and household servant. Further evidence for the pervasive Nahua influence is the fact that most of Antequera's Mixtec and Zapotec servants in 1579 spoke Náhuatl in addition to their native tongue. [79]

Thus by 1580 there was a developing urban Indian culture, primarily Nahua in orientation but strongly conditioned by the demands of Spanish colonialism, to which a migrant from the hinterland had to adapt. Regardless of his particular niche in the system, be it that of a household servant, artisan, or day laborer, the migrant was constantly in association with other Indians and was forced to acquire a working knowledge of Náhuatl (and some Spanish as well) in order to survive. The obvious question arises of whether, in the process, a migrant lost his identity as a Valley Mixtec or Zapotec, becoming instead simply another "urban Indian." In my own view, it seems unlikely that a migrant would have undergone a complete identity transformation even if he did learn Náhuatl and a new trade or craft. The reasons behind the decision to leave one's native village and make a new life in the Spanish city can be better understood in terms of "push" rather than "pull" factors. Most Indian newcomers to Antequera and Jalatlaco during this period viewed the city as a refuge from the problems that plagued the countryside: epidemic disease, harsh tribute quotas, the destruction of crops by Spanish livestock, and the abuses of the encomenderos and corregidores. As the possibility of leading a satisfying life in the Indian communities became increasingly remote, many families were drawn to Antequera in the hope of establishing a patron-client relationship with a vecino that would lead to favored treatment and possibly even an escape from the exigencies of tribute. Under these conditions, a change in identity from "Mixtec" or "Zapotec" to "urban Indian" probably did not occur, or at least did not occur so straightforwardly as that. For first-generation migrants, the process can be viewed primarily as the acquiring of a new situational identity specific to city roles that complemented rather than replaced the migrant's former identity.

By the end of the sixteenth century Mixtec and Zapotec migration was beginning to have an impact on the social structure of Jalatlaco, and traditional forms of organization were being threatened by the rising tide of newcomers.* In 1590 the Mexicanos, Colhuacanos, and Tlatelolqueños of Jalatlaco lodged a complaint that Mixtec- and Zapotec-speakers from the "sierra and other places" had settled in their midst, and had created considerable animosity because of their refusal to perform the communal duties required of all residents (such as tequio labor, alguacil service, and care of the parish church).[80] This was not an isolated incident, but rather evidence of an ongoing process of sociodemographic change that had important consequences for community organization.

One of the best measures of ethnicity and group solidarity available for the colonial period is found in parish marriage registers, which permit the calculation of rates of endogamy and exogamy. The earliest surviving records from Jalatlaco date from 1611, and a breakdown of the 380 identifiable marriages recorded there in the ten-year period 1611–20 is presented in Table 3. What is most immediately striking in the table is the proliferation of barrios since 1565, and especially barrios bearing the names of Valley Zapotec towns (Etla, Teozapotlan, Teotitlán, Coyotepec) or the generic name Mixtlán, "place of the Mixtecs" in Náhuatl. Meanwhile, we see that two Nahua barrios—Cholula and Huejotzingo—had disappeared, though a new one with a Náhuatl-derived name—Tetlamacazcau—had come into existence. The barrio San Juan, the artisan community formed in 1563, was also populated primarily by Náhuatl-speakers.

Lacking other kinds of supporting evidence, it is difficult to determine the settlement pattern of these barrios, though in all probability those with Nahua place names and Mixtlán en los Solares made up the core of the community, with the others distributed in sujeto fashion around the periphery. The references to the barrios of Ejutla and Coyotepec are probably erroneous and applied only to

---

* Not all of these came to reside permanently. There were significant numbers of Indians who lived in the urban areas for 4 to 6 months each year, returning to their communities for the remainder. I thank William B. Taylor for this information.

TABLE 3

Jalatlaco Marriages, 1611–1620

Barrio	Males marrying within barrio		Males marrying into other barrios		Males marrying out of community		Total number of marriages
	No.	Percent	No.	Percent	No.	Percent	
Zapotec names							
Etla	69	71.9%	19	19.8%	8	8.3%	96
Teozapotlan	14	50.0	11	39.3	3	10.7	28
Teotitlán (del Valle)	11	73.3	4	26.7	—	—	15
Ejutla	1	100.0	—	—	—	—	1
Coyotepec	1	100.0	—	—	—	—	1
Mixtec names							
Mixtlán de Diego García	22	66.1	7	19.4	7	19.4	36
Mixtlán en los Solares	10	38.5	13	50.0	3	11.5	26
Mixtlán de Alonso Martín	11	64.7	4	23.5	2	11.8	17
Mixtlán	6	85.7	1	14.3	—	—	7
Mixtlán Toctlan	1	50.0	1	50.0	—	—	2
Mixtlán en las Huertas	1	100.0	—	—	—	—	1
Nahua names							
Tepeaca	15	60.0	4	16.0	6	24.0	25
Tlaxcala	15	75.0	3	15.0	2	10.0	20
Colhuacán	14	60.9	7	30.4	2	8.7	23
Mexicapan[a]	14	60.9	7	30.4	2	8.7	23
Tetlamacazcau	11	64.7	4	23.5	2	11.8	17
Tlatelolco	9	75.0	2	16.7	1	8.3	12
Other							
San Juan	10	66.7	4	26.7	1	6.7	15
Guatemala	7	46.7	8	53.3	—	—	15
TOTAL/ AVERAGE	242	63.7%	99	26.1%	39	10.3%	380

SOURCE: Archivo Parroquial de Jalatlaco, *Libro de Casamientos*, 1611–31.

NOTE: In some of these cases, the man may have been only a part-time resident, but the records do not reflect that fact, and there is no way to control for this factor in calculating the rates of endogamy and exogamy. Fifteen unidentified marriages have been excluded.

[a] Presumably the barrio formerly identified by the authorities as Tenochtitlán (see Table 2).

individual migrants from those towns, and the names Mixtlán, Mixtlán Toctlan, and Mixtlán en las Huertas were probably alternative designations for the other three Mixtec barrios. Though no population figures are available for this period, it is fair to assume that most of these men stayed on in their barrios, and so the number of grooms from each barrio may serve as a rough indication of size. It is clear that the Nahua barrios by 1620 represented a smaller proportion of Jalatlaco's total population than they did in the sixteenth century. By far the largest barrio was Etla, with 182 marriage partners represented. Next in size, with a total of forty partners or more, were Teozapotlan, Mixtlán de Diego García, Mixtlán en los Solares, Tepeaca, Tlaxcala, Colhuacán, and Mexicapan.

Table 3 shows that there was a significant degree of endogamy (expressed as the percentage of males who married within the group) in Jalatlaco at both the barrio and the community level. Most difficult to interpret are the rates of endogamy for the barrios, which ranged from 38.5 percent in Mixtlán en los Solares to 75 percent for the barrios of Tlatelolco and Tlaxcala. In most cases, however, the rate is above 50 percent, and the overall percentage of men who married within their own barrio is 63.9 percent. These figures can be interpreted to mean that the barrios of Jalatlaco at their inception coincided with recognized ethnic divisions based on place of origin and maintained by a rule of preferential endogamy. By 1611, however, ethnic boundaries no longer coincided with geographical divisions; a degree of barrio endogamy was still present, but it was in the process of changing. From the place of origin recorded for several of these Jalatlaco residents, it is clear that migrants had arrived from many areas, and that the traditional barrio organization was breaking down. The process of the reduction of an ethnically diverse population into a minimally differentiated urban Indian proletariat would continue well into the eighteenth century.

Though the barrios were losing their original distinctiveness, Jalatlaco as a whole had acquired other characteristics that set it off sharply from the Indian settlements in and around the city. This was reflected in the high rate of community endogamy. Only 10.3 percent of the males in 1611–20 married out of Jalatlaco; over half of these took their wives from Antequera, and the rest married women from nearby villages. The most reasonable explanation for this pattern is that most Jalatlaqueños had become essentially urban dwellers engaged in nonagricultural pursuits, and viewed themselves as quite different from the other Indians on the outskirts of Antequera. In 1630 Jalatlaqueños identified themselves as the bakers, shoemakers, and tailors of the city of Antequera;[81] no other Indian community could make such a claim.

Jalatlaco was changing in another way as well, and this change, too, reflected its urban orientation. By 1630 it contained small numbers of mestizos, free mulattoes, and Negroes (who were accused of various unnamed offenses against the community's Indian craftsmen).[82] The presence of these non-Indians in the community was apparently a new phenomenon, for only three of the men whose marriages were recorded in the entire 1611–20 period were identified as mestizos; all the rest were designated as Indians.

Hispanic Society

The years after 1550 marked an important turning point in the social structure of Antequera. As the city acquired a degree of stability through the rise of the silk and cochineal trades and the tapering off of antagonistic relations with the Marquesado del Valle, its population increased and the social structure became more complex. By the 1560's there were several indications that the "crystallization" of Spanish colonial society in the Valley was well under way. Growth in the number and kinds of occupations generated by population increase and the dyeing and weaving industries provided a basis for a greater range of variation in socioeconomic status than had previously been the case. At the same time, the social boundaries that had made three distinct groups of the Spaniards, Indians, and Negroes were becoming blurred with the appearance of more and more castas, the progeny by and large of extramarital relations between Spanish men and Indian or Negro women and between Negro men and Indian women. As the numbers of these castas grew, it became increasingly difficult to accommodate them within the three groups, and the racial factor came to be an important criterion of social status, supplementing those of language, culture, religion, and the possession (or lack of it) of noble title. These key economic and racial factors, which were of only minimal importance in the early decades of settlement, now emerged as the primary criteria of social differentiation; and this development marked the solidification, or crystallization, of colonial urban society in Antequera. Once these characteristics became important in fixing a person's place in society, all the essential elements of the colonial stratification system were present, and changes in the system during the remainder of the colonial period can be explained by altered conceptions that placed a different emphasis on these criteria.

A crucial part of the crystallization process was the rise in Antequera during the second half of the sixteenth century of a small non-encomendero elite whose members, unlike the encomenderos, corregidores, and other appointees, did not depend directly on royal favors or the colonial bureaucracy for the legitimation of their status. Though encomenderos and officials were not excluded from this group, the major source of power and wealth lay in landholding and ranching. The evidence that this was the new avenue to economic and political power is found in various petitions to the Crown from several white vecinos of Antequera for licenses to establish *mayorazgos* (entailed estates).* The first known request was filed by Luis de Aguilar in 1560. In the next twenty years or so, several others follows: from Lope de Maya (1567), Pedro Sánchez de Chávez (1569 and again in 1575), Alonso de Canseco (1570), Rodrigo de Vegil (1578), and Bartolomé de Zárate (1583).[83] Detailed accounts of the property of all of these men are not available, but we do have information for two of them. Rodrigo de Vegil was said to own "much movable and landed property, including cattle ranches, many parcels of land, horses, and many other possessions with a total value of more than 40,000 *ducados*."[84] Luis de Aguilar at the time of his death in 1586 owned several ranches and garden plots, over 5,000 head of sheep, thirty or more donkeys, and several houses in Antequera.[85] With the exception of Aguilar, none of these men were successful in establishing mayorazgos, but their petitions

---

* Buildings, livestock, and land were eligible for entailment and once so declared were inalienable and not to be mortgaged. Primogeniture was the rule. If there was no legitimate son, the estate passed on to the nearest blood relative, with preference given to males. Clerics and mentally deranged heirs were excluded from succession, and the founder's family name had to be retained. (William Taylor, *Landlord and Peasant*, p. 153.)

reveal that they controlled substantial amounts of property. Of the six mayorazgos founded in the Valley during the colonial period, five were established before 1630 and the sixth in 1677. The Mayorazgo de Bohórquez at the time of its entailment in 1624 included various buildings in Antequera plus the Hacienda Valdeflores north of Santa Ana Tlapacoya, with five Negro slaves, seventeen teams of oxen, 470 head of cattle, and 3,500 sheep and goats.[86]

Most of Antequera's elite families during this period held a seat on the cabildo and protected their holdings and prerogatives through the exercise of political power. Luis de Aguilar served as regidor from 1564 to 1583; his son Cristóbal Ramírez de Aguilar held the same post from 1586 to 1623. Alonso de Canseco, Rodrigo de Vegil, Bartolomé de Zárate, Pedro Sánchez de Chávez, and Bartolomé de Bohórquez all served as alcaldes ordinarios at various times. The oligarchic nature of the cabildo reflected the pervasive influence of Antequera's elite in the economic and political affairs of the city. For the period 1564–1640, for which records are available, the same names reappear in the membership lists year after year. Some, if not all, of the regimientos (there were eight until about 1580, when the number was increased to ten) were purchased from the Crown, and it was not unusual for a regidor to serve ten years or more; a few in fact held on for as long as thirty years. It was also common for a man to be elected to the office of alcalde ordinario several times during the course of his life.[87]

The arrogance and ostentation characteristic of the elite in the late sixteenth century were symbolized most dramatically by one practice in particular: the one that saw the wealthy Spanish women conveyed about the city in litters resting on the shoulders of slaves and Indians.[88]

Equally important in the formation of colonial society in Antequera was the emergence of groups of racially mixed heritage as identifiable elements in the social structure. In the mid-sixteenth century the terms mestizo (applied to persons of mixed Spanish and Indian descent) and mulatto (applied to those with some evident degree of African ancestry) came into common usage, and the broader

category of castas was developed by the Spaniards to refer generally
to all people of mixed racial heritage. As was described in Chapter
3, for a time the offspring of mixed unions were assimilated easily
enough into the ranks of the Spanish, Indian, and Negro groups,
since they were few in numbers and did not represent a serious
threat to Spanish colonial power or the estate-based Iberian view of
society. A case in point was the family of the Antequera encomendero Bartolomé de Astorga, who never married but had two daughters by an Indian woman. Because they were openly recognized
by their father, both daughters were regarded as españolas and
eventually married two of Antequera's most prominent citizens.
In 1548 one of the daughters, Isabel de Astorga, married the encomendero Rodrigo de Vegil, who in subsequent years managed to
amass a considerable fortune. Isabel's sister made just as good a
match, marrying Antonio de Villarroel, also an influential encomendero, who served twice as alcalde ordinario in the city's cabildo.[89]

Soon afterward, however, the increasing numbers of miscegenated persons who were identified as such, and the castas as a
whole, came to be seen as a threat—groups whose claims might well
upset the hierarchical estate society. In the words of Lyle McAlister, "Their existence was deplored. They really were not supposed
to exist. In the eyes of most of the white population they were lazy,
vicious, irresponsible, and a threat to social and political stability."[90] No early written accounts have been found that tell us specifically how Spanish vecinos felt about the castas, but a letter of 1552
to the king from an Augustinian friar in Mexico City sums up the
alarm that was undoubtedly prevalent among the white elite:

The low and wretched peoples and the slaves have caused the most tyrannical and cruel disturbances and revolts. It makes one think about where this
land is headed, now that it is becoming populated by a mixture of such a
bad people. It is clear that this land is full of mestizos, who are very badly
inclined; it is full of Negroes, who are slaves; it is full of Negroes who marry
Indian women, who in turn give birth to mulattoes; it is full of mestizos who
marry Indian women, engendering a diverse group [casta] of great numbers. And from all these mixtures are derived other diverse mixtures that
are not good.[91]

The socioracial categories elaborated by the Spaniards to classify all members of colonial society were more socially than biologically determined. They were ostensibly based on skin color and descent, it is true, but they also rejected the white colonists' attempt to preserve their power by denying other groups access to it. A further defining criterion for the castas in the sixteenth century was the stigma of illegitimacy. The word mestizo at that time was virtually synonymous with "illegitimate," and biological mestizos born in wedlock and recognized by both parents were commonly defined as creoles (or rather, as españoles, the term in use at the time).[92] The lack of correspondence between genetic and social mestization is seen in the fact that the numbers of mixed-bloods in the census records for Antequera remained relatively small during the entire colonial period. Without exception, the "creoles" always constituted the largest segment of the city's population despite the very extensive miscegenation. The implications of this imbalance between biological process and social categorization for a theory of social stratification in New Spain will be discussed in subsequent chapters.

Discrimination against the miscegenated found its justification in the Spanish doctrine of *limpieza de sangre* (purity of blood). In sixteenth-century Spain, at certain levels of society the preoccupation with establishing the orthodoxy of one's lineage had become almost fanatical. Proof of descent from Old Christian stock, free of the "taint" of Moorish or Jewish blood, was a precondition not only for noble status but for membership in artisan guilds, religious and military orders, and municipal councils.[93] Any person who could not demonstrate such a claim was thought to be inherently and morally inferior. Racist as this doctrine was, with its emphasis on blood as the medium through which superiority or inferiority was transmitted, its ultimate justification was religious. Once transferred to the New World, however, the concept became more patently racial as the threat to orthodoxy shifted from religion to race. Thus people of mixed racial ancestry were thought to have "bad blood" that made them inherently inferior beings. Most damaging of all was evidence of black ancestry, for in addition to the stigma of slavery with which Negroes had to cope, they were regarded by the Spaniards as physically repugnant. Mulattoes therefore ranked below the mestizos in prestige, and like Negroes were eligible for slavery and royal tribute whereas the mestizos were not.

We have two sets of figures on the numbers of castas in Antequera in the latter half of the sixteenth century. One is the rough estimate of Bishop Albuquerque, who in 1568 stated that a third of the city's vecinos were mestizos or mulattoes. Another, more detailed estimate made the following year put the count at 350 Spanish vecinos, 150 slaves, 50 mestizos, and 30 mulattoes.[94] This would appear to conflict with the bishop's estimate, but when we also take into account the wives of the vecinos, it becomes clear that the castas may well have composed one-third of the city's non-Indian population, which is what the bishop's statement can be interpreted to mean. Surely many of the Spaniards had mestizo or mulatto wives or mistresses, and we may safely surmise that few of the mestizo and mulatto vecinos had Spanish wives. So of the estimated 980 non-Indians in Antequera in 1569, it is reasonable to classify 326 of them as castas.

As the mestizo and mulatto groups emerged as identifiable elements in the social structure of New Spain, they became the target of a number of legal decrees that attempted to limit their social and economic mobility and permanently exclude them from positions of power and authority. Taken together, these laws do not add up to a coherent definition of the place of these groups in society, but can be seen as merely stopgap measures to preserve the powers and privileges of the colonial elite.

The first legal restriction on the freedom of the mestizos and mulattoes was issued in 1549, when Charles V decreed "that no mulatto, mestizo, or man of illegitimate birth be permitted to hold Indians [in encomienda] or royal or public office without a special license from the Crown."[95] Several years later Philip II informed the viceroy and Audiencia of New Spain that he was aware of the growing numbers of Negroes, mulattoes, and mestizos in the colony but was not sure how to deal with the problem.[96]

Mestizos came to be legally regarded as superior to the mulattoes since they were unaffected by slavery and had no Negro blood. Nevertheless, in the 1570's they were excluded by law from the positions of Protector of Indians, Notary Public, and cacique, and were forbidden to live among the Indians. In 1643 they were also prohibited from becoming soldiers.[97] Furthermore, in many towns they were barred from becoming *maestros* (masters) in the municipally organized artisan guilds.[98] Yet the stance of the law and Spanish colonial officials toward the mestizos was frequently ambivalent, a fact that reflected the heterogeneity of the mestizo group itself. This is well illustrated in the following report to the Crown by the Royal Secretary Juan de Ledesma in Mexico City in 1574:

> New Spain has a large number of mestizos who are all permitted to ride on horseback. In this they are quite agile, and they are very bold people. For entertainment they go to the cattle ranches and run the cows and young bulls till they drop. They are a people extremely given to vice, and the caciques follow their example in riding on horseback. No one has looked into this, or considered the difficulties and dangers that could arise from this situation. . . . With regard to the licenses that are given to some [mestizos] to carry arms, I have them come before me and give them to understand that I consider them as Spanish as the Spaniards, provided they live in a virtuous and Christian manner; and [instruct them] that on all occasions they must identify themselves with the Spaniards, and never with the Indians, mulattoes, or Negroes. . . . The Spaniards are so defenseless and careless that it would be wise to decree two things: (1) that no Indian or mestizo be permitted to own horses or ride on horseback, and (2) that mestizos and Negroes be forbidden to own or carry arms. It should also be decreed that all Spanish vecinos of New Spain be equipped with arms and horses and be prepared, for there are many who do not even have swords.[99]

This statement expresses two contradictory views that were widely held at the time. On the one hand, all mestizos were regarded as inherently vicious and dangerous and a threat to the established order. On the other, those mestizos who were able to obtain special privileges, such as the right to carry arms, were somehow different and were in fact regarded as Spaniards. This meant that despite the legal restrictions, the possibility of upward social mobility did exist and in some cases was even encouraged. Whether this was a rare occurrence or not in Antequera is difficult to say. Clearly, some of the city's mestizos succeeded in getting privileges. In 1563 two of them were granted licenses to carry swords "for the defense of their persons," though they were expressly forbidden to possess firearms; and another such license was granted in 1583.[100] Four years later, in 1587, a mestizo named Diego Núñez Sedeño was licensed to carry a sword and dagger, "notwithstanding any provision that forbids sons of Spaniards and Indian women to carry arms, since don Juan de Guzmán, *alcalde mayor* . . . of Oaxaca [Antequera], certifies that he is an honorable and virtuous man and the son of a conquistador."[101]

Other mestizos were less successful in realizing their ambitions, however, particularly those who sought to enter the priesthood. In 1568 Philip II prohibited mestizos from becoming ordained priests, though twenty years later he relented to the extent of permitting ordination if the man could prove his legitimacy.[102] The Church authorities in Antequera took the matter seriously and in 1582 sought the Crown's advice on whether the prohibition also applied to sons of Spaniards and mestizas.[103] But the advice, it seems—the reply was negative—was not what the Antequera clergy wanted to hear, and they strove to maintain the Church's exclusivity. In 1602 two sons of the Antequera vecino Martín Alonso were denied entrance to the clergy because their father was a mestizo and their mother's mother a mestiza. The two brothers challenged the decision, and a hearing with witnesses was held before an alcalde ordinario in which it was stressed that the brothers' parents were legally married and were both of Old Christian stock.[104] The outcome of the dispute is not known, but the difficulties encountered by the two brothers show that legitimacy by itself did not necessarily permit a mestizo to pass as a Spaniard.

Mulattoes in the late sixteenth and early seventeenth centuries were socially and economically more homogeneous than the mestizos, and ranked below them in prestige. Their chances of upward mobility were even more limited, not only by reason of their skin color but also by reason of their eligibility for slavery. As in other parts of Latin America, mulattoes in New Spain were subject to the same laws as Negroes. "In addition to the restrictions imposed on the mestizos, they were liable to pay tribute like the Indians. They might be sent to forced labor in the mines, but should then work apart from the Indians to prevent them from abusing the natives. Their movements were restricted, their dress was regulated, and they were strictly prohibited from owning firearms."[105]

Viceregal decrees forbade mulattoes and Negroes in New Spain to form religious sodalities (*cofradías*) of their own, to gather together in large groups, or to possess their own homes if they were unemployed. Women were not to dress in silk clothing or wear jewelry made from gold, silver, or pearls. Those persons of color who were unemployed were ordered to work as household servants of "known masters" on pain of 200 lashes and five years of forced labor in the Philippines. Finally, no more than two Negroes or mulattoes could accompany a Spaniard in public, though there was no such restriction placed on mestizos or Indians.[106]

Little specific information is available on the status of mulattoes in Antequera during this period. Taking the Negro and mulatto populations together, however, it is clear that in 1569 the large majority were slaves: by the census count there were 150 adult males held in slavery against only 30 (presumably free) mulatto vecinos.[107] Like mestizos, free mulattoes could apply for licenses to carry arms, and two cases have been found for Antequera. In 1620 an illegitimate mulatto son of Luis Ramírez de Aguilar, a wealthy hacendado and cabildo member, was licensed to carry a sword and a dagger; and in 1632 Marcos de Matos, a mulatto married to a creole woman, had received a license for a sword and dagger but was rebuffed by the viceroy when he requested permission to carry firearms.[108]

Most free mulattoes and mestizos in Antequera worked as household servants, artisans, peddlers, or unskilled laborers. Outside the city, some found employment on Spanish ranches and at the Chichicapan mines. Valley Indian towns occasionally lodged complaints about abuses committed by Negroes, mulattoes, and mestizos, though only four instances are known for the period 1576–1638.[109] Moreover, *mestizaje* in the Valley was primarily an urban phenomenon, and the vast majority of the castas identified more with colonial Spanish society than with the Indian sector. Despite their generally low socioeconomic position, they were nevertheless held to be *gente de razón* and were considered part of the Hispanic community as opposed to Indian society.

Social differentiation was further complicated in this period by the growing rift between peninsular Spaniards (*españoles europeos*) and creoles (*españoles americanos*). Though all the Spaniards of Antequera were identified simply as españoles in the documentation, the distinction between the two groups was well established by the early seventeenth century, as shown by an incident witnessed by the English traveler Thomas Gage in 1626:

Oaxaca . . . is of so temperate an air, so abounding in fruits, and all provision requisite for man's life, so commodiously situated . . . that no place I so much desired to live in whilst I was in those parts as in Oaxaca, which certainly I had attempted as I travelled by it, had I not understood that the Creole or native friars were many and as deadly enemies unto those that came from Spain as were the Mexicans. And this their spite and malice they shewed whilst we were there, to an ancient and grave old friar, Master in Divinity, who living had been for learning the oracle of those parts.

This old man died when I was there, and because when he lived they could pick no hole in his coat, being dead they searched his chamber, and finding in a coffer some moneys which he had not made known to his Superior when living (which they would reduce to a sin against his professed poverty, called propriety, and subject to the censure of excommunication), they reported that he had died excommunicated, and might not enjoy their Christian burial in the church or cloister, and so ignominiously buried their old divine, and with him his credit and reputation in a grave made in one of their gardens. A thing much talked on as scandalous to all the city and country, which they salved with saying he was excommunicated; but the truth was, he was of Spain, and therefore at his death they would shew their spite unto him. . . . With this which we saw with our eyes, besides what with our ears we had heard of discords and factions amongst them, we thought Oaxaca was no place for us to live in; so after three days we made haste out of it, and departed toward Chiapa.[110]

By this time the creoles had developed their own variant of Iberian culture, heavily influenced by native Mesoamerican society and the colonial situation. Cultural differences and the friction arising from the frequent exclusion of creoles from offices in the colonial bureaucracy and high positions in the Church hierarchy now so separated the peninsular and native-born Spaniards that from this period on they must be viewed as two distinct ethnic groups.

Finally, there was also increasing socioeconomic differentiation among the creoles themselves. To be a creole did not automatically imply inclusion in the local elite or a prestigious occupational standing. On the contrary, many creoles were employed as lower-status artisans, and by the mid-seventeenth century they often worked side by side with mestizos and mulattoes at the same jobs. In short, the outlines of a more complex mode of stratification based on the intersection of racial and economic criteria were well in evidence by the mid-seventeenth century, a development we shall look at more closely in the next chapter.

CHAPTER FIVE

Continuity and Change, 1630-1750

The Economy

Beginning about 1630 and continuing through the first half of the eighteenth century, the Spanish exploitation of land by means of Indian labor became the basis of the regional economy of Antequera. This was the age of the hacienda, a new kind of colonial estate devoted to ranching and agriculture with an Indian labor force held in bondage through the institution of debt peonage; and ownership of land was now the key to positions of wealth and power in the city. Mining was of little importance in the Valley after 1650, trade was still very rudimentary and locally oriented (with the single exception of the cochineal traffic), and manufactured items for export were largely confined to cotton textiles produced in Indian towns and in a small number of *obrajes* (sweatshops) in Antequera. The city's population remained small during the seventeenth century—probably below 6,000—and though it increased somewhat during the first half of the eighteenth century, appreciable growth did not occur until the cochineal and weaving boom began in the 1740's.

The most noteworthy aspects of the development of Spanish landholding in the Valley were, first, the instability and relative smallness of the estates, and second, the fact that it did not entail any great losses of land or agricultural self-sufficiency on the part of the Indian communities.[1] The Indians held onto the bulk of their lands throughout the colonial period, and only a few communities became dependent on Spanish haciendas or on sharecropping arrangements. Against this background of Indian resistance and self-sufficiency, the Spanish haciendas emerged about 1630 as the Spaniards moved to meet the growing demand for food in the city at a time when the size of the Indian population had reached its lowest point.

By 1643 the Valley contained forty-one haciendas. Most were cattle estancias with a few tracts of cropland. Horses, sheep, and goats were also often raised, and the principal crops were corn and wheat; sugarcane was grown occasionally, and some hacendados experimented with small amounts of beans, fodder, watermelon, and cochineal. The Valley estates differed considerably in size, but most were relatively small, encompassing less than 3,000 acres, and only a handful achieved any degree of political and economic independence comparable to that of the large haciendas of northern Mexico.[2]

Great amounts of land were concentrated in the hands of a few families after 1630, and individual Spaniards and creoles owned more land in the seventeenth century than they did in the eighteenth. Six families possessed large entailed estates, or mayorazgos, that flourished during the seventeenth century: the Ramírez de Aguilars, the Jaúregui Pinelos, the Maldonados, the Bohórquezes, the Lazo de la Vegas, and the Guenduláins. The mayorazgo estates came closest to resembling the large haciendas of northern Mexico, and their perpetuation within family lines, primarily by means of primogeniture, was ensured by the laws of entailment. The holders of entailed estates succeeded in maintaining their position among the elite even when their resources were declining. They were prominently represented in the cabildo and the Church hierarchy, and their social rank gave them a degree of influence independent of the offices they held.[3]

The mayorazgos, however, were more the exception than the rule. Most Valley estates were much more modest, and few of them were stable properties transferred through inheritance. The hacendados on the whole showed little concern for primogeniture in the transfer of non-entailed estates. Holdings were often divided among several relatives, and many owners chose to sell their properties rather than preserve them for their heirs. Nor was it uncommon for estates to be heavily mortgaged. Thus Antequera's landowners did not represent a closed, homogeneous, self-perpetuating group, and most new owners were not wealthy men.[4]

In sum, privately owned Spanish estates in the Valley tended to be relatively small and unstable, were often unproductive, and were closely tied, both politically and economically, to Antequera, where most of the landowners resided. The estates did not follow a course of steady expansion during the colonial period, but were subject to dramatic fluctuations in productivity and value and changed hands frequently. This precariousness of agricultural and ranching activity had a significant impact on Antequera. Spanish estates developed in order to meet the demand for foodstuffs in the city, but at least during the seventeenth century they were not wholly able to do so.

Droughts and the monopolistic activities of corregidores and various entrepreneurs were in part to blame for the haciendas' lack of success, but their own inability to produce a significant surplus and the Indians' unwillingness to plant more cash crops were fully as much to blame. In 1632 Antequera's supply of corn and wheat reached such a critical level that the alcalde mayor requested that he be given jurisdiction over the land within a ten-league radius of the city in order to force the Indians to produce more.[5] Another wheat crisis occurred in 1642, when several Spaniards were buying up grain in the Villa de Etla and San Juan del Rey and reselling it at highly inflated prices.[6]

The decade of the 1680's was especially grim for the people of Antequera who suffered through shortages and high prices year after year. In 1681 the Virgen de la Soledad was paraded through the streets in an effort to secure divine intervention to increase the food supply; the following year corn was imported from Puebla to meet the city's needs. Blaming the city's plight on the lack of rainfall and the monopolistic practices of several of the merchants, some cabildo members argued for the establishment of a municipally controlled grain market (*alhóndiga*). One perceptive regidor, who opposed the idea, emphasized that other Spanish cities did not face the same problem as Antequera, with its heavy dependence on the indigenous population for its foodstuffs:

Those that supply this city are the Indians from nearby towns, who come on Saturday, the designated market day, with their loads of corn and sell them at very reasonable prices. If they were compelled to come to an *alhóndiga*, the hardships of these poor and wretched people would only increase at the hands of those who meddle with the distribution of the corn. . . . It would be different if the city was supplied by Spaniards [i.e., haciendas], as in other cities that have *alhóndigas*, since [hacendados] have no other market for their products and can sell them easily [in the cities] without being exploited.[7]

Another regidor concurred, noting that Valley haciendas produced little apart from their owners' subsistence needs, and that the small surplus they sold in Antequera was not enough to warrant the administrative costs of a grain market. In the end, however, the proponents won out, and an alhóndiga was established soon after 1690.[8]

It is clear, then, that during the seventeenth century Antequera continued to rely heavily on Indian production for its food supply, and that most Valley haciendas were not especially productive.* The Indian population continued to form the basis of the regional economy as it had in the sixteenth century, the principal difference being that the mechanisms of exploitation had changed and were now more closely tied to the market system. The role of the Indian in the colonial economy is vividly illustrated by a practice that became institutionalized among the corregidores and alcaldes mayores in the seventeenth century: the *repartimiento de efectos*. This was

---

*The supply of meat, however, was always in Spanish hands. Contracts for the meat supply were awarded each year to one man by public auction. But even here, by all evidence, the Valley hacendados were often unable to meet the city's requirements. In 1703–4, for example, a large share of the cattle that were slaughtered for urban consumption were brought from the isthmus of Tehuantepec. Some 20 years later, in 1722, no rancher would have anything to do with the contract, and the cabildo was forced to take on the job itself, ordering a herd of cattle beef raised on pastureland rented from nearby Indian communities. (Colección Castañeda Guzmán, *Libro de Despachos*, fols. 111v–116r; Archivo General de la Nación, Mercedes 70: 116v, and Hospital de Jesús 348, exp. 21.)

the practice by which political officials (and often hacendados as well) forced the Indians to accept money or basic goods in order to establish a bond of obligation and create a captive market for certain products.[9] The amounts of cash and the prices paid were of course determined by the Spanish official. Thus the Indians were forced to part with their products for prices considerably below the market level and at the same time were obliged to buy certain goods at highly inflated prices. This artificially induced system of supply and demand came to be a mainstay of the colonial economy and was virtually foolproof as long as the Indians continued to accept it without violent protest.* Very often the official acted as an intermediary for a peninsular merchant, who in return provided the money for the *fianza* that the official had to pay to the Crown for his post.[10]

This form of exploitation was present in the Valley in incipient form in the late sixteenth century and became full-blown as early as the 1640's. In 1647 the bishop of Oaxaca accused the alcalde mayor of Antequera of monopolizing commerce in the region and taking advantage of Indians and Spaniards alike.[11] In 1669 Indians from Tlalixtac, Tlacochahuaya, Zaachila, and San Martín Tilcajete complained to the bishop of recent repartimientos forced on them by the alcalde mayor. Those of Tlalixtac had been required to buy 60 pesos' worth of soap, a barrel of wine, and 50 yoke of oxen at prices ranging from a third to a half above the going rate. In addition they were given eighteen *arrobas* (about 450 pounds) of cotton that they were to spin into thread and sell back to him for a third of its normal market value. The Indians of Tlacochahuaya were likewise obliged to spin cotton and buy oxen, soap, chocolate, candles, and wine; by their claims the alcalde mayor's profit margin figured to be at least 200 percent.[12] Similar protests were lodged by the Indians of San Miguel Chichicapan and Coyotepec.[13] A slightly different form of the repartimiento was employed in the mid-eighteenth century by

---

* Refusal to comply was not unknown. In 1660 the harsh repartimientos of the alcalde mayor of Tehuantepec sparked a rebellion in which he lost his life. The revolt then spread to the towns of Nejapa, Ixtepeji, Villa Alta, Teutila, Teococuilco, and Huajuapan, and on into the Puebla and Tlaxcala regions. See Basilio Rojas, *La Rebelión de Tehuantepec*.

the alcalde mayor of the Cuatro Villas jurisdiction, who ran a store in the Villa de Oaxaca that all the Indian communities within the confines of the Marquesado were forced to patronize. The items sold consisted of such staples as tobacco, sugar, cacao, candles, cinnamon, salt, cloth, and machetes. Collective debts owed to the store by some communities in 1751 ranged as high as 264 pesos for the Villa de Oaxaca and 218 pesos for Santo Tomás Xochimilco.[14]

These practices had little effect on the Indian marketing system, however, and the indigenous network of trade in the Valley remained strong. The largest Indian markets in the late seventeenth century were located at San Juan Chilateca and the Villa de Etla; both not only drew Indians from many areas, who came there to trade in cochineal, cotton mantles, and other local products, but also attracted white merchants from the city, who put Castilian goods up for sale.[15] In 1717 Mitla was authorized to hold a weekly market with the expectation that it too would serve as an outlet for some city traders. Other Valley Indian markets were held at San Andrés Huayapan, Tlacolula, and Ocotlán.[16] Of the non-market towns, Francisco de Burgoa singled out Teotitlán del Valle and Coyotepec as being the most commercially oriented. Both contained substantial numbers of traders, who dealt in such items as knives, machetes, scales, cloth, fish, and salt. The weaving of woolen blankets and zarapes continued to be an important activity in Teotitlán, while Coyotepec produced substantial quantities of lime, pottery, metates, and pulque.[17] Many other Indian towns also had strong local industries. Tlalixtac and Tlacolula produced pulque and mezcal both for local consumption and for the taverns of Antequera; weaving was important in Santo Domingo del Valle (now Díaz Ordaz), Tlacolula, Mitla, and Macuilxóchitl; Santa Cecilia produced wooden spoons; Azompa was a major pottery center; and several towns on the edge of the Valley sold firewood and charcoal in local and regional markets.[18]

Despite the vitality of the Valley trade, Antequera continued to play only a limited role in interregional commerce during the seventeenth century. The city experienced a degree of social and economic isolation after 1630, as mining activity in the Valley ground to a halt and the outside demand for cloth and hides declined.[19] The silk industry had long since collapsed, and the Pacific port of Huatulco was little used after 1600. Manufactured items for trade were limited to small quantities of yarn, thread, cotton cloth, and cotton mantles.[20] Even then, not all of these articles were produced in Antequera; many of the mantles and much of the yarn and thread for export were manufactured in Indian communities under threats from political officials. Textile sweatshops in the city were few, and they rarely employed more than four or five workers. Among the 426 men who married in Antequera between 1693 and 1700 for whom occupations were listed, there were only four weavers and three dyers.[21] In 1698 a guild of obraje workers (including spinners, weavers, and carders) that was centered in Xochimilco but drew its membership from the city as well had just forty-one members.[22]

Because of its geographical location, Antequera continued to serve as a way-station for Guatemalan indigo dye and cacao en route to Mexico City and Veracruz.[23] Other articles important in local commerce about 1670 were vanilla, wheat, corn, chick-peas, beans, chile peppers, fruit, flowers, medicinal roots, lumber, and annatto.[24]

The single exception to the diminished trading activity of the seventeenth century was cochineal, which continued to be Oaxaca's chief export and the most lucrative trading commodity. Burgoa estimated that about 10,000 arrobas (250,000 pounds) left the bishopric each year in the late 1660's; most of it was funnelled through the hands of a small number of Antequera merchants, one of whom shipped as much as 25,000 pounds annually.[25]

In accord with the sluggish economy of this period, urban growth and population increase were slow, and Antequera attracted few migrants. Of the 1,257 persons of known provenance who married in the city between 1693 and 1700, only 153 (12.2 percent) were born outside of the Bishopric of Oaxaca (including 60 peninsular Spaniards and 14 Negro slaves). Fully 72.3 percent of the non-Indians in the group were born in Antequera. Of the 464 persons born outside of the city, Indians constituted the single largest group, accounting for 40.7 percent of the total.

Woodrow Borah has described the seventeenth century in New Spain as a century of depression, caused primarily by the catastrophic decline of the Indian population at a time when the non-Indian population in the cities was growing.[26] Though P. J. Bakewell has recently questioned this hypothesis, particularly for the silver-mining region of Zacatecas, where he found no evidence of a long-term labor shortage,[27] the data from Oaxaca tend to support it. The question then arises of how far into the eighteenth century these conditions persisted in Oaxaca and whether they were partially alleviated or intensified. William Taylor has discerned an economic decline in the Valley during the first half of the eighteenth century as evidenced in the slight downward trend in the numbers of livestock on the haciendas and an overall increase in the mortgage values of Spanish estates.[28]

It seems that the economic doldrums of the seventeenth century carried on and even intensified in the Valley until the beginning of the cochineal boom in the 1740's. As Taylor points out, the area was hit by a series of natural disasters in the early eighteenth century, notably "droughts, frosts, wheat blight, and a fatal epidemic among cattle and sheep."[29] And then we also know, from several references, that the Valley had a vagamundo problem in the late seventeenth and early eighteenth centuries.[30] Many of these rootless people preyed on Indian communities; some were no doubt out-and-out thieves, but others were desperate men unable to find work in the city in a time of economic contraction. In the 1730's the city jail was overflowing with "vagabonds" and "idle people," and in 1742, 108 prisoners were transferred to Veracruz for lack of space. In the group were forty-two Indians, twenty-four mestizos, twenty-one creoles, eighteen mulattoes, and two Negroes; the background of one person is uncertain.[31]

The Urban Indians

What little population increase the city saw during the seventeenth century resulted primarily from the in-migration of Indians from the Valley and the surrounding region. This process brought a further deterioration of ethnic distinctions among the urban Indians and a blurring of the division between principales and macehuales. Antequera's service needs created a demand for the Indians' skills and labor, and they assimilated to Spanish urban society with little difficulty, though they continued to form a relatively closed and highly exploited ethnic group. Apart from a small number of caciques and principales, Indians uniformly ranked at the bottom of Antequera's social hierarchy. Though by now a number of the residents of the Villa de Oaxaca, Xochimilco, and Trinidad de las Huertas can be characterized as urban in terms of their occupations and ties with the city, we have few data for these towns during this period, and our discussion must necessarily focus on Jalatlaco and the city proper.

Counter to the trend in most Valley towns in the late sixteenth and early seventeenth centuries, the population of Jalatlaco increased steadily during this period and after, in keeping with its role as a reception center for Indian migrants. In general, Jalatlaco's population increased steadily until the early eighteenth century, turned down after that, and dropped precipitously after 1748. Precise data are not available for all periods, but the population figures available for the cabecera are summarized in Table 4.

Population growth was accompanied by the founding of new hamlets dependent on the cabecera. Jalatlaco became an independent pueblo administratively separate from Antequera sometime before 1680, and in the following two decades the offshoot settlements of Santa María Ixcotel and Santa Cruz Amilpas were recognized as sujetos.[32] Trinidad de las Huertas, another sujeto, was elevated to the status of pueblo in 1706, when it had about 100 families.[33]

The barrio organization within the cabecera also changed significantly during the seventeenth century. As the process of ethnic homogenization proceeded, the number of named barrios diminished. Those of Teotitlán, Ejutla, and Coyotepec, if they ever existed, had been absorbed into other units by the end of the seventeenth century, and the independence of Trinidad de las Huertas (formerly San Juan) left the cabecera with twelve barrios (see Table

TABLE 4
The Population of Jalatlaco, 1564–1777

Year	Units counted		Multiplier	Population estimate	Source
1564[a]	310.5	tributaries	2.9	900	AGN, Hospital de Jesús 398, 4: 19v
1565[a]	120	tributaries	3.3	396	AGN, Hospital de Jesús 285, 98
1609	477	tributaries	2.9	1,383	AGN, Tierras 2942, 53
1646	690.5	tributaries	?	?	AGI, Patronato 230B, ramo 9: 255r
1661[b]	1,075.5	tributaries	?	?	AGI, Patronato 230B, ramo 9: 256r
1729	2,029	adults	—[c]	3,277	Jalatlaco, *Padrón de 1729*
1748	415	families	5	2,075	Villaseñor y Sánchez, *Theatro americano*, 2: 114–15
1777	54	households	—	303	AGI, Audiencia de México 2589, ramo 38

[a] The possible explanation for the discrepancy between these figures is discussed in Chapter 4.
[b] The same source cites another count of 1,605.5 tributaries for this year (fols. 254v–255r), but that figure seems exaggerated. It probably includes a large number of nonresidents; and there may also be some truth in the claim of Jalatlaco officials that many people were counted twice.
[c] Children under 14 were not counted in the census; I have added 2 children for each married couple to obtain the population estimate.

6). The barrio of Mixtlán Toctlan in 1691 was referred to simply as Toctlan, and only two barrios still carried the generic Mixtec name —Mixtlán Oaxaca and Mixtlán Solar. By 1729 the barrios of Tepeaca, Tetlamacazcau, and Teozapotlan had disappeared, and the number of units was reduced to nine (see Table 5).

Politically, Jalatlaco was organized along similar lines as other Indian communities in the Valley. In the early eighteenth century its cabildo was composed of a gobernador, two alcaldes, four regidores, an alguacil mayor, a *fiscal* (treasurer), and an escribano.[34] The hereditary basis of cacique succession was apparently still in effect, though the cacique in 1729 lived in Antequera and seemingly had little influence in community affairs.[35] Though the barrios had lost most of their ethnic character, they continued to exercise political functions, and there is some evidence that each controlled rights to certain property, most likely common lands or religious paraphernalia. Each had one or more tequitlatos, a *tepixque*, a *topil*, and a *mayordomo*. Universally in the Valley, tequitlatos were minor Indian officials (usually macehuales) charged with the house-to-house collection of royal tribute. Mayordomos de la Communidad were generally responsible for community (in this case, barrio) properties, such as common lands, and any other possessions.[36] Lowest in the political hierarchy were the topiles, who in Valley towns in the eighteenth century served as menial assistants to the alcaldes of the community.[37] Of the four barrio offices, only that of tepixque was unique to Jalatlaco; its precise nature is not known, but in all probability it was a low-status position held by macehuales.[38]

Though the positions of topil and tequitlato plainly derived from the pre-Hispanic calpulli organization of central Mexico,[39] the widespread presence of these same offices in non-Nahua towns throughout the Valley cautions against viewing Jalatlaco's political organization as uniquely Nahua. This is not to say that the authority

TABLE 5
The Population of Jalatlaco, 1729

Place of residence	Population estimate
Barrios of the cabecera	
Etla	733
Oaxaca	665
Mexicapan	532
Toctlan	409
Tlaxcala	391
Colhuacán	215
Mixtlán Solar	164
Guatemala	95
Tlatelolco	73
SUBTOTAL	3,277
Sujetos	
Santa María Ixcotel	197
Santa Cruz Amilpas	488
SUBTOTAL	685
Residence unidentified	226
TOTAL	4,188

SOURCE: Archivo Parroquial de Jalatlaco, *Padrón de 1729*.
NOTE: Children under 14 were not counted in the census; I have added 2 children for each married couple to obtain the population estimate.

TABLE 6

Jalatlaco Marriages, 1691–1701 (Except 1698)

Barrio	Males marrying within barrio		Males marrying into other barrios		Males marrying out of community		Total number of marriages
	No.	Percent	No.	Percent	No.	Percent	
Etla	44	46.3%	36	37.9%	15	15.8%	95
Teozapotlan	4	25.0	9	56.3	3	18.8	16
Mixtlán Oaxaca	8	30.8	17	65.4	1	3.8	26
Mixtlán Solar	1	5.3	18	94.7	—	—	19
Toctlan	7	28.0	18	72.0	—	—	25
Mexicapan	8	25.0	21	65.6	3	9.4	32
Colhuacán	—	—	11	91.7	1	8.3	12
Tlatelolco	1	16.7	5	83.3	—	—	6
Tlaxcala	7	21.2	22	66.7	4	12.1	33
Tepeaca	1	16.7	2	33.3	3	50.0	6
Tetlamacazcau	3	25.0	8	66.7	1	8.3	12
Guatemala	1	11.1	8	88.9	—	—	9
Other exogamous marriages					3		3
TOTAL/ AVERAGE	85	28.9%	175	59.5%	34	11.6%	294
Females who married out of Jalatlaco							76

SOURCE: Archivo Parroquial de Jalatlaco, *Libros de Casamientos*, 1691–1701.

NOTE: Records for 1698 have been destroyed. In 3 instances, the records reveal no more than that the men married exogamously; these marriages are included in the table. Sixty-four unidentified marriages are excluded. The barrio of Trinidad de las Huertas, while still part of Jalatlaco at this time, no longer belonged to the same parish and therefore is not represented in these records.

structure of the community had no indigenous elements, but only to suggest that it did not differ in its essentials from that of Zapotec and Mixtec communities. Yet Jalatlaco was certainly quite different politically from other Valley Indian towns in important respects. For one thing, it had less political autonomy than they had because of its dependence on the urban economy and occupational structure. And for another, it had to cope with a stream of newcomers. Gaining the allegiance and cooperation of the numerous migrants who arrived from a variety of regions and communities was no small problem, as we have seen.

Náhuatl continued to be the predominant language in Jalatlaco through the first half of the eighteenth century, though by 1716 the cabildo claimed that all Jalatlaqueños were fluent in Spanish as well. [40] The ethnic bifurcation between Nahuas and non-Nahuas was still in effect, but the various sub-Nahua identities based on ancestral place of origin were no longer of any significance. Analysis of marriage records from the late seventeenth century shows that the original correspondence between ethnic group and barrio of residence, already eroded by 1611, had ceased to exist. Table 6 shows that most men now took wives from barrios other than their own. Only in the largest barrio, Etla, did endogamy prevail to any great extent, and even there more than half the men took wives from the outside. Mating behavior in the late seventeenth century appears to have been almost totally random with respect to barrio divisions.

One possible indicator of internal ethnic divisions during this period was the continued use of indigenous names by some numbers of the settlement's Nahuas. In the early colonial period many of the Valley's Indians, Mixtecs and Zapotecs as well as Nahuas, had customarily been identified by their Spanish names and surnames followed by a *sobrenombre*, or indigenous name. In Jalatlaco this practice persisted well past the early colonial days (until at least 1730) and was limited to those of Nahua descent. One source from 1662 suggests that the use of sobrenombres was widespread in the community, though a census taken in 1729 by the local priest gives them for only twenty-eight persons, all of them Nahuas and fifteen of whom lived in the barrio of Mexicapan. [41] This seems to say that Nahua identity continued to be of some importance in Jalatlaco. *

---

*An interesting case that illustrates the importance of Nahua identity in Jalatlaco is the furor that arose over the election of Miguel Nuñes to the office of alcalde in 1718. With the "help" of Antequera's alcalde mayor, Nuñes had been elected as gobernador in Jalatlaco in January 1718. But he was accused by fellow villagers of being a mestizo (and hence ineligible for the position), and a month later was removed from office and ordered out of the pueblo. What is more, Nuñes was also accused of aiding the alcalde mayor in an illegal repartimiento de efectos in Jalatlaco in which horses and cattle were forced on the people at high prices. Nevertheless, in April 1718 Nuñes was still in Jalatlaco, and when one of the town's elected alcaldes died, the alcalde mayor of Antequera succeeded in having Nuñes "elected" as a replacement. Four months later, in response to another accusation that he was ineligible for office because of his supposed mestizo ancestry, Nuñes took legal action to keep his position as alcalde. Appearing with witnesses before the alcalde mayor in Antequera, he presented evidence that he was not only an *indio puro*, but a descend-

Ethnicity can also be discussed in another context. The marriage records presented in Table 6 show that though endogamy was no longer characteristic of the barrios, it was still present to a significant degree at the community level. Of the 294 cabecera males in the group, only 11.6 percent took wives from outside Jalatlaco. Though the rate had increased slightly since 1611–20 (see Table 3), endogamy remained significantly high. Furthermore, only seven men in the group were identified as non-Indians (mestizos or mulattoes), essentially the same pattern that prevailed some 90 years earlier. It is interesting to note that twice as many women as men married out of the community, a fact that perhaps reflects their desirability as mates for Indian migrants to Antequera.

Despite its elevation to the rank of pueblo in the middle of the seventeenth century, Jalatlaco always suffered from a shortage of land and never had many inhabitants who relied exclusively on agriculture for their livelihood. In the eighteenth century the community had little more than the legally established minimum of the 600-vara townsite.[42] As in earlier times, most of the residents were artisans or engaged in small family businesses. Judging from late-seventeenth-century sources, hatters and potters predominated among the artisan group, which also included carpenters, shoemakers, masons, tailors, bakers, rosary-makers, gilders, chandlers, guitar-makers, and producers of fireworks.[43]

In summary, it is appropriate to discuss the concept of ethnicity and ethnic identity in Jalatlaco at three different levels, each with distinct referents and each operating in its own situational context. In the most fundamental sense, the bulk of the town's residents considered themselves to be indios and were so regarded by others. This identity was a prerequisite to full membership in the community, and those who did not qualify were regarded as outsiders, as the case of Miguel Nuñes has shown. The determinants of Indian identity were multiple, and its boundaries were defined by a subtle

---

ant of Tlaxcalan conquerors as well, stressing that only descendants of the "Tlaxcalan and Mexican nobles" who founded Jalatlaco should be permitted to hold public office in the community (this was evidently the custom in Jalatlaco since the time of its founding). Ultimately, the case went to the viceroy, who ruled in Nuñes's favor. (Archivo General de la Nación, Indios 43, exp. 21, 41, 79.)

interplay of phenotype and dress, language, descent, and culture. Indian identity was mobilized mainly in the context of dealings with Spaniards and creoles in Antequera and in formal legal proceedings in which the status of indio entitled a claimant to certain prerogatives and special treatment.

Interaction between Jalatlaqueños and rural Indians brought a second identity into play, one that we may call "urban Indian." In this case the referents were the ability to speak Náhuatl and subcultural differences arising from long-term participation in Spanish urban life. Finally, a third, still more narrow ethnic distinction can be described that operated within the urban Indian category: the distinction between Nahuas and non-Nahuas. The boundaries between these two categories were not as rigid as those of the others, but the persistence of Náhuatl sobrenombres indicates that a Nahua identity, defined mainly in terms of descent, was still meaningful.

Traditionally, the internal political organization and authority structure of Jalatlaco were controlled by Nahuas, and membership in the class of principales was acquired only by birth into the Nahua group. As in many other Valley towns, however, the division between principales and macehuales was being eroded by the possibilities for achievement set in motion by Spanish colonial policy. Social and economic mobility was now possible for some macehuales, particularly those involved in the urban economy, and legal confirmation of *principal* status in the absence of noble birth could be achieved through devious means. In 1680 the principales of the barrio Colhuacán protested that some macehuales, "dressing in Spanish clothes, not only pass for *principales*, but on this pretext excuse themselves from paying the royal tribute, participating in public works projects, working the community lands, and other obligations. They also fail to show the obedience and respect that they owe to their officials and superiors."[44]

Traditional modes of organization were also threatened by the increasing numbers of non-Indians taking up residence in the community. Mestizos, mulattoes, and creoles never represented more than a small minority in Jalatlaco before the late eighteenth century, but their importance as a source of change far outweighed their numbers. Only 100 of the 2,029 adults in the census of 1729 were identified as non-Indians; and by the statistics compiled by Villa-señor some twenty years later, there were 380 Indian families in 1748 against only thirty to forty families of creoles, mestizos, and mulattoes.[45] In terms of occupational specialties and levels of wealth there was little difference between the Indian and non-Indian residents of Jalatlaco, but the non-Indians were clearly different in cultural orientation and ethnic identification, and were perceived by the Indians as a threat to village autonomy and indigenous social organization. Non-Indians were accused of stirring up discontent among the macehuales, usurping political offices customarily reserved for Nahua principales, and ignoring traditional duties and obligations expected of all members of the community. Whether by force or consensus, a mulatto was elected alcalde in 1678 and a mestizo the following year. The 1718 case of the alleged mestizo Miguel Nuñes is also relevant, though in the end he was able to legitimate his claim to Nahua status.

Antequera's Indian population, unlike Jalatlaco's, increased steadily through the whole of the colonial period. A census taken in the city in 1661 found a total of 398 Indians eligible for tribute, including 123 married couples.[46] Allowing two children for each married couple we arrive at 644 as a conservative estimate of the city's Indian population. The total number of Indians was undoubtedly higher, since the figures do not include caciques, people who were exempt from tribute for various reasons, and all those who managed to evade the census taker.

Of the 398 Indians counted, 186 were born outside of Antequera. Most were from Valley towns (over 43 percent) or from the Sierra Zapotec region (28 percent), particularly from the area around Villa Alta. Eleven Indians were native to the Mixteca Alta, and thirteen came from other, widely scattered parts of the bishopric. Only eleven Indians in the census were born outside the Bishopric of Oaxaca.

At least 58 percent of the Indians in the census lived in houses they did not own, a fact that reflects their frequent employment as household servants. This was particularly true of the Indian migrants; 135 of the 186 resided with others, against only 97 of the Indians native to Antequera. All the other Indians (51 migrants and 115 city natives) were listed by barrio and presumably owned their own homes or rented from other members of the urban lower class. Most of them were concentrated in the Barrio de China and the Barrio de Coyula (both located in the southwest portion of the traza), or in a haphazardly arranged settlement on the northern bank of the Atoyac River (see Table 9 in the following section). Clearly, the Spanish worked very hard to seal off the Indian quarters from the rest of the community. Most of these Indians were shunted into the least desirable location in the city—what was then a marshy area close to the river—and virtually none lived among Spaniards and creoles in the more prestigious neighborhoods. Mestizos and mulattoes were never subjected to residential segregation in this degree.

Indians in Antequera were employed in a wide variety of trades and crafts, though almost without exception they were among the least prestigious and remunerative of all urban occupations. Though far from conclusive, a list of occupations of 64 Indian males culled from late-seventeenth-century marriage records shows a high proportion of Indians working as masons, bakers, tailors, and shoemakers. Fully 22 percent of the sample (14 men) were masons involved in the construction of private and public buildings, replacing in part the manpower once provided by the repartimiento system.* Scattered sources indicate that Indians also formed an integral part of the city's craft guilds.[47] *Gremios* were organized for all the major crafts and trades in Antequera (as in other cities in New Spain), and were empowered to regulate membership and production and set quality standards.[48] Most Indian craftsmen were employed as oficiales and worked in shops owned and managed by non-Indian maestros (though there were certainly some Indian maestros, especially in the masonry and candle-making trades).

---

*There were 8 tailors, 8 bakers, and 5 shoemakers. Other categories in which more than 1 man was employed were muleteers, hat-makers, and farmers (3 each) and tanners, button-makers, traders, candlemakers, and potters (2 each). Rounding out the group were a cap-maker, a rosary maker, a sacristan, a painter, a water carrier, a stonecutter, a shopkeeper, a chair-maker, a butcher, and a herdsman. (Archivo Parroquial del Sagrario, *Libros de Casamientos*, 1693–1700.)

The most valuable data on the status of the Indians of Antequera in relation to other sectors of the population are found in the marriage registers for the Sagrario parish housed in the cathedral of present-day Oaxaca. These records contain the names and socioracial designations of virtually every person in colonial Antequera who married in the city, for Church marriage was the only form of legal matrimony at the time. I chose for my sample the years 1693–1700, during which 860 marriages were performed. Of the 1,720 men and women involved, 321 (18.7 percent) were Indians (or more precisely, macehuales; there were eight caciques and ten cacicas in the sample as well), making them the third largest group after the creoles and free mulattoes (see Table 8 in the following section). Only 28.4 percent of the Indians (commoners) were born in Antequera; the rest came mainly from Valley towns (about a third) or elsewhere in the Bishopric of Oaxaca.

Significantly, of all the socioracial groups in the city, the Indians exhibited the highest degree of closure with respect to choice of marriage partners (see Table 10). Three-quarters of the males (104) took Indian wives; only three married creole women and twenty-one married mestizas or castizas. Indian women were slightly more inclined to marry non-Indians. Of 176, five married creoles, sixteen married mestizos or castizos, twenty-three married free mulattoes, and thirteen married black or mulatto slaves. The high rate of legitimacy among the urban Indians is further evidence that they formed a very tightly bounded ethnic group. In a sample of 180 only 10 percent were found to be of illegitimate birth. All the other groups except the peninsular Spaniards exhibited significantly higher rates of illegitimacy.

The marriage records tell us little about internal ethnic distinctions among the urban Indians of Antequera, but one is left with the impression that such distinctions were not as important as in Jalatlaco. In only a small number of the marriages between Indian men and women did both partners come from the same town. It was not uncommon for husband and wife to be from widely divergent geographical and linguistic areas, and no recognizable patterns emerge from the data. Similarly, Indians born outside of Antequera were just as likely to marry non-Indians as were those native to the city. Most of the immigrants had resided in Antequera a considerable length of time before marriage, the average being thirteen years.

In sum, it is clear that in both Antequera and Jalatlaco the Indians continued to form a tightly bounded ethnic group vis-à-vis other sectors of the urban population through the early eighteenth century. Marriages with non-Indians were few, and internal differentiation in terms of power and wealth was minimal. The ethnic distinction between Nahuas and non-Nahuas was of some importance in Jalatlaco, where it was closely linked to *principal* status and political office-holding, but it had little meaning in Antequera, where there was no Indian power base to aid in maintaining the division. Indians ranked at the bottom of the hierarchy of social prestige and were economically exploited as servants and construction workers, and in other sorts of low-status jobs. This is not to say, however, that they were in any sense marginal to city life or unassimilated into Spanish colonial society. Indeed, the reverse was true: despite the many differences separating Indians from other members of society, urban Indians often attended the same churches, held the same jobs, and worked in the same shops as many non-Indians. They formed an integral part of the urban milieu, though in a decidedly inferior position, and without them the city would have been unable to function.

In this and other ways the Indians' situation had changed substantially since the late sixteenth and early seventeenth centuries. The term naboría, so frequently used by Spaniards in the sixteenth century to refer to the urban Indians, is rarely encountered in the late-seventeenth-century documentation, and its fall into disuse seems to denote a shift in attitude on the part of the white elite. As naborías, Indians were looked on primarily as a source of labor; they were *in* the city but not *of* the city. By the end of the seventeenth century, however, they had become an accepted feature of the urban scene and were no longer regarded as something foreign to the white colonists' ideal of city life.

The seventeenth century also witnessed the collapse of the various sub-Nahua identities based on place of origin. Already breaking down by 1630, the boundaries separating these groups could not hold up under the demands of Spanish colonialism, particularly since the groups were small and were not replenished from the outside. Finally, the Nahuas, once the core of the urban Indian population, now became an increasingly smaller minority in the face of migration from the hinterland. Náhuatl was still widely spoken, to be sure, and the Nahuas were still politically dominant in Jalatlaco; but they had lost their earlier superiority in urban trades and skills and were gradually being absorbed into the broader urban Indian culture.

It is important to note that these remarks apply solely to Indian commoners, who constituted the overwhelming mass of the native population. In a separate category altogether—in both Indian society and the Spanish city—were the caciques, direct descendants of the pre-Hispanic native nobility. Unlike the nobles of Tarascan Michoacán and the Valley of Mexico, who were virtually indistinguishable from macehuales in status and wealth by the mid-seventeenth century, the Valley caciques retained large landholdings and high social status throughout the colonial period.[49]

As was generally the case in all New Spain, the Indian nobility in the Valley was granted recognition by the colonial administration as a means of gaining control over the mass of the native population. Nobles were quick to accept Spanish ways and were rapidly acculturated during the sixteenth century. They spoke fluent Spanish and dressed in European clothes, and by 1600 most caciques who could afford it lived in Antequera.[50] Many caciques also received licenses that permitted them to display the trappings of Spanish nobility—a sword and a mount. Most of these licenses were granted in the second half of the sixteenth century and the first decades of the seventeenth, falling off rapidly after 1630. This trend correlates well with the decreasing Spanish reliance on caciques as intermediaries once the Indian commoners began to be exploited by a variety of colonial economic institutions rather than by the exclusive use of force embodied in the encomienda and the repartimiento labor system. Furthermore, though the position of cacique remained a rank of prestige in the Valley, there was a general decline in wealth and political power among the nobility in many towns in the seventeenth century as the macehual class gained more political control and legal privileges.[51]

These observations pertain specifically to the Indian nobility of the Valley of Oaxaca. When attention is focused on Antequera alone, other factors enter into a characterization of the cacique group, since the city contained many Indian nobles who had migrated from other areas. Only seven of the nobles in the marriage records of 1693–1700 were native to the Valley; the others came from widely scattered areas of the bishopric. The marriages of these eighteen nobles, eight men and ten women, are shown in Table 10. Though it is difficult to draw conclusions from such a small sample, it is nonetheless significant that only two of the men married Indian women of noble birth. Three married Indian commoners, one a mestiza, and one a castiza; the background of the wife of the eighth man is uncertain. Similarly, of the ten cacicas, only two married Indian nobles. Most of the others married creoles, but two married Indian commoners and one married a mestizo.

It is clear that by the end of the seventeenth century many of Antequera's caciques were no longer ranked with the Spanish elite. Thus one cacica from Santa Cruz Mixtepec married a creole blacksmith, another married a mestizo cowpuncher, and a third, from Tehuantepec, married a commoner sacristan from Tlacochahuaya. Likewise, among the men in the sample, we find a Mountain Zapotec cacique from Santo Tomás Ixtlán who made his living as a tailor. And then there was Francisco Santiago de Carrasco, a city-born cacique who worked as a baker and who on his death in 1758 left as his only property his house and a small number of possessions collectively valued at just 2,085 pesos.[52] On the other hand, some caciques were able to maintain their status as nobles and found a degree of acceptance among the white elite. Thus in 1725 a son of don Lorenzo Martínez de la Fuente, cacique of Santa Catarina Quiane, was ordained as a priest, a position that was normally closed to Indian commoners at that time.[53]

By the late seventeenth century, then, the identity of cacique or the claim of direct lineal descent from a pre-Hispanic ruling family did not automatically imply a position of power and prestige in Antequera. The city's caciques did not in any sense form a closed, homogeneous group, but were in fact quite heterogeneous in terms of wealth, social status, and political influence in their native communities.

Race and the Urban Social Structure

Non-Indians in seventeenth-century Antequera were formally classified by eight socioracial terms: *español europeo* (peninsular Spaniard), *español* (creole), *castizo* (offspring of mixed Spanish and mestizo descent), *mestizo* (of mixed Spanish and Indian descent), *mulato libre* (free mulatto), *mulato esclavo* (mulatto slave), *negro libre*, and *negro esclavo*. These categories were not, of course, unique to Oaxaca but were widely used in colonial Spanish America and were reinforced by written law that sought to define the rights and obligations of Spaniards, mestizos, mulattoes, and Negroes.[54]

Descriptive terminologies for persons of mixed racial heritage have attracted considerable attention because of their exotic quality and sheer variety. Lengthy erudite classifications based on different combinations and permutations of Spanish, Indian, and Negro "blood" became a favorite intellectual exercise in the late eighteenth century, and regional variations in terminology further stimulated the imagination of many white elitists. Joaquín Roncal, who studied the question in the 1940's, found forty-six terms in use in New Spain alone, but insists that only ten had any importance, judging from parish registers and tax lists:[55]

1. *español*	6. *mulato* (español + negro)
2. *indio*	7. *morisco* (español + mulato)
3. *negro*	8. *lobo* (indio + negro)
4. *mestizo*	9. *coyote* (indio + mulato)
5. *castizo*	10. *chino* (indio + lobo)

Terms like lobo, coyote, and chino are rarely mentioned in the documentation for Antequera, though they must have been common in everyday speech. Parish priests in the seventeenth century occasionally distinguished between *mulatos blancos* (light mulattoes) and *mulatos prietos* (dark mulattoes), or used the euphemistic expression *de color pardo* (of brown color). Racial slurs could also take a variety of forms, such as *perro mulato* or *perro chino*. For classificatory purposes, however, most deviations from the basic terms were mere embellishments on the standard categories; for example, *mulatto achinado* or *indio amestizado*.[56] This is not surprising since the function of this classification system, or sistema de castas as it is often called, was to define social strata in the colonial society as perceived by the white elite, and the use of the more obscure and erudite terms in administrative contexts would have made this impossible.

The sistema de castas as a "folk," or cognitive, model of the white elite was by far the most complex schema for hierarchical social categorization (and the one with the most internal contradictions), but it was not the only one. There was first of all the legal distinction between tributaries and non-tributaries, which in part cut across racial divisions: Indians, Negroes, and mulattoes were all required to pay royal tribute, while other groups were exempt. Two other, similarly simple binary divisions also existed and also cut across racial lines. One was the distinction between gente de razón (literally, rational people) and indios, which was essentially a cultural classification designed to set off the members of Hispanic society based in the cities from the culturally alien Indian populace. The other, socioeconomic in character, drew a line between *gente decente* (respectable people) and *la plebe* (the populace, or common people), and was unquestionably derived from Europe. This classification is more directly applicable to the urban setting and represents an emerging concept of socioeconomic classes.

Racial designations were thus important but not all-powerful in determining relative social position in the minds of colonial Oaxaqueños. Indeed, the only forms of documentation from Antequera in which socioracial terms were consistently employed were parish marriage registers, censuses taken by Church officials, and transcripts of Inquisition trials. In the secular documentation they appear less often (with the exception of the designation indio), and their usage was determined by circumstance. We are left with a number of interesting questions. What meaning attached to the various racial terms in Antequera and what kinds of people did they refer to? How was a particular label bestowed on a person and what did it imply for his personal and social identity? To what extent did people act and categorize others in terms of this rigid classificatory system in everyday life?

The categories of peninsular Spaniard, Indian, and Negro were of course the most well defined in the system and need no further explanation. The creole group, though technically composed of the New World offspring of European Spaniards, was in fact quite heterogeneous. Creoles were always the single largest racial group in Antequera. Given the limited number of Spanish women, it seems obvious that the many creoles were the products of race mixture. Most of them were biological mestizos and some showed traces of Negroid traits, though what distinguished them as a group was their preponderantly white phenotype. In the words of Gonzalo Aguirre Beltrán, "It is possible that there were some pure creoles, true American Spaniards, but their number was surely insignificant." [57]

The term mestizo was reserved for those of mixed Spanish and Indian ancestry whose skin color and physical features more closely approximated the Indian rather than the Spanish phenotype. There was also a small number of castizos (technically, of mestizo and creole parentage), who in skin color and social status occupied an intermediate position between the creoles and mestizos. Finally there were the mulattoes, the darkest of all the miscegenated and the most anomalous in terms of racial composition. This category took in all persons of dark phenotype with obvious signs of Negro ancestry. It thus included those of mixed white and Negro origin, of mixed Indian and Negro origin, or some combination of the three.

All of these categories were ranked in a hierarchy of social prestige that was generally agreed on by all members of society:*

*This ranking for Antequera is essentially the same as in Magnus Mörner's more generalized scheme (*Race Mixture*, p. 60). I wish to emphasize, however, that the relative positions of Negroes and Indians in the hierarchy varied from place to place in colonial Latin America, probably according to different population proportions.

Peninsular Spaniard
Creole
Castizo
Mestizo
Mulatto
Negro
Indian

But an important question remains, namely, how did a person come to be classified within a particular category? Was an individual's racial identity arbitrarily imposed on him by white officials, or was he (together with his parents) allowed some degree of choice, phenotype permitting? The answer would be easy enough if there was little intermarriage between categories, and each child adopted the classification of his parents. However, as will be shown below, there was a significant degree of intermarriage. How, for example, would the two offspring of a mulatto and a mestiza be classified when one was closer in phenotype to the father and the other closer to the mother?

In most parts of colonial Spanish America children were racially classified soon after birth when they were taken to the church for baptism. Frequently, separate registers were kept for Spaniards, Indians, and castas, each baptism being duly recorded by the parish priest. Roncal has suggested that racial labels were assigned on the whim of the priests, though this did not make them any less valid, since "parish priests were experts in racial classification and were sincere in their judgments."[58] But documents from the late colonial period published by Richard Konetzke cast considerable doubt on this view; they indicate rather that the classifications were based on the declarations of the parties concerned. The archbishop of Mexico stated in 1815, for example, that "to register a baptism, the priests do not receive juridical information but rely on the word of the parties. They do not demand proofs nor do they dispute what they are told. Even if they know that the people belong to another class, they do not shame them by doubting the sincerity of their word."[59]

Blacks were more likely to occupy the bottom rung of the prestige ladder in areas where they substantially outnumbered the Indians.

TABLE 7
Persons Eligible for Tribute (Including Spouses)
in Antequera, 1661

Classification	Men	Women	Total	Population estimate
Mestizos	38	49	87	
Free mulattoes	101	115	216	
Negroes	5	5	10	
Unidentified (mostly mestizos and mulattoes)	46	106	152	
SUBTOTAL	190	275	465	707
Indians	188	210	398	644
TOTAL	378	485	863	1,351

SOURCE: Archivo General de la Nación, Patronato 230B, ramo 10.
NOTE: I have added 2 children for each married couple to obtain the population estimate.

The surviving baptismal registers in Antequera covering the late-seventeenth and eighteenth centuries do not ordinarily give the racial classification of children or their parents, nor were separate books kept for Spaniards, Indians, and castas.[60] Furthermore, careful study of ecclesiastic and civil censuses for Antequera in the late eighteenth century reveals that children living with parents of different socioracial affiliation were rarely classified at all in the census manuscripts.[61] This information does not suggest that Antequera differed in any significant way from other cities in New Spain, but it does enable us to put the facts in a better perspective. For most persons, their first encounter with the sistema de castas came when they began to become independent from their parents—that is, when they began to work full time or decided to marry. The same priest who found it unnecessary to record a person's racial affiliation at birth rarely refrained from noting it down when he or she married. It would thus appear that there was an element of individual and family choice built into the system that people sought to exploit to their own advantage.

As a rule, a person's racial classification was contingent on what he could get away with, and the consistently large number of "creoles" in Antequera and elsewhere in New Spain compared with the other categories is evidence that many learned to play the game successfully.[62] A man regarded his racial identity not so much as an indicator of group membership or even as a badge of self-definition within a static and rigid social system, but rather as one component of his personal identity that could be manipulated and often changed. Other important components were his occupation (or that of his spouse) and his economic status. The mutually reinforcing relationship between economic and racial factors and their effect on social rank and behavior will be discussed shortly.

No accurate census data exist for seventeenth-century Antequera, but the rough outlines of the population and the overall proportions represented by the various socioracial categories can be discerned from other sources. A tributary census taken in 1661 is summarized in Table 7.* Allowing two children per married couple yields an estimated tributary population of 1,351 at that time. This seems low when we consider Andrés Portillo's estimate of 3,000 for the total population in 1660 (see Table 1), and the main problem appears to be an underrepresentation of Negroes and mestizos. The relative size of socioracial groups can be more accurately gleaned from the Sagrario marriage records. A breakdown of the 1,720 persons married between 1693 and 1700 (see Table 8) reveals a quite different picture. We now find creoles accounting for a little under a third of the total, mestizos for 14.5 percent, and Indians (commoners) for 18.7 percent. The castizo and Negro groups are both quite small. One further source is available for a check on the inherently biased nature of marriage records: the classification of 1,778 male patients in the Hospital of San Damián and San Cosme during the years 1703–10.[63] Essentially the same categories were used here as in the parish registers, though a few persons were classified as lobos and chinos who would show up in the marriage registers as mulattoes. In terms of overall proportions, the main differences are the lower percentage of creoles (25.5 percent) and the higher percentage of mestizos and mulattoes (23 percent and 27 percent, respectively) among hospital patients.

---

*This count was made under the supervision of the oidor Juan Francisco de Montemayor y Cuenca in the aftermath of the Indian uprising of Tehuantepec. Mestizos were not ordinarily subject to royal tribute, and the oidor's decision to include them in the tax list was soon overridden by the Audiencia. The count does not include persons married to Spaniards or creoles, or those exempt from tribute (e.g., children, the infirm).

TABLE 8

Racial Composition of Marriage Partners
in Antequera, 1693–1700

Classification	Men	Women	Total	Percent
Peninsulars	58	2	60	3.5%
Creoles	258	278	536	31.2
Castizos	9	17	26	1.5
Mestizos	123	127	250	14.5
Free mulattoes	172	174	346	20.1
Mulatto slaves	24	14	38	2.2
Free Negroes	6	2	8	0.5
Negro slaves	21	6	27	1.6
Caciques	8	10	18	1.0
Indians	145	176	321	18.7
Miscellaneous	3	3	6	0.3
Unidentified	33	51	84	4.9
TOTAL	860	860	1,720	100.0%

SOURCE: Archivo Parroquial del Sagrario, *Libros de Casamientos*, 1693–1700.

A consistent and striking pattern in all of these data is the dispro-
portionate number of mulattoes for the size of the Negro population. There is no evidence that the Valley ever had a substantial
number of Negroes during the colonial period, though most Valley
Negroes lived in or around Antequera.[64] The best explanation for
the inordinately large size of the mulatto group is that (1) Negro
genes were largely confined to the city because most blacks were
employed as household servants; and (2) Negroid traits were highly
visible, and the stigma attached to black ancestry by the whites
severely limited the mulattoes' chances for social mobility and
"passing" as mestizos or creoles. Notice, in contrast, the relatively
low proportion of mestizos in the population. On purely biological grounds, we would expect the mestizo group to be much larger
given the small numbers of Negroes and Spaniards in the Valley
during the sixteenth and seventeenth centuries. The key here is the
large size of the creole group, which suggests that many "mestizos"
were in fact able to pass as creoles, where the mulattoes often could
not. The difference in the percentages of mestizos in the hospital list
and the marriage records lends credence to this hypothesis. Marriage was an important means of social mobility, so that people had

every reason to present themselves in the most favorable manner. When checking into a hospital for medical care, however, the reasons for the "upgrading" of one's racial status were perhaps less compelling.

After the demise of the Chichicapan mines in the mid-seventeenth century, Antequera and its immediate vicinity became virtually the only locus of extensive race mixture in the Valley of Oaxaca. Indian towns remained for the most part racially and ethnically homogeneous, and I have found only scattered references to the penetration of non-Indians into indigenous communities during the period 1630–1750.* An investigation in 1686 to determine the number of creoles, mestizos, and mulattoes living within the jurisdiction of the Villa de Etla located just sixteen non-Indians among 850 Indian tributaries.[65] Most rural mestizos and mulattoes lived on the fringe of Indian society as administrators or laborers on Spanish estates or as sharecroppers or small farmers on rented land.[66]

Within the city itself there was much less residential segregation among mestizos and mulattoes than among the Indians. Table 9 summarizes fragmentary data from the 1661 tributary census on the barrios of residence of non-whites in Antequera. Many of them, as we see, were concentrated in the Barrio de Coyula and various locations on the edge of town, but it is clear that some numbers of mestizos and mulattoes lived among the whites in neighborhoods where Indians were barred. In 1673 a mulatto woman ran a rooming house patronized by non-whites on the plaza opposite the cathedral. The Church condemned the establishment as a haven for "vagabonds" and vice, and tried for two years to have the woman evicted, though without success.[67] Apart from the Indians, residential patterns appear to have been determined more by socioeconomic factors than by strictly racial or ethnic considerations. Some barrios were of course more prestigious and wealthy than others, and as always the white elite tended to cluster near the central plaza mayor. But there

---

*This applies to the cacique lineages as well as to the mass of Indian commoners. As William Taylor points out, the Valley is an exception to Magnus Mörner's statement that "the efforts of the Crown to maintain the exclusively Indian character of the native leadership had failed completely." (Taylor, *Landlord and Peasant*, p. 39; Mörner, "La Infiltración mestiza," p. 160.)

TABLE 9
Barrios of Residence of Tributaries in Antequera, 1661

Barrio or other address	Mestizos, mulattoes and Negroes	Indians native to city	Other Indians	Total
(In the house of . . .)[a]	228	97	135	460
Barrio de Coyula	40	30	9	79
Barrio de China	7	28	8	43
Next to Atoyac River	—	27	—	27
Barrio de la Merced	15	—	—	15
Calle de San Pablo	14	—	—	14
Barrio de Santa Catalina de los Indios	5	3	5	13
Barrio del Cerro	10	—	—	10
Barrio de la Soledad	9	—	—	9
Barrio de la Veracruz	8	—	—	8
Barrio de San Agustín	2	3	—	5
Barrio de San Francisco	5	—	—	5
Miscellaneous	52	21	24	97
Unknown	70	3	5	78
TOTAL	465	212	186	863

SOURCE: Archivo General de la Nación, Patronato 230B, ramo 10.
[a] In these cases the owner of the house was given, but not its location.

is no evidence that any barrio tended toward racial homogeneity, or that barrios as units had any special significance for social organization.

If the Sagrario marriage records do not tell us all that we would like to know about the relation between race, ethnicity, and socioeconomic status in late-seventeenth-century Antequera, we can nevertheless learn much from them; for the choice of marriage partners is one of the best available indexes of ethnic boundaries and may also be assumed to be related to socioeconomic status. Some scholars have expressed doubt about the value of such records for the study of race mixture, pointing out that it was usually the result of extra-marital and informal unions.[68] This is certainly true of the unions involving Spaniards, Indians, and Negroes, but it ignores the fact that there was extensive secondary race mixture, involving persons of miscegenated background, that was sanctioned by marriage and openly recognized by all. The records from Antequera are well suited for this type of study, since all marriages performed in the city took place in one spot—the cathedral. Moreover, as Borah and Cook point out, "although informal and irregular union was a prominent feature of custom in the Spanish [colonial] cities, it should not be forgotten that most of the people did marry in accordance with church requirements and that Spanish law obtained in all the rigor of its requirements of formal marriage and legitimate birth for inheritance, the taking of holy orders, and the holding of office."[69]

The marriage patterns revealed in a study of the 860 marriages performed in Antequera between 1693 and 1700 are shown in Table 10. The creole and Indian groups showed the least propensity for intermarriage, roughly 75 percent of each marrying within the group. Better than 13 percent of the creole men married mestizas or castizas, and about 8 percent married free mulattoes; five men married cacicas, and five married Indian commoners. Creole women were somewhat more likely to marry outside the group because of their desirability as wives for peninsular Spaniards. Few Spanish women emigrated to Antequera before marriage; there were only two in these records. As is clear from the table, women in general were more upwardly mobile than men in the sistema de castas.

Nearer the bottom of the social hierarchy, the free mulattoes exhibited a much higher rate of intermarriage, with 40 percent of the men marrying non-mulatto women. Some 14 percent married Indians, and 25 percent married into more prestigious categories: 15.7 percent married mestizas or castizas, and 9.6 percent married creole women. Mestizos and castizos (who are included with the mestizos because of their small number) were the most heterogeneous of all the categories; only 37.5 percent of them married within the group.* On the whole, mestizos tended to marry beneath their position on the prestige scale more often than above it (reversing the

---

*The sample contains only 26 castizos, 9 men and 17 women. Of the 6 men whose wives' backgrounds are known, 5 married creole or peninsular women, and only 1 a castiza. Six of the 17 women took creoles as husbands, 4 took mulattoes, and 3 took peninsular Spaniards. In 4 cases the husband's background was not identified.

TABLE 10

Marriage Patterns in Antequera According to Church Records, 1693–1700

(Percentages based on 776 marriages in which both partners' origins are known)

Men	Women										Total	Inter-marriage rate
	Peninsulars	Creoles	Castizas and mestizas	Free mulattoes	Mulatto slaves	Free Negroes	Negro slaves	Cacicas	Indians	Unident. and misc.		
Peninsulars												
Number	1	40	6	—	—	—	—	—	—	11	58	
Percent	*2.1*	*85.1*	*12.8*	*—*	*—*	*—*	*—*	*—*	*—*	*—*		*97.9%*
Creoles												
Number	—	178	33	19	2	—	—	5	5	16	258	
Percent	*—*	*73.6*	*13.6*	*7.9*	*0.8*	*—*	*—*	*2.1*	*2.1*	*—*		*26.4%*
Castizos and mestizos												
Number	1	29	48	30	3	—	—	1	16	4	132	
Percent	*0.8*	*22.7*	*37.5*	*23.4*	*2.3*	*—*	*—*	*0.8*	*12.5*	*—*		*62.5%*
Free mulattoes												
Number	—	16	26	95	4	1	1	—	23	6	172	
Percent	*—*	*9.6*	*15.7*	*57.2*	*2.4*	*0.6*	*0.6*	*—*	*13.9*	*—*		*40.4%*
Mulatto slaves												
Number	—	—	3	12	3	—	—	—	5	1	24	
Percent	*—*	*—*	*13.0*	*52.2*	*13.0*	*—*	*—*	*—*	*21.7*	*—*		*34.8%*
Free Negroes												
Number	—	—	—	4	—	1	—	—	—	1	6	
Percent	*—*	*—*	*—*	*80.0*	*—*	*20.0*	*—*	*—*	*—*	*—*		*80.0%*

Negro slaves											
Number	—:	—	1	6	—	—	5	—	8	1	21
Percent	—	—	*5.0*	*30.0*	—	—	*25.0*	—	*40.0*	—	*75.0%*
Caciques											
Number	—	—	2	—	—	—	—	2	3	1	8
Percent	—	—	*28.6*	—	—	—	—	*28.6*	*42.9*	—	*71.4%*
Indians											
Number	—	3	21	6	2	—	—	2	104	7	145
Percent	—	*2.2*	*15.2*	*4.3*	*1.4*	—	—	*1.4*	*75.4*	—	*24.6%*
Unidentified and miscellaneous	—	12	4	2	—	—	—	—	12	6	36
TOTAL/ AVERAGE	2	278	144	174	14	2	6	10	176	54	860	*41.6%*

SOURCE: Archivo Parroquial del Sagrario, *Libros de Casamientos*, 1693–1700.
NOTE: Percentages have been rounded. Marriages between slaves and non-slaves of the same racial affiliation are not counted as intermarriages.

pattern among the mulattoes) since 39 percent of the males took free mulattoes, slaves, or Indians as wives.

As always, little can be said about Antequera's Negro population except that it was small, and that evidently very few Negroes were legally married. Many black and mulatto slaves who did marry were upwardly mobile, over 80 percent of them taking free wives. It appears that there were more mulatto than black slaves. A sampling of the sales of slaves recorded for the entire eighteenth century, taking one year in each decade, produced a total of 89 persons, 58 percent of whom were mulattoes.[70]

What kinds of conclusions may be drawn from these data? The frequency of intermarriage across socioracial lines is striking indeed, with 41.6 percent of the males taking wives of different racial affiliations than their own. In-group marriage was a well-defined pattern among the creoles and Indians, but even in these cases there was a degree of race mixture that was openly recognized and formalized by marriage bonds. Most interracial marriages took place between members of adjacent categories, though there were more than 100 exceptions to the rule (at least 14 percent of the known marriages). The almost random mating behavior among large numbers of mestizos and mulattoes is sufficient to show that the stratification system cannot be adequately described as a rigid hierarchy of racially defined castes or estates composed of a series of clearly defined ethnic groups. As much as the Spanish and creole elite tended to view their society in this manner, the departure of so many of the non-elite from the expected pattern of behavior forces us to recognize another aspect of reality.

The marriage records show that non-racial factors were often involved in the selection of a mate. They also show the pitfalls of viewing the mulatto and mestizo populations as ethnic groups with distinct social identities. Mestizos did not constitute a group in the sociological sense, and their high intermarriage rate indicates that they did not share a common identity. Whether or not the mulattoes constituted an ethnic group is highly problematic. One would expect that their eligibility for slavery and royal tribute would have provided a basis for group solidarity and a common identity. Yet by

the mid-seventeenth century the tribute system had ceased to operate effectively, and the tax rolls showed only thirty-seven free
mulattoes and Negroes within the jurisdiction of Antequera in 1661
prior to the oidor Montemayor's investigation.[71] On the other hand,
there is some evidence that mulattoes came together as a group in
the domain of religious activity. The late-seventeenth-century Cofradía de las Nieves (organized to finance the construction of the
church of the same name) was composed of mulattoes, as was the
Cofradía de la Sangre de Cristo.[72] In addition, Burgoa tells us that
the church of Nuestra Señora del Carmen was founded by "mulatos
y ladinos," and that the hospital run by the Dominican nunnery
Santa Catalina de Sena ministered primarily to Negroes and mulattoes.[73] Questions of ethnicity aside, the patterns of intermarriage
show that the Hispanic community of Antequera was racially quite
fluid, and that by the late seventeenth century the terms mulatto
and mestizo did not necessarily imply illegitimate birth. More than
half of the mestizos and mulattoes in the marriage records, in fact,
were born in wedlock.

That recognized racial divisions did not coincide neatly with social
strata in the functioning social system can also be inferred from the
distribution of occupations. The marriage records list occupations
for approximately half the males in the group, and the correlation
between occupation and socioracial status is presented in Tables 11
and 12. In Table 11 I have grouped occupations into closely associated categories in order to show the relative participation of the
racial groups in different sorts of economic activity. The source is of
course inherently biased toward young men, and there is no way to
correct for this deficiency, but the overall distribution does not depart radically from the late-eighteenth-century pattern based on
more reliable data (see Chapter 6).

A striking feature of the distribution is the inclusion of all the
groups except the peninsular Spaniards in most of the occupational
categories. It is clear that almost all the non-whites were found in
the less prestigious manual occupations, but equally important, so
were many of the creoles. More than half the creoles were employed as artisans; many of them worked not only at the same jobs as

TABLE 11

Occupations of Bridegrooms in Antequera, 1693–1700

Occupations	Peninsulars		Creoles		Mestizos and castizos		Free mulattoes		Indians		Total	
	No.	Percent	No.	Percent	No.	Percent	No.	Percent	No.	Percent	No.	Percent
Landowners	1	7.1%	23	14.0%	5	5.6%	3	3.2%	3	4.7%	35	8.2%
Merchants	9	64.3	2	1.2	—	—	—	—	—	—	11	2.6
Professionals and administrators	1	7.1	12	7.3	2	2.2	1	1.1	—	—	16	3.8
Artisans												
Gilders, silversmiths, painters, and sculptors	—	—	13	7.9	6	6.7	3	3.2	1	1.6	23	5.4
Confectioners, bakers, and butchers	1	7.1	1	0.6	1	1.1	—	—	9	14.1	12	2.8
Masons	—	—	1	0.6	7	7.8	10	10.6	14	21.9	32	7.5
Other	1	7.1	87	53.0	62	68.9	63	67.0	27	42.2	240	56.3
Traders and peddlers	1	7.1	14	8.5	2	2.2	3	3.2	2	3.1	22	5.2
Millers, wranglers, and shepherds	—	—	3	1.8	2	2.2	9	9.6	1	1.6	15	3.5
Muleteers	—	—	7	4.3	2	2.2	1	1.1	3	4.7	13	3.1
Miscellaneous	—	—	1	0.6	1	1.1	1	1.1	4	6.3	7	1.6
TOTAL	14	100.0%	164	100.0%	90	100.0%	94	100.0%	64	100.0%	426	100.0%

SOURCE: Archivo Parroquial del Sagrario, Libros de Casamientos, 1693–1700.
NOTE: 432 grooms whose occupations are unknown are not included in the table. The records do not list occupations for any of the 27 Negros or for the 8 caciques. One mulatto slave was a shoemaker, and another was a silversmith. Percentages do not always total 100 due to rounding.

TABLE 12

*Racial Composition of Selected Artisanal Occupations
in Antequera, 1693–1700*

Occupation	Peninsulars	Creoles	Mestizos and castizos	Free mulattoes	Indians	Total
Gilders	—	7	4	—	—	11
Blacksmiths	—	19	6	10	—	35
Farriers	—	9	1	—	—	10
Carpenters	—	19	4	5	—	28
Shoemakers	—	2	14	9	5	30
Tailors	1	8	12	7	8	36
Chair-makers	—	1	5	12	1	19
Tanners	—	5	4	6	2	17
Potters	—	4	2	2	1	9
Hat-makers	—	1	4	1	3	9
TOTAL	1	75	56	52	20	204

SOURCE: Archivo Parroquial del Sagrario, *Libros de Casamientos*, 1693–1700.

mestizos and mulattoes, but side by side with them, and this was often true in the case of Indians as well. Even such a menial occupation as muleteer (*arriero*) was held by a significant number of whites. Creoles were also well represented in the middle and upper ranks of the economic hierarchy, as evidenced by the clusterings in the categories of professionals and landowners. The landowner group was not economically homogeneous but included virtually any kind of landowner who derived his livelihood from agriculture or ranching. Nevertheless, as we have seen, most large landowners in the Valley resided in Antequera, and it is clear that creoles made up the majority of this group.

Peninsular Spaniards, on the other hand, had little interest in acquiring land, nor were they employed as professionals or artisans. The overwhelming majority of them were involved in commerce, and they dominated the city's merchant class. Antequera's wealthiest residents in the seventeenth and eighteenth centuries were merchants of European origin who rarely invested in Valley lands.[74] Indeed, one such merchant, Pedro Cañón de Anaya, died in 1689 leaving a store and warehouse inventory valued at over 14,000 pesos, considerably more than the value of many haciendas.[75] Merchants must be sharply distinguished from the tratantes, traveling merchants or peddlers who dealt in much smaller volume on a more precarious basis. Significantly, a majority of these traders were creoles.

Table 12 gives a breakdown of the most common occupations in the artisan group. It is impossible to identify the race of the masters, journeymen, and apprentices in the various trades. Many maestros were creoles, yet many of the whites must have worked as oficiales, for a city with as few as 5,000–6,000 inhabitants clearly could not have supported the number of workshops that would have existed if each creole artisan had run his own business.

The marriage patterns and occupational distributions we have discussed suggest that economics as well as race determined a person's social position in Antequera by the late seventeenth century. Behavior (as well as the perceptions of many of the non-elite) cannot be adequately accounted for with a model of racially defined estates based on the legal system and the outlook and biases of the white elite, or with a model of economic classes based solely on occupations and levels of wealth. Indeed, the system was more complex than either of these models alone would allow, and was based on the intersection of racial and economic criteria.

Positions of power, wealth, and authority in Antequera were invariably held by persons classified as socially "white"—either creoles or peninsular Spaniards. People in other categories were rarely able to enter the ranks of the elite and were excluded from positions in the Church and the government. But of all the socioracial groups, the creoles were by far the most heterogeneous in status and wealth, and many of them ranked with the non-whites on the occupational and economic scale. The creole group was constantly expanded by the absorption of upwardly mobile mestizos and mulattoes. Those who took light-skinned marriage partners increased their chances of having themselves labeled as creoles in the parish registers, and their children would thus become españoles as well. The introduction of the term castizo into the racial lexicon of the seventeenth century was one result of this process.

By 1700 the ongoing race mixture could no longer be interpreted by members of the society as an aberration in an otherwise "normal" system of ethnically defined estates of Spaniards, Indians, and Negroes. The white elite ceased to view the mulatto and mestizo groups as illegitimate misfits beyond the pale of Spanish colonial society, and incorporated them as defined strata in a larger system of socioracial stratification. New classifications were devised, both erudite and utilitarian, in an effort to reconcile observed behavior and social change with the ideal estate system inherent in written law and the colonial mentality of the elite. As we shall see, this process reached a culmination in the late eighteenth century as the internal contradictions in the sistema de castas became glaringly apparent.

The discussion has focused in large part on the late seventeenth century, though the terminal date for this chapter is 1750. Data for the first half of the eighteenth century are thin, but there is no reason to believe that there were any fundamental changes in the basic structure of race and class during this period. All indications are that urban population growth proceeded slowly until the 1740's, and there were apparently no major changes in the agriculturally based economy. Not until 1750 did Antequera embark on its Golden Age, ushered in by a cochineal boom and by an increase in trade and manufacturing encouraged by the Bourbon commercial reforms. During the late eighteenth century the city's population increased significantly, the textile industry was revived, and merchants grown rich from the cochineal trade dominated Antequera as never before.

CHAPTER SIX

The Late Colonial Period, 1750-1812

Economic and Population Growth

The 70-year span between 1750 and 1820 has frequently been called, and with some justification, Oaxaca's Golden Age.[1] During these years the city of Antequera reached the peak of its power and wealth, assuming a greater importance among Mexican cities than at any other time in its history, either before or since. Though its relative isolation prevented the town from attaining the importance of such cities as Puebla, Veracruz, and Guadalajara, during the course of the eighteenth century Antequera was transformed from a small, inward-looking agro-town into a highly commercial export center of considerable size.

This spurt in development was in keeping with trends in the viceroyalty as a whole. Cities all over New Spain thrived with the initiation of important economic reforms during the reign of Charles III (1759–88), and according to the best estimates, the colony's population increased from about 3,336,000 in 1742 to 6,122,000 in 1810, a dramatic rise of 83 percent due in large measure to the resurgence of the Indian population.[2] The Valley of Oaxaca's population did not rise quite so spectacularly, but the rate of growth was far from neg-

The analysis of the 1792 Antequera census and related materials, which occupies much of this chapter, was carried out in collaboration with William B. Taylor.

ligible: the number of inhabitants rose 57 percent, from an estimated 70,000 in 1740 to some 110,000 by the 1790's.[3] Population
figures for Antequera during the first half of the eighteenth century
are lacking, but in the year 1700 the city could not have had much
more than 6,000 inhabitants. By 1777 the population had risen
threefold, to 18,558; it then declined somewhat, to stand at 18,008
in 1792.[4]

Economic growth and an increase in trade characterized many
parts of Spanish America in the eighteenth century as the Bourbon reforms revamping the antiquated and restrictive commercial
policies of the Hapsburgs made themselves felt. During the first
two decades, import duties in the colonies were lowered and in
some cases eliminated altogether. In 1765 the Cádiz trading monopoly was ended, and merchants in other Spanish cities were permitted to trade with the Americas; after the 1770's the colonies
themselves were allowed to engage in reciprocal trade with Spain.
Furthermore, the *intendentes* and *subdelegados* who replaced the
alcaldes mayores and corregidores soon after 1786 were under instructions to encourage the growth of industry and trade. These
measures had the effect of eliminating much of the contraband
trade provoked by the Spanish government's economic strictures,
and also stimulated an increase in the volume of commerce. Antequera and other small Spanish towns in New Spain benefited significantly from the Bourbon reforms. As Brian Hamnett observes,
the freeing of restrictions on trade, the establishment of intendentes in the provincial capitals, and the founding of the two new
consulados (merchant guilds) of Veracruz and Guadalajara in 1795
severely weakened the political and economic dominance of Mexico
City over the rest of the viceroyalty.[5]

Antequera's response to this new economic and administrative
climate took the form of a substantial increase in the cochineal trade
and a revival of the textile industry. The boom began in the 1740's
and continued, subject to periodic fluctuations, into the second decade of the nineteenth century. During this period large amounts of
wealth came to be concentrated in the hands of a small number of

peninsular merchants who had close contacts in Mexico City and who succeeded in wresting control of Antequera's political and economic affairs from the local landowners. Hamnett suggests that the economy of New Spain, and of Antequera in particular, was more closely linked to worldwide trends than has previously been supposed. Not only did the contraband trade establish links with northern Europe, but the merchants of Seville and Cádiz often acted as middlemen for American goods on their way to points north. This was especially true in the case of cochineal, which had long been highly coveted in Europe. Once the trade restrictions were lifted, the demand for the dyestuff increased appreciably in the textile factories of France, Holland, Britain, and Spain.[6]

As in earlier years, cochineal was New Spain's second-most-valuable export (after silver) in the eighteenth century, and between 1745 and 1854 production was almost entirely confined to the Bishopric of Oaxaca.[7] The actual cultivation of the insect continued to be carried out by the Indians, sometimes for their own profit, but more frequently under the coercion of political officials, priests, or powerful Antequera merchants. Cochineal registration figures in Antequera for 1758–1826 suggest that a large part of the dyestuff produced in the bishopric passed through the city before being sent to Veracruz for export (see Table 13). Between 1758 and 1782 the cochineal trade was subject to periodic but regular fluctuations. Overall, however, this was a time of growth in which the volume of trade steadily rose, with the base level of each cycle settling at an increasingly higher figure. The peak production year was 1774, when 1,558,125 pounds were registered; after 1782 a substantial decline set in, never to be reversed. Hamnett ascribes the decline to four things: (1) the attempts of the Church to raise the tithe (for whites) on cochineal from 4 percent to 10 percent; (2) a cutback in production because of the threat of a reform of the *alcabala* (sales tax), which would have made transactions more costly; (3) the widespread famine and inflation that plagued New Spain in 1785–87; and (4) the establishment of the intendancy system and the prohibition of the repartimiento de efectos commonly practiced by political officials. In the nineteenth century the cochineal trade collapsed al-

TABLE 13

Cochineal Registration Figures for Antequera by Decades, 1758–1826

Period	Pounds	Value in pesos
1758–67	8,413,874	18,157,924 : 4
1768–77	9,809,540	27,122,412 : 5½
1778–87	7,911,812½	16,452,162 : 4
1788–97	4,513,512	8,136,267 : 6
1798–1807	3,869,162½	10,428,179 : 5½
1808–17	3,383,764½	11,661,338 : 6¼
1818–26	3,025,674½	7,857,797 : 6¾

SOURCE: Brian R. Hamnett, *Politics and Trade in Southern Mexico, 1750–1821* (London, 1971), p. 171.

together in the face of competition from Guatemala after 1821 and the use of cheaper, chemical dyes after the 1850's.[8]

There is good reason to believe that the vecinos of Antequera took substantial control of the cultivation end of the industry in the 1780's. Between 1784 and 1789 the amount of cochineal tithes collected by the Church each year in the bishopric exhibited an increase quite independent of the total amount of dyestuff registered. Since Indians were exempt from these tithes, this can only mean that production was being increasingly taken over by non-Indians, almost all of whom lived in Antequera.[9] This development was related to the revival of the weaving industry in Antequera, which used large quantities of cochineal in the manufacture of silks, cottons, and linens. Intendant Antonio de Mora y Peysal reported in 1793 that there were seven silk looms and 500 cotton looms in the city. The second figure was almost certainly an overestimate, since a survey made by the weavers' guild a decade earlier turned up only 152 cotton looms.[10] Still, the industry must have flourished in the next several years, for a military survey of the city in 1792 showed a healthy number of non-Indian men employed as tailors (359), weavers (284), hat-makers (114), and button-makers (51).[11] Most of this growth was registered in the clothing industry, stimulated by the demand for cheap cotton goods among the Indians and the urban poor. Among the favorite items were *rebozos* (shawls), striped mantles of all colors, blue ribbon, and *chiapanecos* (Chiapas-style man-

TABLE 14

Employment of Non-Indian Males in Antequera by Sectors, 1792

Sector	Number	Percent
Clothing and textiles	1,083	30.6%
Metal, wood, and		
wax working; pottery	583	16.5
Church	416	11.7
Commerce	366	10.3
Agriculture and ranching	207	5.8
Food and drink	176	5.0
Professional	158	4.5
Servants[a]	93	2.6
Government	91	2.6
Construction and housing	91	2.6
Skins and hides	87	2.5
Transport	58	1.6
Other manufactures	54	1.5
Fine arts, entertainment	30	0.8
Mining	14	0.4
Miscellaneous	34	1.0
TOTAL	3,541	100.0%

SOURCE: Archivo General de la Nación, Padrones 13; Tributos 34, 7.

[a] There were in addition at least 300 non-Indian female servants and 120 male and female Indian servants working in convents and monasteries. There are no figures available on the numbers of Indian servants working in private homes.

tles).[12] The clothing and textile industries in fact were by far the most important economic activities in the city, employing by 1792 over a quarter of the male non-Indian work force (see Table 14).

Cotton textiles had become important in the local economy at least by 1757, when the guilds of silk and cotton weavers split, and the cotton weavers received their ordinances from the weavers' guild of Mexico City.[13] Between 1793 and 1796 the number of looms in Antequera increased dramatically, and the textile industry reached its peak around the turn of the century. Antequera cottons lost their competitive advantage, however, with the introduction of cheaper, machine-produced imports from Europe, and by 1828 the city had only 50 cotton looms.[14]

Though the textile industry provided work for many creoles, mestizos, mulattoes, and Indians, few if any fortunes were made in that activity. The wealthiest citizens of Antequera in this period were the peninsular merchants who dealt in cochineal and imported goods. In 1792 only some 30 percent of the city's 144 merchants (excluding apprentices) were creoles. All the rest were peninsular Spaniards, who also accounted for 80 percent of the 72 apprentice merchants (*cajeros*). Wealthy creoles invested their money in land more often than not, a commodity of little interest to the peninsulars. Among the 191 non-Indian landowners in Antequera in that year, there were only twelve peninsulars, compared with about 104 creoles.[15]

The Valley landowners and ranchers fared far better in the second half of the century than in the first, when they had been hard hit by natural disasters and the faltering urban economy; yet very little land was added to Spanish estates at this time. Indian communities and their caciques clung to their holdings and continued to resist the efforts of the hacendados to draw them into debt peonage. Consequently, there was no letup of the labor shortage on Spanish estates despite the recovery of the Indian population. Writing in 1776, the alcalde mayor of Antequera, don Diego de Villasante, lamented the conditions of slavery that obtained on the haciendas and the unwillingness of independent Indians to hire on as agricultural laborers.

In light of the misery of the Indian peons, one might conclude that those in debt should be freed and permitted to pay back what they owe little by little. But there is a great danger in this. If one peon were allowed to leave, then the rest of them would want to do the same, and there would be no one left to do the farming. Consequently, the public would suffer from a lack of corn and other products. One might argue that the hacendados can hire labor when they need it from the Indian towns, but experience has taught us that the Indians do not want to go. Several hacienda owners have discussed this problem with me, and I have issued orders to the Indians that they go to work for a daily wage of two *reales* [approximately double the salary of the indentured peons]. But the Indians say they cannot do it, some because they have their own crops to tend and others because they are cultivating cochineal. Therefore I do not insist that they go, since I believe that their own concerns come first.

If conditions here were the same as in the Archbishopric of Mexico and the Bishopric of Puebla, where the villagers can be forced to work on the haciendas when necessary, then the indentured peons could be set free. But this would be difficult to put into practice and the outcome very doubtful, since most of the Indians in this bishopric grow their own crops, whereas those in the bishoprics of Mexico and Puebla do not.[16]

An added difficulty in securing temporary agricultural labor was the fact that wages for day laborers in the city were higher. At best, a day laborer on a hacienda could earn only two reales for twelve hours of hard work, whereas an unskilled worker in the city got at least two and a half reales, and the work and conditions were often more favorable.[17] Thus the hacendados of the late eighteenth century found it just as difficult to control the Indian population as their predecessors had a century before. Not so the merchants, however. Once the cochineal boom began, they were in a better position to coerce the Indians into work, since cultivating the insects did not require the Indians to leave their communities or neglect their own crops.

In many ways Antequera in the late eighteenth century was a quite different city than it had been in the years prior to 1740. A 1777 plan of the city reveals that the layout of the streets and the location of public buildings were essentially the same as they are today.[18] By this time the city's population had tripled, commerce and manufacturing were strong and had involved Antequera to a much greater degree in the world economy, and the provincial landed aristocracy had lost much of its power to wealthy peninsular merchants with contacts in Mexico City, Veracruz, and Europe. In 1792 more than 40 percent of the employed non-Indian males were involved in some capacity in commerce or the textile industry. Apart from these activities, however, the distribution of occupations had changed little since the late seventeenth century. As Table 14 shows, most of the labor force was employed in the service sector of the economy or engaged in manufacturing basic commodities for local consumption. Though the profile is somewhat distorted due to the exclusion of Indians and women, the broad outlines of the occupational structure are clear. If those groups had been included in the survey, we would see greatly increased numbers of workers in the clothing, metal, wood, and construction trades.

The Urban Indians

Growth in the urban Indian population kept pace with the development of Antequera during the second half of the eighteenth century. Indian migration to the city continued as the rural population recovered from its disastrous decline and the need for cheap labor increased in the obrajes, the construction industry, and a variety of trades and crafts. In purely numerical terms, Antequera became a more "Indian" city during these years, its indigenous population accounting for 27.9 percent of the total in 1792 (see Table 15 in the next section). However, there are no discernible signs that the ethnic boundaries separating the urban Indians from the other sectors of the population had changed to any great extent. With the exception of a handful of caciques, few Indians managed to escape their status as members of an oppressed minority forced into the most menial of urban occupations.

There were significant changes in social differentiation and identification within the Indian sector itself, however, though they went largely unnoticed by the white administrators who produced so much of the documentation on which this study depends. The curate of Jalatlaco provided the first clue in 1777, when he observed that Náhuatl was no longer spoken publicly in Jalatlaco or the Villa de Oaxaca, and that only a few Indian families commonly used it within the household.[19] Similarly, in 1804 Father Ybarra of the Villa de Oaxaca wrote that Náhuatl, once so widely spoken in his parish, had virtually ceased to be used around the middle of the eighteenth century in the Villa de Oaxaca, San Juan Chapultepec, San Martín Mexicapan, and San Jacinto Amilpas. Mixtec was still to be heard in Santa María Azompa, San Pedro Ixtlahuaca, and San Andrés Ixtlahuaca, he noted, but Náhuatl was all but dead: no one born in his parish during his twenty-nine years of residence could speak a word of it.[20]

The demise of Náhuatl in and around Antequera in the mid-eighteenth century is a strong indication that Nahua identity, which was still important in the urban Indian sector as late as 1730, had become virtually meaningless. In Jalatlaco, though residents remembered that the town was founded by Nahua allies of Fernando Cortés, and though a few of the old barrio names were still extant (notably, Tlaxcala, Tlatelolco, Mexicapan, Mixtlán Solar, and Guatemala), there is no evidence that their residents traced their ancestry through the Nahua line.[21] Nor did Nahua sobrenombres appear in a 1777 parish census as they had in a similar count in 1729.[22]

The disappearance of the Nahua identity was but one facet of the continuing deterioration of the boundary between the *principal* and macehual classes in urban Indian society, for we have seen that in Jalatlaco in the early eighteenth century the statuses of Nahua and *principal* were virtually synonymous. The squabbles over the participation of the macehuales in Jalatlaco's cabildo ceased after 1750, and one may infer that the Indian population had become more homogeneous.* Indeed, by 1765 there were even a few mestizos in Jalatlaco who claimed *principal* status.[23] Both the Villa de Oaxaca and Jalatlaco had Indian caciques in 1777, though the one in Jalatlaco, an unmarried assistant to the local priest, had very little influence.[24]

Closely tied to the demise of Náhuatl and Nahua identity was the decline of Jalatlaco as a populous urban Indian town and labor pool for Antequera. From an estimated population of 2,075 in 1748, the number of residents in the cabecera had fallen to a mere 303 by 1777. Many of the barrios of the settlement had disappeared or lost their former significance, and many houses were abandoned and in ruins. The parish priest blamed this decline on the town's loss of water rights to the adjacent Jalatlaco River and its lack of land.[25] Whatever the causes, many Jalatlaqueños were drawn to Antequera as spinners and weavers in the obrajes, and as masons, bakers, and

---

* Distinctions in status and wealth between principales and macehuales continued longer in many rural areas of the Valley. Though the question of political participation was generally resolved by the late eighteenth century, the 2 groups still differed in their dress and eating habits in 1777 in San Pablo Huitzo, San Martín Tilcajete, and Santa María Ayoquesco. (Biblioteca Nacional [Madrid], 2449: 256r, and 2450: 7r, 14r.)

artisans. As the city expanded, it became increasingly difficult for Jalatlaco to maintain a separate existence, tied as it was to the city economy.

Moreover, by 1777 Jalatlaco could no longer even be called an Indian settlement, for more than half of its 303 inhabitants (171, or some 56 percent) were non-Indians. Along with this influx of outsiders into the community came a much greater propensity toward intermarriage by the Indian residents. Twenty of the forty-eight married couples in the cabecera in 1777 were of mixed background. As many as a third of the Indian husbands were married to mestizas, mulattoes, or creoles.[26]

Significantly, Jalatlaco was the only satellite town of Antequera that underwent such an extensive mestization process during the colonial period. All the other nearby communities remained almost wholly Indian, as did the Valley's population in general. The 1777 census, which covered 88 Valley towns (in addition to Antequera), listed non-Indians in only forty-two of them.[27] The eight sujeto towns in the parish of Jalatlaco, which had a combined population of 1,893, had only twenty-four adult non-Indian residents; and Santo Tomás Xochimilco, directly north of Antequera, had just seven non-Indians among its 176 inhabitants.[28] Similarly, there were only 94 non-Indians in the seven towns in the parish of the Villa de Oaxaca to the west and south of the city.[29]

With few exceptions, the occupations held by urban Indian males differed little from those that had been open to them a century before, and there is little indication of any pattern of Indian occupational mobility.* The marriage records for 1793–97 reveal the occupations of 216 of the 228 Indian men who married in Antequera in those years, and we find that most worked at the more menial, less-skilled jobs, such as weaving, masonry, hat-making, baking,

---

*This statement applies only to those who fell into the social category indio. Though the definition of this category had changed little since the late seventeenth century, movement upward into the mestizo group by individuals may have increased in the late colonial period. Very often such a move was linked to occupational mobility. However, the relatively small size of the mestizo group recorded in the 1792 census indicates that it was harder to move out of the Indian category than to move from mestizo to creole rank.

shoemaking, and pottery manufacture. There were only three men in the relatively prestigious trades: two silversmiths and one blacksmith.* Two important changes since the seventeenth century are clearly related to changes in the local economy: the large increases in the number of weavers and cultivators of cochineal. The increase in the number of urban farmers is also noteworthy and was probably due to the development of intensive farming in the area of Trinidad de las Huertas to the southeast of the city.

As we would expect, these records also suggest that a much higher percentage of the Indians in Antequera were city-born than in the previous century: 63.5 percent of the Indian brides and grooms were born in the city compared with fewer than 30 percent in 1693–1700. Most of the others came from the same places as in the earlier group; well over a third came from Valley towns, and many of the rest came from the Sierra Zapotec region.

The Indian marriages presented in Table 19 (see the following section) show some interesting contrasts and parallels with those of the seventeenth century. Of the 847 marriages that took place in Antequera during 1793–97, only four involved caciques or cacicas (one married a peninsular Spaniard, two married creoles, and one married an Indian commoner), an indication of the shrinking size of the urban Indian nobility. Of the 285 Indian commoner grooms whose partners are known, 36.1 percent married outside the group, against an intermarriage rate of 24.6 percent for the seventeenth-century group. Most of the increase was due to the jump in the number of unions between Indian men and creole women: 32, compared with just three such unions in the years 1693–1700. When we consider that a full century had elapsed between the two samples, not to mention the many important social and economic changes in the colony itself, this change in the rate of intermarriage seems surprisingly small. As for the increased intermarriage between Indian men and creole women, it was probably due more to

*Archivo Parroquial del Sagrario, *Libros de Casamientos*, 1793–97. The breakdown on the other 213 is as follows: weavers, 27; masons, 23; hat-makers, 23; bakers, 21; cultivators of cochineal, 19; farmers, 18; shoemakers, 10; potters, 9; butchers, 8; tailors, 6; button-makers, 5; candle-makers, 4; unskilled laborers, 4; dyers, 2; brickmakers, 2; confectioners, 2; shopkeepers, 2; stonemasons, 2; carpenters, 2; other, 24.

the downward mobility of many creoles (and the ambiguity surrounding the category español in the eighteenth century) than to the upward mobility of the Indians. In any case, there was little change in the ethnic boundary between creoles and urban Indians, whose position in colonial urban society remained essentially the same as it had been 100 years before.

The virtual disappearance of the Nahua language, identity, and hegemony within the urban Indian population; the breakdown of the boundary between nobles and commoners; and the greatly reduced size of the urban Indian nobility clearly indicate that the process of proletarianization among Antequera's Indians had reached its final stage by the late eighteenth century. Two and a half centuries of Spanish rule had transformed a highly differentiated colonized population into a relatively homogeneous mass of urban workers who identified more with the city than with their Zapotec and Mixtec neighbors. That such should be the result of a prolonged colonial experience is not surprising. Indeed, the remarkable feature of this homogenization process is that it took so long in reaching its culmination.

Race and Social Identity

Racial identity and the nature of racial and economic differentiation in Antequera can be studied in greater detail for the late eighteenth century than for any other period. By far the single most valuable source is the census of 1792, which not only identifies the major part of the urban population by name, age, sociracial category, marital status, and street address, but also gives the occupations of the adult males. Because the government conducted this survey solely for the purpose of conscription, Indians and slaves were not included, since they were not legally eligible for military service. An Indian head count was taken, however, and recorded in the summary of the census drawn up in 1793; these figures are included in Table 15.[30]

According to this census, the population of Antequera in 1792 was 18,008 (excluding a small number of black and mulatto slaves) as shown in Table 15. This figure is 233 less than the total given in the

TABLE 15
The Population of Antequera, 1792

Classification	Male	Female	Total	Percent
Peninsulars	261	13	274	1.5%
Creoles	3,041	3,640	6,681[a]	37.1
Castizos	433	371	804	4.5
Mestizos	1,228	1,284	2,512	13.9
Moriscos or pardos	95	118	213	1.2
Mulattoes	911	980	1,891	10.5
Afromestizos[b]	185	198	383	2.1
Negroes[c]	15	12	27	0.1
Indians	2,644	2,374	5,018	27.9
Unidentified	82	123	205	1.1
TOTAL	8,895	9,113	18,008	99.9%

SOURCE: Archivo General de la Nación, Padrones 13; AGN, Tributos 34, 7: 51r.
NOTE: Percentages do not sum to 100 due to rounding.
[a] This figure includes members of the religious orders: 138 males and 177 females. Though the census does not give their racial classifications, miscellaneous sources suggest that most were creoles.
[b] An artificial category that does not appear in the census itself.
[c] Does not include most of the Negro slaves.

manuscript, but the discrepancy is not a serious one and is probably due to faulty arithmetic on the part of the census takers. There is a significant difference, however, between the racial categorizations of people in the census totals and the ones appearing in Table 15. Most children living with their parents were not racially identified in the body of the census, though no one was left unclassified in the manuscript totals. Rather than eliminate a large group from the study, we have calculated the racial affiliation of each child on the basis of its parents' background. In the cases of mixed marriages, the children's identities were largely arrived at through the standard formulas of the sistema de castas as employed in the census itself; one category, afromestizo (i.e., the child of a mestizo man and a mulatto woman), had to be artificially created to account for all of the offspring.

Two socioracial designations were used in this census that were not used in the seventeenth century: *morisco* and *pardo*. These new terms both came into use in the mid-eighteenth century to designate light-skinned mulattoes, frequently the offspring of creole and mulatto parents.[31] (Morisco designated those with the lightest skin color and pardo those of somewhat darker color.) This expansion of the socioracial lexicon was analogous to the creation of the category castizo in the seventeenth century and was symptomatic of upward social mobility and the ongoing integration of the mulattoes into the creole group. For the census takers (who almost certainly were local residents), however, these categories were plainly not well developed, since morisco was used only twenty-three times and pardo only twenty-six. Employing the standard formula, we have classified 213 persons as moriscos or pardos. This group is mostly composed of offspring living with their parents: 94 percent were age thirty or under and 60 percent were age ten or under. The census takers were far more comfortable with the designation castizo, which is used 535 times in the manuscript. Our calculations yielded 804 castizos, 77 percent of whom were age thirty or younger.

It should be stressed that just as there was no one "correct" folk model of the social structure of Antequera, neither was there always one correct racial identity for many of its inhabitants. The data indicate that the boundaries of the peninsular, Indian, and black groups were fairly rigid and well defined throughout the entire colonial period. Membership in these groups was for the most part a matter of ascription at birth. The categories for people of mixed racial heritage (including the creoles), however, were less clear in the minds of the people, and there was considerable latitude for variation according to circumstance and individual preference and prejudice. A comparison of the classifications employed in the 1792 census with those found in the marriage records for 1793–97 illustrate the ambiguity and irregularity inherent in the sistema de castas as a terminological and cognitive system (see Table 16). In the marriage records, socioracial terms were used in a more precise manner than in the census, with finer distinctions being made (by the priests or by the marriage partners themselves) within the mulatto group on the basis of visible traces of African ancestry. In the census, the term mulatto was applied almost universally to persons of such ancestry, whereas in the marriage registers, moriscos, pardos, and mulattoes were represented in equal proportions. The best explanation for discrepancies of this sort is that people were categorized (or

TABLE 16

Racial Composition of Marriage Partners
in Antequera, 1793–1797

Classification	Men	Women	Total	Percent
Peninsulars	22	—	22	1.3%
Creoles	220	261	481	28.4
Castizos	23	22	45	2.7
Mestizos	129	161	290	17.1
Moriscos	12	38	50	3.0
Pardos	32	19	51	3.0
Mulattoes	23	27	50	3.0
Negroes	2	—	2	0.1
Caciques	2	2	4	0.2
Indians	313	228	541	31.9
Mestindios	1	6	7	0.4
Unidentified	68	83	151	8.9
TOTAL	847	847	1,694	100.0%

SOURCE: Archivo Parroquial del Sagrario, *Libros de Casamientos*, 1793–97.

categorized themselves) in different ways in different situations, maximizing or elevating their racial status whenever and wherever they could.

The incidence of mulattoes "passing" as creoles is suggested by the age distribution for the mulatto category in the 1793 census summary.[32] Unlike the standard age pyramid, which finds most of the population under the age of sixteen, the mulatto age distribution shows a marked underrepresentation of children below the age of seven (15.5 percent of the total). Though the age distribution for the population as a whole does not indicate a generally low fertility rate at this time, it is possible that fertility was especially low among mulattoes and in Spanish-Negro unions. A more satisfactory explanation of the abnormally low number of mulatto children, however, is that a significant number of mulatto adults were marrying "up," with the result that their children would be classified as españoles (evidence that this was indeed the case is revealed in the marriage data for 1793–97, discussed below). A demographic factor, as well as the pattern of increasing social mobility, helps to account for such a trend at this time: there was a substantial imbalance of the sexes in the combined español-castizo-mestizo population among different age groups. In the under-sixteen group there were 2,248 males and

1,620 females; in the sixteen-and-over group the distribution was reversed, with 3,880 females and 2,675 males. This left many males in the under-sixteen group and many females over sixteen available for marriage outside their category when they came of age. With these trends in mind, we would expect that the mulatto category would virtually disappear from social ranking in Antequera by the mid-nineteenth century.

Socioeconomic Groups

The variety of occupations found in Antequera in 1792 (in coding the census we identified 141 different occupations) suggests a complex social and economic system, with special concentrations of activity in commerce, textile and clothing production, and the administration of public affairs, both secular and religious. Table 17 presents an occupational breakdown of Antequera's adult male population, with the employed males divided on the basis of size of income or estate, regularity of employment, and "employment status" (skill and prestige) into three primary socioeconomic groups: the elite, preindustrial middle groups, and lower groups. Since information on income and wealth is generally limited to the elite and must be supplemented with status considerations at all levels, we use the term socioeconomic groups rather than classes for the three main groupings, even though the occupational and ethnic patterns imply a developing system of preindustrial economic classes.[33]

The census information does not always allow for easy placement of occupations into elite, middle, and lower categories. The 191 men listed as *labradores* (or farmers) and hacendados are especially difficult to classify in socioeconomic terms, since these categories lump together holders of entailed estates, large landowners, small landowners, sharecroppers, and farm laborers. Some owners of rural estates were prominent figures in the government and society of the city; but except for the few who came from the wealthiest or oldest families and owned other property or productive capital, such men were wholly dependent for their prominence on the productivity of their land, a most precarious resource. With many estates sold on the death of their owners, the prestige of a landed family was rarely ascendant for more than a generation. Owing to the

TABLE 17

Socioeconomic Groups in Antequera, 1792

(Adult males)

Elite			**Lower Groups**		
Merchants	217		Low-status artisans		
High royal officials	72		Bakers	54	
High clergy	20		Blacksmiths and		
Large estate owners	19	328	farriers	135	
Preindustrial Middle Groups			Butchers	76	
Professionals			Button-makers	51	
Secular clergy	91		Carpenters	136	
Members of			Cart-makers	22	
religious orders	138		Chair-makers	39	
Minor royal			Confectioners	27	
officials	18		Fireworks-		
Physicians	7		makers	33	
Lawyers	10		Hat-makers	114	
Schoolteachers	19		Masons	37	
Scribes	39		Potters	25	
Students	102		Shoemakers	232	
Other	15	439	Stonecutters	19	
High-status artisans			Tailors	359	
Barber-surgeons	56		Tanners	80	
Druggists	6		Turners	75	
Gilders	10		Weavers	284	
Graneros	16		Other	251	2,049
Musicians and			Muleteers		15
music teachers	26		Peons		2
Painters	36		Servants		93
Practical surgeons	4		Unemployed		102
Silversmiths	106		Indians		1,543
Other	24	284			
Small landholders,					
sharecroppers,			**TOTALS**		
and farm laborers		172	Elite		328
Traders		127	Preindustrial Middle		
Shopkeepers		18	Groups		1,054
Miners and			Lower Groups		3,804
mineralogists		14			5,186

modest size, heavy indebtedness, and frequent sale of estates owned by non-Indians, the landowning class of Antequera was not a closed, homogeneous, self-perpetuating, or especially powerful group. The limited information in the census on the occupations of sons of labradores and hacendados suggests that many children of landowners moved down the social ladder into craft groups, such as weavers, carpenters, and silversmiths, or became petty merchants.

Three measures allow us to make a rough division between the elite and the non-elite within this important group. First, William B. Taylor's work on the value of estates in the Valley of Oaxaca provides a rough measure of the wealth of an important segment of the landholding group residing in Antequera.[34] Only fifteen estates in the Valley were valued at over 15,000 pesos in the late eighteenth century. Of these, five belonged to the religious orders, six were entailed properties, and the remaining four had an average net value (assessed value minus mortgages) of 4,864 pesos. An additional eighteen private estates were worth between 5,000 pesos and 15,000 pesos (averaging 5,791 pesos). If we use 5,000 pesos as a somewhat arbitrary cutoff figure, twenty-eight families holding land in the Valley of Oaxaca would qualify as elite. Actually, we can only say with certainty that the holders of the six entailed estates with a net worth over 15,000 pesos belong in the socioeconomic elite. Members of the Guenduláin, Ramírez de Aguilar, and Bohórquez families in particular are frequently mentioned in colonial records as "leading citizens"—as indeed they were bound to be, for not only did the entails of these families carry with them the title of *regidor perpetuo*, but from time to time individual holders of these estates secured other political and religious offices as well. Some were positions of substantial authority, such as corregidor, alguacil mayor, alcalde ordinario, and *promotor fiscal del obispado*; others, such as *alférez real*, were largely honorific. The social rank of holders of entailed estates gave them subtle influence in political matters even when they did not hold office. Their friendship and advice frequently was sought by political officials of lower social standing. In 1711, for example, the community of Teotitlán del Valle complained that owing to Joseph de Guenduláin's close ties with the local alcalde mayor the boundary between Teotitlán and the Guenduláin hacienda had been faultily measured.[35]

A second measure of elite status for landowners is the prefix "don," a mark of prestige that is attached to thirty of the 107 labradores who headed households in the 1792 census. As with the 5,000 pesos standard, the "don" title is a somewhat arbitrary measure that gives an overgenerous estimate of elite landowners. At the end of the eighteenth century the title did not necessarily signify nobility and wealth. For example, there were three French shopkeepers in Antequera in 1792 who carried the "don" but were classified as *plebeyos*, or commoners.[36] The term seems to have been a sign of status based somewhat vaguely on respectability and wealth rather than a legally designated rank. In other words, all men in the elite were dons, but not all of the dons were members of the elite.

A final measure of elite status within the landholding group comes from the accounts of donations for the defense of Antequera against the Independence forces of José María Morelos in 1812.[37] With few exceptions, Loyalist supporters in Antequera two years into the Independence wars were reduced to the economic and social elite, the group that had most to lose from a change in government. Though these events occurred twenty years after the census, the donation record is our one clear example of elite behavior and is probably the most accurate measure of the landholding elite in the city. A total of nineteen landowners residing in Antequera gave to the Loyalist cause in 1812. Of the five landowners who gave more than 66 pesos, three headed families holding entailed estates in the Valley. In short, the landholding elite, by any measure, falls far short of the total labradores residing in Antequera in 1792. A range of nineteen (donor labradores in 1812) to thirty (labradores carrying the don title in 1792) is our best estimate of the landholding elite near the end of the colonial period.

Though we can make a satisfactory distinction between elite and non-elite cultivators, we cannot further divide the non-elite cultivators into smallholders, sharecroppers, and farm laborers. We have placed all 172 non-elite cultivators under the small landholder heading, recognizing that this inflates the middle groups and undervalues the lower groups, where sharecroppers and farm laborers should properly go; but the distortion is probably small, since few farm laborers are known to have resided in the city and commuted to the fields (there are only two men in the peon category in the census), and Taylor's work on land tenure suggests that most of the relatively small number of Valley sharecroppers resided in rural villages rather than in the city.

There are also problems of classification with Indians, high royal officials, apprentice merchants, and craftsmen. All adult Indian men have been placed in the lower group because from what information we have we know that urban Indians were likely to make their living in the clothing, metal, wood, and construction trades or as servants. There were certainly exceptions, however. For example, many of the Indian nobles who lived in the city enjoyed landed wealth and higher status, and small numbers of Indians worked in the more prestigious trades and held positions in the clergy.[38] There may also have been a few very wealthy Indian residents following in the footsteps of Luis Sánchez (d. 1766), an Indian noble from San Martín Tilcajete, who possessed extensive rural properties and owned a boisterous tavern in the city, where he sold the pulque produced on his estates.[39] Moreover, the 1,543 total for Indian men is merely an approximation derived from the census manuscript summary plus the count on the monastic servants and two individuals mentioned in the body of the census. This figure is undoubtedly less accurate than the totals for other ethnic groups, since Indians were not systematically recorded in the census, and there were significant numbers of Indians who resided in the city only part of the year.

Cajeros (apprentice merchants) have been put in the elite even though these young men presumably did not enjoy independent wealth at this stage of their careers. Many of them were nephews of the owners of merchant houses, and according to the pattern described for Guanajuato, would eventually inherit the business.[40] The high royal official group contains some minor functionaries because the census taker listed them along with important officeholders such as the customs officials. Our classification of craftsmen into high-status and low-status groups is based on the skill and training required or on the prestige accorded to a particular artisan group, such as silversmiths and gilders who worked with precious metals. Traders and graneros have been included in the middle group on the assumption that their incomes were substantially greater than those of low-status artisans. Finally, we suspect that such low-status artisan groups as blacksmiths, cobblers, and carpenters disguise substantial unemployment in the city. We base this suspicion on the fact that many of the 102 men classified as unemployed in the census were old or disabled rather than sturdy beggars, and the further knowledge that vagabondage was a frequently reported problem in Antequera at the end of the colonial period.

With these qualifications and adjustments in mind, the relative size and distribution of the three socioeconomic groups can be summarized. In broad terms, this was a society with a small, wealthy elite, a large semi-skilled and unskilled work force, and a well-developed middle layer of professional and skilled occupations. The elite, representing 6 percent of the adult men classified, was composed of cochineal and textile merchants, high royal officials, the high clergy, and large estate owners. Within the elite, the merchants were the most numerous by a wide margin. The great personal fortunes of Antequera were in the hands of leading merchants, and all but two of the merchants (apprentices excluded) enjoyed the prestigious don before their names. As David Brading has noted for Guanajuato and the Bajío region, the landholding elite in Antequera was smaller and relatively less powerful than is usually supposed.[41] The middle groups, composed of various professional and business occupations, skilled and high-status artisans, miners, and small landholders, were considerably larger than the elite. Accounting for 20 percent of the employed males, these intermediate occupations provided at least the potential for significant numbers of people to move up and down the social scale. The lower groups, representing 73 percent of the male work force, were especially numerous in the semi-skilled and low-status trades, occupations that served the merchant elite. Over 50 percent of the low-status artisans were textile and clothing workers.

Race and Stratification

Table 18 and the accompanying figure summarize the information on the racial distribution of occupations in Antequera according to the 1792 census, arranged by the socioeconomic groupings discussed in the preceding section. These summaries indicate that the peninsulars' place in the socioeconomic hierarchy is just what one would expect, but there are many more low-status creoles and sig-

TABLE 18

Racial Distribution of Socioeconomic Groups in Antequera (Excluding Slaves and Indians), 1792

(Adult males)

Group	Peninsulars	Creoles	Mestizos and castizos	Mulattoes[a]	Total
Elite					
Number	191	132	3	1	327
Percent	*58.4%*	*40.4%*	*0.9%*	*0.3%*	
Professionals (includes shopkeepers)					
Number	15	275	11	6	307
Percent	*4.9%*	*89.6%*	*3.6%*	*2.0%*	
High-status artisans (includes traders)					
Number	8	295	71	37	411
Percent	*1.9%*	*71.8%*	*17.3%*	*9.0%*	
Low-status artisans (includes muleteers)					
Number	4	816	702	536	2,058
Percent	*0.2%*	*39.7%*	*34.1%*	*26.0%*	
Servants and peons					
Number	—	18	46	31	95
Percent	—	*18.9%*	*48.4%*	*32.6%*	
TOTAL	218	1,536	833	611	3,198

NOTE: The totals on the socioeconomic groups do not match those in Table 17 in every case. The racial designations of one political official in the elite group, of 12 men in the professional group, and of 6 men in the low-status artisans group are unknown; and the 138 members of the religious orders have been omitted from the professionals for lack of precise information on their ethnic backgrounds. Percentages do not necessarily sum to 100 due to rounding.

[a] Includes moriscos, pardos, and afromestizos, and also free Negroes.

nificantly more high-status mestizos and mulattoes than one would predict from the racial hierarchy. Only vestiges remained of a former precapitalist society and economy that had once been simple enough to organize in estate-based terms. Creoles were well represented in all five social strata and were not particularly concentrated at the upper levels. Whereas more than four-fifths of the peninsular group were members of the elite, only 8 percent of the employed creole men attained that status—a strikingly low figure for a group that accounted for a third of the city's population. In absolute terms, the creoles were most numerous in the low-status artisan group (53 percent of the employed creole men were in that category), a clear departure from an estate system based on race. Mulattoes, mestizos, and other castas, meanwhile, though only marginally represented in the elite and professional categories, were spread across the high-status artisan, low-status artisan, and servant categories. Roughly 17 percent of the high-status artisans were mestizos or castizos, and 9 percent were mulattoes or related castas. This racial distribution of occupations suggests that Antequera's "ambiguous middle layer" was not confined to the mestizo group, but included the creoles, and to a lesser degree, the mulattoes and the other casta groups.

Another test of the extent to which race and social position were related is provided by status positions within the artisan occupations. The position of master in the numerous craft guilds was an achieved status that could be acquired through personal skill and business acumen, and for many craftsmen served as a means of up-

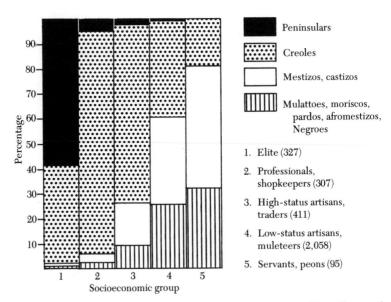

Racial Distribution of Socioeconomic Groups in Antequera, 1792. *Note*: Slaves and Indians are not included.

ward mobility. Though the 1792 census does not identify the rank of craftsmen, we have a detailed list of guild elections for 1790–94. The racial classifications and marriage patterns of twenty-nine masters from twelve guilds have been determined by matching the names of the men listed therein with the census data on them.[42] Eleven of the twelve guilds represented in this sample are in the low-status category: shoemaker, carpenter, confectioner, blacksmith, button-maker, weaver, pork-butcher, stonecutter, tailor, potter, and hat-maker. The one high-status trade represented is that of the painter.

The racial distribution of this sample does not follow the estate-like pattern limiting access to master status to men classified as españoles—peninsulars or creoles.[43] Creoles, mestizos, castizos, and mulattoes are all represented by at least three masters, and just as we saw in the general pattern of racial distribution across occupations in Antequera, we find creole masters in the same guilds with mestizos and mulattoes rather than being confined to certain "Spanish only" trades. Eleven of the masters were classified as creoles, ten as mestizos, four as castizos, three as mulattoes, and one as a pardo. The creole masters were found in the shoemakers, blacksmiths, tailors, painters, carpenters, confectioners, and weavers guilds; the mestizos in all but the weavers and confectioners guilds; the castizos in the carpenters, button-makers, pork-butchers, and weavers guilds; the mulattoes in the blacksmiths and tailors guilds; and the pardo in the potters guild. The marriage pattern of this group of master craftsmen finds most marrying within their racial classification. Of the twenty-one married men, only two married down the racial scale (one creole-mestiza couple; one mestizo-mulata couple) and three married up (two mestizo-creole couples, one pardo-mestiza couple). As we see, only the mestizos married across three groups, taking wives in both the creole and mulatto groups, as well as their own. There were only three men in the full group who were masters in the higher-status painters guild; two were creoles, and the third was a mestizo. All three were married, and all three had taken creole wives. Though this sample of twenty-one married masters is too small to permit any firm conclusions, the high-status trades probably came closer than the low-status ones to approximating the estate model of Spanish masters with Spanish wives, allowing of course for significant miscegenation in the creole classification.

In three respects, race did continue to dictate social status. The elite clearly was dominated by the peninsulars, a racially designated group that is absent, or nearly so, from the other four social strata. Some 88 percent of the employed peninsulars were engaged in occupations of elite status: wholesale merchants and their apprentices, government officials, large landowners, and priests. Fully 72 percent of the peninsulars were involved in commerce, but only two of them were tratantes, or petty traders, whose ranks were dominated by creoles. A second social stratum that carries a strong relationship to racial designations is the professional group, where 90 percent of the sample was designated as creole. It appears that certain occupations, such as lawyer, doctor, notary, clergyman, student, and schoolmaster, were still associated with Spanishness, and that the overwhelming majority of professionals at least passed as white. Third, mulatto status continued to carry socially inferior meaning even though many mulattoes had escaped the lowest socioeconomic ranking. Here are three representative cases of negative association with mulatto status: in 1754 a Spanish woman from Antequera, in charging a local man with cursing at her, called his outburst "mulatto talk"; in 1789 the parents of Joaquín Camacho y Ybañez brought a civil suit against their son to keep him from marrying a mulatto woman, alleging "inequality of rank"; and in 1790 a man from Coyoacán (near Mexico City) assaulted a public official after telling him to "Go to hell! . . . I'm no mulatto who has to pay tribute."[44] It is hardly surprising that anyone who could escape the label was likely to do so.

Yet a further test to assess the significance of eighteenth-century socioracial categories in Antequera and their relationship to social identity and stratification is found in marriage patterns. For reasons to be discussed shortly, the 1792 census is not a good source for the study of marriage patterns, and we prefer to rely instead on statistics culled from parish records for the years 1793–97. The marriage patterns in Table 19 show some interesting parallels and contrasts with the seventeenth-century data presented in Table 10.

As in the preceding century, one of the striking features of the data is the lack of marriageable peninsular women (in this sample, there are none at all), and the overwhelming propensity of peninsular males to take creole wives. The 1792 census reveals that the peninsular population was distinctly different from all other groups in three important respects: it was nearly all male (261 of 274); 22 percent of the men and women were over fifty years old compared with slightly less than 7.5 percent for the general population; and over half of the men (55.8 percent) were listed as unmarried. The very high proportion of unmarried peninsulars in 1792 has a clear legal explanation. At this time, no peninsular could declare himself married in Spain and remain in the New World without his family. In 1784, eight years before the census, the bishop of Oaxaca, with the aid of a cédula, saw to it that nineteen "unmarried" peninsulars living in the bishopric were sent back to Spain to be reunited with their families on the grounds that "their souls are more important than their wealth and positions in America."[45] The large bachelor population further suggests that peninsular Spaniards at the end of the colonial period expected to return to their homeland and were not inclined to establish deep roots in the American colonies. Those who did stay and marry, however, almost always wed creole women, who were also defined as socially white.

Looking at the marriages of all the socioracial groups in Table 19, we find an overall intermarriage rate of 44.8 percent, only a slight increase over the seventeenth-century figure of 41.6 percent. Creoles and Indians also continued to exhibit a marked predilection for in-group marriage, at the rate of 68.2 percent and 63.9 percent, respectively. Nor was there any substantial change in the kinds of mates sought by mestizos and castizos, though a slightly higher percentage now took creole wives (25.4 percent, compared with 22.7 percent a century before).

Though the broad outlines of the system remained essentially the same, the society was nevertheless far from static during the eight-

TABLE 19

Marriage Patterns in Antequera According to Church Records, 1793–1797

(Percentages based on 714 marriages in which both partners' origins are known)

Men	Women								Total	Intermarriage rate
	Peninsulars	Creoles	Castizas, mestizas	Mulattoes[a]	Negroes	Cacicas	Indians	Unident. & misc.		
Peninsulars										
Number	—	19	1	—	—	1	1	—	22	
Percent	—	*86.4*	*4.5*	—	—	*4.5*	*4.5*	—		*100.0%*
Creoles										
Number	—	144	48	12	—	1	6	9	220	
Percent	—	*68.2*	*22.7*	*5.7*	—	*0.5*	*2.8*	—		*31.8%*
Castizos, mestizos										
Number	—	35	55	28	—	—	20	14	152	
Percent	—	*25.4*	*39.9*	*20.3*	—	—	*14.5*	—		*60.1%*
Mulattoes[a]										
Number	—	15	18	13	—	—	8	13	67	
Percent	—	*27.8*	*33.3*	*24.1*	—	—	*14.8*	—		*75.9%*
Negroes										
Number	—	—	2	—	—	—	—	—	2	
Percent	—	—	*100.0*	—	—	—	—	—		*100.0%*
Caciques										
Number	—	1	—	—	—	—	1	—	2	
Percent	—	*50.0*	—	—	—	—	*50.0*	—		*100.0%*
Indians										
Number	—	32	45	26	—	—	182	28	313	
Percent	—	*11.2*	*15.8*	*9.1*	—	—	*63.9*	—		*36.1%*
Unident. & misc.										
Number	—	15	14	5	—	—	10	25	69	
TOTAL/ AVERAGE	0	261	183	84	0	2	228	89	847	*44.8%*

SOURCE: Archivo Parroquial del Sagrario, *Libros de Casamientos,* 1793–97.

NOTE: The slave population cannot be broken down in this table, as it was in Table 10, because the eighteenth-century records do not consistently distinguish between slave and free mulattoes and Negroes. Percentages have been rounded.

eenth century. Creoles were still reluctant to take Indian or mulatto wives, as they were a century before, but now fully one-fifth of the creole grooms married mestizas. By far the greatest changes, however, had occurred within the mulatto group. That the creation of the categories morisco and pardo for light-skinned mulattoes was symptomatic of heightened social mobility and the ongoing integration of the mulattoes into white society is borne out by their marriages. The proportion of mulatto males marrying within the group declined from a little over half to less than a quarter during the course of the eighteenth century. The change was unmistakably upward: by the 1790's close to 28 percent of the mulattoes were taking creole wives, and fully a third married mestizas or castizas. Less than 15 percent married Indian women, roughly the same proportion as prevailed for the free mulatto group in the previous century.*

Though the 1792 census lists many more married people than the 1,694 newlyweds in the church records, the census data are of questionable value. For one thing, there are no statistics on Indian unions. But worse still, from the point of view of our present concern, racial designations were assigned to persons after the marriages had taken place, thus increasing the chances of husband and wife being "lumped" together in the same category. The total intermarriage rate (44.5 percent) is about the same as in the parish records, and so is the pattern of the creole marriages. But this lumping problem is evident in the case of mulatto marriages because of the format of the census itself. The mulatto population was counted and recorded separately, with the result that there is a systematic bias in favor of in-group marriage. Thus 55.9 percent of the mulatto males were said to have mulatto wives (compared with 24.1 percent in Table 19). There were 9 percent fewer mulattoes with creole wives than in the church sample, 8 percent fewer with mestiza wives, and almost 10 percent fewer with Indian wives. Similarly, the census shows 8

---

* Further evidence that the mulattoes as a group were blending into white society is found in the fact that whereas they accounted for 22.3 percent of the marriage partners in the seventeenth-century group, the combined mulatto population (including moriscos and pardos) accounted for only 9 percent of the identifiable partners in this group.

percent fewer mestizos with mulatto wives, and their in-group marriage rate is correspondingly higher. Furthermore, though some 20 percent of the marriages in the parish records involved partners from non-adjacent categories in the socioracial hierarchy (a substantial increase over the 14 percent in the 1690's), the corresponding figure for the census data is only 14.3 percent.

Taking the parish records as the more reliable of the two sources, we see a clear trend toward marrying upward among the mestizos and mulattoes, and a corresponding downwardly mobile trend among the creoles. Significantly, the one marriage between a peninsular man and an Indian woman recorded in the parish registers was performed in secret, unannounced to the general public because of the "risks involved and the consequences that could result." Creoles who were not members of the elite or the professional group were more likely to marry women of color.

Theory and Practice

Despite the high degree of miscegenation and intermarriage in the eighteenth century and the increased acceptance of people of color by many of the whites, the Spanish legal system remained all but impervious to change when it came to regulating social relations. By 1774 the *Recopilación de leyes de los reynos de las Indias*, promulgated in 1680 as the first attempt to codify Spanish colonial law, was in its third edition. Yet, significantly, in all this time few changes had been made in respect to the rights and duties of the traditional colonial categories of Indians, mestizos, mulattoes, and blacks. Almost all of the laws in the new edition dated back to the late sixteenth and early seventeenth centuries. Nevertheless, there were two general trends in colonial legal and social thought that affected the castas: (1) a growing acceptance of the mestizos and a frequent willingness to grant them legal parity with whites; and (2) the laxity with which the laws were enforced and the greater frequency with which exceptions were made for particular individuals or groups.

The authorities in Spain were not oblivious to these trends. Stimulated by a petition concerning a pardo from Venezuela in 1806, the Council of the Indies in Madrid reflected on past developments in the policies toward mestizos and mulattoes. With regard to mestizos, the council noted how their eligibility for the priesthood had changed since the days of the conquest. Up to about 1580 mestizos had been categorically excluded from both public and religious office on the grounds that they were "vicious, illegitimate neophytes with bad customs" who were incapable of shouldering the duties of office. This policy had been relaxed somewhat in the succeeding decades because of the lack of priests who could communicate effectively with the Indians, though the council noted that the ordination of mestizos had never been a common practice. Now, in this "third epoch," the Crown was finally ready to acknowledge that mestizos were indeed useful to the Church, and the bishops accordingly were ordered to ordain them, though with "scrupulous care." [46]

But if the council was prepared to make concessions to the mestizos, it drew a rigid line between them and persons with visible traces of African ancestry. The mulattoes as a whole, under whatever label, were felt to be the most "spurious, adulterous, and illegitimate" of all groups, people whose added taint of Negro blood made them "notably inferior to and different from legitimate whites and mestizos." Mulattoes were considered to be antagonistic to the colonial government, and were to be placed in a class apart from the whites and mestizos. "Mestizos who prove themselves to be legitimate sons of Spaniard and Indian may obtain all the rights, jobs, and offices open to Europeans and Americans [creoles]", the council ruled. "As to the *morenos* and *pardos*, they must prove with documents (not with witnesses) their free and legitimate descent over four generations in order to be eligible for such offices and positions." [47]

These distinctions were known to administrators in the Valley of Oaxaca at least by the 1770's. In 1779 Bishop Alonso de Ortigoza instructed the local priests to follow a directive from the Audiencia that discouraged the intermarriage of Indians with mulattoes, Negroes, and *coyotes*. There was no specific objection to marriages between Indians and mestizos or castizos.[48] Legal proceedings conducted in the second half of the eighteenth century to certify limpieza de sangre also show that the status of castizos and mestizos had improved by this time. A person no longer had to establish a claim to pure Spanish ancestry to be legally of *casta limpia*. Frequently proof of castizo or mestizo heritage would do just as well, and it appears that the mestizo, castizo, and español categories were becoming consolidated in the minds of many people.[49]

Still, as we have seen, mulattoes were able to obtain dispensations from the various legal restrictions by in some way qualifying as members of a select group. One such method was to enter the army. For lack of manpower, special militias of mulattoes were formed in New Spain in the late-seventeenth and eighteenth centuries, and members of these groups were exempt from tribute and permitted to carry arms.[50] In the late eighteenth century the Crown instituted a mechanism by which mulattoes could purchase a license that made them legally white and entitled them to all the rights and prerogatives of Spaniards.* Finally, though even free Negroes and mulattoes were required to pay royal tribute, we have seen that collection in urban New Spain was far from systematic from the mid-seventeenth century on, and many tributaries successfully escaped it with a minimum of effort.

All told, the posture of Spanish law toward the separation of the races relaxed a little in the eighteenth century but did not change fundamentally. The dividing line between creoles and mestizos became somewhat fuzzy, but mulattoes and Indians by and large were subject in theory to the same sort of legal discrimination as they had endured during the previous two centuries. The legal system and the Spanish colonial elite continued to view society in terms of a hierarchy of racially defined strata, each endowed by law with certain rights and duties (or lack of them) in much the same manner as the estate-based social system of feudal Europe. That the society

* Magnus Mörner, *Race Mixture*, p. 45. No instances of this have been found for Oaxaca.

was in fact operating on different principles, and had been for quite a while, was apparent to some, but their reaction was invariably to tighten restrictions or devise new racial categories in an effort to restore the "old" system and preserve the basis of Spanish colonial power.

Contrary to what one would expect if the socioracial labels designated actual ethnic groups in all cases, the proportion of mestizos and mulattoes in Antequera's population declined over the course of the eighteenth century. In 1700 mestizos accounted at best for 15–20 percent of the population, and free mulattoes for some 20–27 percent. By 1792 the mestizos and mulattoes each accounted for less than 15 percent of the populace despite the high degree of miscegenation. Most of the slack was taken up by a 5–10 percent increase in the proportion of creoles and an 8–11 percent jump in the Indian sector. With the exception of the Indians, these proportional shifts cannot be explained solely in terms of geographical mobility. The non-Indian population of the Bishopric of Oaxaca was very small, and it is doubtful that the only groups that the cochineal boom attracted to the city were creoles and Indians. Many areas to the north were thriving as well, and jobs were not in short supply. Though the information on places of origin in the 1792 Antequera census was found to be unreliable, a similar count made in the city of Guanajuato in the same year revealed that 77.7 percent of the adult non-Indian males were born in the city or in nearby mining villages and ranchos. Only among the elite, and especially the merchant class, was there a significant degree of immigration.[51]

As the marriage records indicate, the most probable explanation for the small size of the casta population is the assimilation of large numbers of mestizos, castizos, and mulattoes into the creole group. This process frequently occurred in cases where the children of, say, a mulatto and a creole woman were identified as creoles. Furthermore, it was not uncommon for castas to attain the status of creole during their lifetimes as a result of the accumulation of wealth or strategic marriage alliances. Gonzalo Aguirre Beltrán has found similar evidence of passing for many parts of New Spain, and if Antequera differed at all from the general pattern it was merely in respect to the time depth of the phenomenon. The passing that Aguirre Beltrán believes to have been characteristic of the breakdown of the sistema de castas in the late colonial period was very much in evidence in Antequera in the seventeenth century.[52]

The inevitable result of this social mobility on the part of the miscegenated was the absorption of many Negro and Indian genes into the segment of society culturally defined as Spanish and white. Thus during the eighteenth century there was a gradual change in the phenotypical standards associated with membership in the creole group as darker individuals became eligible for "white" status. There was a slow but steady darkening of what H. Hoetink calls the "somatic norm image" of colonial society, "the complex of physical (somatic) characteristics which are accepted by a group as its norm and ideal."[53] This white somatic norm, of course, was implanted and maintained by the dominant Spanish elite. Discrimination tended to be strongest against individuals and groups whose phenotypes deviated most sharply from the norm and mildest toward those who most closely approximated it. Observed from the individual's point of view, the phenomenon of social mobility amounted to what some have called a process of "bleaching," or racial upgrading, that was an important element in the functioning of the sistema de castas from its inception.

The most notable change in the socioracial system of eighteenth-century Antequera, apart from the reduction in the proportion of the mulatto population, was the subdivision of that population into the three classifications of morisco, pardo, and mulatto. The lighter-skinned moriscos and pardos were the product of ongoing miscegenation between whites and mulattoes, and the creation of these new categories signified an attempt by the Spanish elite to preserve its power base and social status from the threat of dilution. The application of these new socioracial terms decreased their bearers' chances of attaining white status, and buttressed the somatic and social distance between españoles and the remainder of the population on which the Spanish colonial system depended. The category of castizo had been created in much the same way in the early seventeenth century when the perceived threat to Spanish power and privilege lay in the mestizo group.

Paradoxically, the sistema de castas as a terminological system became more complex in the late eighteenth century, and the white elite more overtly preoccupied with it, at a time when race alone was no longer a reliable index to social rank. This does not mean that the stratification system was becoming more rigid, but only that the elite was making a belated effort to maintain its position as a dominant white minority. Race mixture had long since blurred the social boundaries between the colonizers and the colonized, but for the elite to have psychologically accepted this fact would have been tantamount to undermining its own justification for colonial domination. Inasmuch as the elite clung to its racist view of society as embodied in the sistema de castas, it is clear that socioeconomic factors, operating to an extent independently from racial ones, had become quite important as determinants of rank by the late eighteenth century.

Many mulattoes did manage to penetrate the creole status group, as evidenced in their marriage patterns. This was a common phenomenon in eighteenth-century New Spain, and Aguirre Beltrán has observed that parish baptismal records frequently show evidence of erasures and the substitution of the word español for the word mulatto.[54] In Antequera the process must have been relatively easy, since racial designations were not ordinarily recorded in the baptismal registers.[55]

An interesting case in point is that of Manuel Yllanes, a master blacksmith who was born in Antequera and lived in the town of Zimatlán in 1791. In that year Yllanes was compelled to go before the authorities to verify his status as an español in order to avoid having his name listed on the mulatto tribute roll. He presented four witnesses, all of whom testified that he was of pure Spanish ancestry, of Old Christian stock, and free of any Indian, Negro, Moorish, or Jewish blood. Soon thereafter his status was confirmed by the city's procurador mayor. The following year, however, the official in charge of tribute collection in Zimatlán became suspicious and had the curate check the marriage certificate of the blacksmith's daughter and the record of his father-in-law's death. According to the church documents, both Yllanes and his wife were pardos, and it was also learned that the blacksmith had intentionally falsified his wife's surname in the 1791 limpieza de sangre proceedings in an effort to conceal her mulatto heritage. In keeping with the ambiguity surrounding mulatto-español status in this period, even with this information the tribute collector was unable to make a decision and solicited the advice of the intendente in Antequera.[56]

The ultimate fate of the blacksmith is unknown, but his situation was not unusual. The tribute collector in the jurisdiction of Huitzo (Guaxolotitlán) in 1799 encountered several "mulatos" who claimed to be "españoles," but since they had no documents to prove their claims their names remained on the tribute roll.[57] In Antequera there were complaints in 1794 about the ploys by which the tributaries who belonged to Antequera's craft guilds avoided their payments. Many of the guilds, the treasury officials charged, had recently revised the racial designations on their membership lists, with the result that great numbers of workers now denied that they were subject to tribute. As of April 1794 only eighteen of the city's thirty-nine guilds had remitted the royal tribute due for the previous year.[58] These sorts of problems were becoming increasingly common in all parts of New Spain. Aguirre Beltrán has brought to light an interesting communication to the viceroy from the supervisor of the 1792 military census of Texcoco:

There is no one who dares to classify the *castas*. Such information, if applied rigorously, would be odious and expose the dark stains, erased by time, in prominent families. The inevitable result would be a number of scandalous charges, which, if converted into lawsuits, would never cease. In my view, the censuses for the establishment of the militias should confer honor, not take it away. I have recorded the *castas* of *español, castizo, mestizo, pardo*, etc., based on the declarations of the people themselves, though some have led me to suspect they were not telling the truth. In the census of Tepetlaoztoc Your Excellency will find a town full of *españoles*. Regardless of what they are, the people live well and honorably, and deserve to be classed with the best *casta*.[59]

The comments of the census taker in Tepeaca are equally interesting:

Usually among the common folk, families leave it up to whoever asks them to decide which class they belong to. They are less worried or more humble than others who pretend to be something they are not. It is necessary to find out what their parents were in order to determine their classification, and they do not care if they are listed as *españoles*, *castizos*, or *mestizos*. They are only concerned that they not be classified as *pardos* or Indian tributaries.[60]

As the case of the Zimatlán blacksmith shows, the legal proceedings necessary to certify one's witness and freedom from tribute were quite straightforward, provided one's papers were in order. Standard procedure in Antequera involved an appearance before the alcalde ordinario with at least three witnesses who knew the claimant's background well enough to testify on his behalf. A priest was brought in to supply copies of the claimant's baptism and marriage certificates, and evidence of the ancestry of his parents and grandparents was to be presented, if not directly from parish registers, then through oral testimony by the witnesses. When the proceedings were concluded, the results were sent to the procurador mayor for his approval. The Audiencia, quite aware of the questionable credibility of the witnesses produced by many claimants, ruled in 1739 that the alcaldes themselves were to select the persons who were to testify, working through local officials if the claimant came from a rural community.[61] This ruling probably had little effect on the outcome of the cases, however, and the uncertainties in the process continued to be weighted in favor of the petitioner.

Since the racial status of an infant and his parents was ordinarily not recorded in Antequera's baptismal registers, virtually all of the evidence submitted on behalf of an unmarried person came from witnesses, who rarely if ever could be expected to place the claimant in an unfavorable light. If he could locate the baptismal or marriage records of his parents, these constituted acceptable written proof of his status. And so was a person's own marriage certificate. But as we have seen, it was often possible to correct any parish register that was found to be "mistaken." In any case, the wording of a small number of limpiezas de sangre that have been located for the late colonial period suggests not only that it was becoming increasingly easy for mulattoes to attain white status, but also that the concept of español itself was coming to mean merely that none of one's forebears had ever been on the tribute rolls. Such documents stand in sharp contrast to the limpiezas of the early and middle colonial period, when the emphasis on racial and religious background was far more explicit and explored in greater depth.

A casta could build on a number of attributes in order to penetrate the ranks of the creoles. In addition to light phenotype, level of wealth, and social connections, the criterion of legitimacy was of some importance. Indeed, one of the fundamental premises of Spanish legal discrimination was that the miscegenated were inferior and unfit for public office because they were usually of illegitimate birth. Though this was true enough in Antequera and elsewhere in the early colonial period, illegitimacy came to be more the exception than the rule as the castas became an accepted element in society. The legitimacy figures for marriage partners in Antequera in the 1790's contrast dramatically with those from the previous century. Between 80 percent and 90 percent of the men and women in all categories claimed legitimate birth. Illegitimacy was actually more common among the creoles than among the mestizos, and the overall rate was only 11.3 percent.

The rising rate of legitimacy among the castas chipped away at the foundations of the colonial legal framework and seriously threatened the sistema de castas, which as a cognitive orientation shared by the Spanish elite was based on many of the same assumptions. The result was a gradual shift away from descent as a criterion of social status and an increasing emphasis on phenotype alone, though the contradictions were never totally resolved. A case in point is a letter to the Crown from the bishop of Oaxaca in 1776 outlining his plans for the founding of a new college in Antequera so that local youth could be prepared for ministry in the Church. The bishop planned to recruit 50 students from "all the classes" of the españoles and the indios. His only requirements were that the students be "needy" (not necessarily poor), that they come from one of these two groups, and that both they and their parents be of legitimate birth. Delving any further back into the students' ancestries would serve no purpose, the bishop felt, for if one went beyond this, "one will encounter obstacles in this land, especially in this bishopric."[62] The bishop's handy rationalization illustrates how the opposing principles of racial discrimination and integration worked together in Antequera. "Negroes, mulattoes, *lobos, coyotes*, and people of other malignant mixtures" were not eligible to study at the college, though expediency counseled against the exclusion of young men only a generation removed from such dubious status. Obviously, the bishop was much more accommodating to social reality than the more distant Council of the Indies, with its 1806 decree that pardos had to demonstrate a history of legitimacy over four generations in order to become legally white. Further evidence that phenotype was overtaking descent as the major criterion of socioracial status toward the end of the colonial era is the frequent appearance of expressions like *de color pardo* and *mestizo según su color* in parish registers and other documents of the period.

As we noted in Chapter 5, the seventeenth-century marriage patterns of the castas and the scarcity of other evidence for any sort of group consciousness among the miscegenated tend to invalidate the application of the concept of ethnicity to this segment of the population even at that stage. The eighteenth-century marriage figures show far more heterogeneity still, especially among the mulattoes, and it can be said with some assurance that by this time there were no well-defined ethnic identities attached to such terms as mestizo, mulatto, and pardo. Indeed, racial status was frequently achieved rather than ascribed, and the term ethnic group should be avoided in discussions of the castas.

Only at the top and perhaps at the bottom of the socioeconomic scale did racial affiliation correspond to ethnic identity and class-like behavior. Preparations for the defense of the city against the Morelos Independence forces in 1811–12 evidence the rudiments of group behavior on the part of the peninsular elite (who stood as one man behind it) and the urban Indians (who showed no interest in either side). The choice in Antequera between loyalty to the Spanish Crown and national independence did not follow a neat vertical cleavage in the urban society, with persons of every social rank in both camps. On the contrary, as we have seen, a detailed list of donations for the defense of the city in July 1812 tells us that the socioeconomic elite was not only united in its support of the Crown, but virtually the government's only defender, at least in economic terms.[63] Merchants, priests, military officers, and state functionaries—mostly peninsulars—accounted for nearly all of the 44,617 pesos collected from 223 individuals, four revenue agencies, and an unknown number of convents and sodalities. The merchants in particular rallied to the Crown's cause: 147 of them contributed 21,182 pesos, or 47 percent of the funds raised; and twenty-one merchants each gave 400 pesos or more. The Church was the other major donor, contributing 12,113 pesos, or 27 percent of the total; 3,410 pesos of this was contributed by forty-eight of the bishopric's secular priests, 7,814 pesos came from the religious orders, and 889 pesos was given by sodalities. Six military officers contributed 3,464 pesos, and various state employees contributed 5,835 pesos. Finally, as discussed earlier, the Loyalist cause was supported by nineteen of the local landowners, but their share of the total amounted to less than 5 percent (2,023 pesos), and only five of them gave more than 66 pesos.

The guiding spirit behind the military and political defense of the city was the peninsular bishop of Oaxaca, Antonio Bergoza y Jordán, who mobilized Church support, formed the Provincial Battalion from priests, sacristans, artisans, merchants, and a few wealthy hacendados, and directed the Junta de Defensa in 1812. The few creole landowners who supported the Loyalists in 1812 (or in 1814, when the city was recaptured from the supporters of Morelos) would qualify as members of the social elite—holders of entailed estates like Captain Manuel Guenduláin, José María Lazo, and José Ximeno Bohórquez, and especially prosperous hacendados like Francisco Monterrubio and Juan José Ruiz.

Beyond this narrow slice of Antequera society—the economic elite and an important part of the priesthood—the urban population was passive at best or openly hostile to the Loyalists. A number of artisans belonged to the Loyalist battalion, but as early as July 1811 they complained that they could not make more financial sacrifices in the king's service.[64] As the Morelos forces closed in on the city in August 1812, Antonio González, a principal Loyalist organizer, complained bitterly of the slow progress in the preparations for the city's defense, and the public's lack of discipline and enthusiasm for the Loyalist cause. The sizable urban Indian population was apparently the least engaged of all, for though the Indians did not figure in any of Bergoza's efforts to organize the defense of the city, they do not appear to have been openly hostile to the Loyalist cause.

Further research is needed on other colonial cities in Latin America before any extended comparisons can be made, though a few concluding remarks on Antequera's distinctiveness are in order. As noted earlier, the colonial Indians in the Valley of Oaxaca differed from their counterparts to the north in that they were able to retain control of a substantial amount of land, at least enough to meet their subsistence needs. This gave them a considerable degree of independence from Spanish society and was directly responsible for the continued influence of the caciques in Oaxaca long after the Indian leaders in other areas had lost their power and prestige. Though we have seen that this did not preclude the steady migration of Indians to Antequera throughout the colonial period, the Indians' retention of their land contributed greatly to the relative smallness and instability of Valley Spanish estates. The frequent sales and transfers of land are a good indication of the instability of the city's elite, especially before 1740 when the cochineal boom began. In the absence of a strong, self-perpetuating elite, status in the upper and professional classes was frequently lost over the course of a few generations, and upwardly mobile newcomers stepped in as replacements. With such constant turnover, it was easier for the miscegenated families of Antequera to penetrate the middle and upper ranks of society while at the same time becoming legally and socially white.

If this interpretation is correct, it would help explain the unexpected fluidity in the structure of race and class described for the seventeenth century. It appears that the "breakdown" of the sistema de castas often associated with the late colonial period began in Antequera at least a century earlier, at the time when it was thought to be strongest.[65]

The discrepancy between theory and practice, policy and action, has long been recognized as fundamental to an understanding of colonial societies. Indeed, the sistema de castas arose out of this basic contradiction, and its very existence as a cognitive and legal system depended on constantly shifting definitions, since it was impossible to press an increasingly mixed population into a predetermined set of categories. Though many scholars have correctly recognized that the boundaries between the various socioracial categories were never impenetrable, and that there had always been some degree of mobility, they have insisted that the hierarchy of estates embodied in the sistema de castas remained the basis of the social structure until the very end of the colonial period.[66] If the social structure is defined as the way the colonial elite perceived their society and their own and others' roles within it, this interpretation is essentially correct. However, it is doubtful that the perceptions and values of the Spanish elite were shared by all members of society. Clearly, we must take into account the values and actions of members of the other social segments in order to understand the colonial social system in its totality. From the viewpoint of the outside observer, we have seen that wealth was a crucial factor in social differentiation, and it is evident that a nascent system of preindustrial economic classes was developing in Antequera toward the end of the seventeenth century.

Property, race, and political power were the three principal determinants of rank in Antequera. In general terms, polar differences in race coincided with the distribution of power and served to demarcate clearly between the Spanish elite and the slaves and Indian proletariat. Racial purity was an important concern for those who could lay some claim to it—Indians as well as Spaniards—but the large miscegenated population relied primarily on its economic situation to define its place in society. The well-known Brazilian adage "money whitens" would have been familiar to many residents of Antequera—in the seventeeth century as well as the eighteenth.

CHAPTER SEVEN

Conclusion

Social stratification in colonial Spanish America has been characterized in different ways by a number of authors with varying degrees of information at their disposal. Ralph Beals speaks of a dual-class system of Indians and Spaniards, which in Mexico and Peru was rapidly transformed into a three-class system with the rise of the mestizo population. Sergio Bagú provides a Marxist analysis that defines three social classes plus a great mass of "marginal" black slaves and Indian peasants excluded from the class system. In a similar vein Luis Chávez Orozco acknowledges that whereas the colonial period in Mexico began with an estate system based on the European model, it soon gave way to a two-class system as capitalism became more entrenched.[1] None of these studies is based on adequate empirical data, however, and they fail to pay close attention to the time dimension and the multiple factors involved in social differentiation.

More useful are the studies of three scholars who have drawn on a substantial amount of research and have attempted to synthesize the work of others. After an extensive archival investigation of the place of the Negro in colonial Mexican society, Gonzalo Aguirre Beltrán has proposed a six-tiered hierarchy of "castes" defined in ethnic or racial terms, suggesting that the Spanish term casta best describes the strata. Magnus Mörner and Lyle McAlister likewise define the principal strata in socioracial terms, but they characterize them as estates and place greater emphasis on the European heritage of the system.*

In light of the data from Antequera, these and similar studies can be criticized on several counts. First, they seek to define and rank the strata of the society, focusing only secondarily on principles of organization. Second, they fail to take rural-urban differences sufficiently into account. Third, they assume, for the most part, that the Spanish elitist point of view and the categories of the *sistema de castas* provide a reasonably accurate description of Spanish colonial society. And, finally, they fail to make adequate use of stratification theory and other concepts that might help to produce more precise and complete explanations.

A large part of the problem has been the lack of adequate data for the building and testing of hypotheses. In the case of Antequera, no single determinant of social differentiation can be said to have predominated exclusively during the entire colonial period, or even at any one point in time. On the contrary, we have seen that socioracial status groupings, occupational and economic divisions, and power blocs were frequently at odds with one another there, and that the relative weight of the various criteria of rank was constantly changing. Yet there was an undeniable unity in the phenomena I wish to account for as they unfolded over the course of three centuries. As James Lockhart has observed, conscious innovation in colonial Spanish America was at a minimum,[2] and the pace of sociocultural change was often tortuously slow after the sixteenth century. We are dealing with a single society through time rather than a suc-

---

*Aguirre Beltrán's 6 strata are as follows: Europeans, euromestizos (persons of mixed European and Indian origin but with predominantly European ethnic and cultural characteristics); afromestizos (mixed bloods with a Negro strain); Negroes; Indians; and indomestizos (European-Indian mixtures but ethnically and culturally predominantly Indian). See *La Población negra*, pp. 245–48, 291–92. McAlister ("Social Structure") finds the trichotomy of Spaniard-casta-Indian most useful for New Spain, whereas Mörner (*Race Mixture*, p. 60) adheres more closely to the colonial view of the Sociedad de Castas and enumerates 6 estates: peninsular Spaniards; creoles; mestizos; mulattoes, zambos, and free Negroes; slaves; and Indians (except caciques).

cession of qualitatively different systems of social relations; at no point did the discontinuities overshadow the common threads engendered by the Spanish colonial experience. Thus any model that seeks to account for the stratification system and the relationship between race and class must be flexible enough to accommodate changes over time while not losing sight of the basic continuities. I believe that Max Weber's threefold distinction of class, status, and power as separate principles of social ranking offers the necessary tools.[3] Before we apply the Weberian model to Antequera, however, let us first examine the concept of estate and consider how it has been applied to colonial Spanish America.

In its original usage the term estate was used to describe the traditional social strata of Western Europe up to the time of the French Revolution in 1789. The European estates were conceived of as fairly rigid strata defined by specific legal rights and obligations deriving from the feudal period; the four basic ones were the clergy, nobility, burghers, and peasants. Membership in an estate was commonly ascribed at birth (with the exception of the clergy), was defined by law, and ultimately rested on economic interests in a precapitalist society based on manorial agricultural production. The functional differences among the estates were legally reinforced by distinctions in such matters as "military service, rates of pay, taxation, right to office, application of the criminal law, opportunity to own property, political representation, [and] various hereditary rights to command the services of other persons."[4] Most scholars agree that if the concept of estate is to be used cross-culturally, primary emphasis should be given to its legal aspect. For comparative purposes, then an estate may be regarded as "a legally defined segment of the population of a society which has distinctive rights and duties established by law."[5]

Thus defined, estate systems tend to be highly rigid, and social mobility, marriage, and status achievement customarily occur within rather than across estate boundaries. This is the kind of social system that Mörner and others have in mind when they claim that the Spanish American *sistema de castas* was created by the imposition of the "estate-based, corporative society of late medieval Castile . . . upon a multiracial, colonial situation."[6]

The data from eighteenth-century Antequera show, however, that the estate model is of only limited value for the description and analysis of the city's complex stratification system when taken as a whole. Indeed, it can be argued that the estate model is inapplicable to colonial societies in general, especially those with a high degree of racial heterogeneity. A functioning estate system is dependent on a set of shared understandings and mutual expectations that help bind together the various strata; unless there is a degree of common acceptance of the legal rights and obligations that serve to differentiate among the strata, such a system is bound to fragment and disintegrate. Almost universally, however, one finds that in colonial situations "precast theories seldom dictated or even strongly influenced practice."[7] Colonial societies are held together more by political coercion and economic interdependence than by a set of shared values and understandings. In a colonial city like Antequera, where race mixture was extensive and frequently legitimized by marriage, and where the phenomenon of passing was endemic, it is not wholly accurate to assert that strata were primarily determined by racial and ethnic criteria when there were so many exceptions. To be sure, the peninsular and Indian groups persisted essentially intact throughout the entire colonial period as a vestige of the estate-like system of the early sixteenth century; but by 1792 the stratification system had become much more complex.

For the case at hand, the problem lies not so much with the recognition of the role of force in the maintenance of the social system, but in the conceptualization of the place of the persons of mixed blood in the society. Some writers have attempted to "explain away" the castas, pointing out that they never occupied a definable position in the social structure and were little more than marginal figures.[8] But to adopt this point of view for Antequera would place undue emphasis on the viewpoint of the law and the elite group. The marriage alliances and occupations of the miscegenated clearly show that far from being marginal figures, most of them were accepted members of the urban proletariat, notwithstanding the social prejudice and discrimination that was leveled against them.

One may legitimately ask to what extent the parish records and census counts reflect the structure of everyday social interaction and the social categories employed by the actors. In reference to Peru, Louis Faron observes, "The semi-technical terms which appear in historical sources, such as *casta, mestizo, mulato*, and so forth, are not (with the limited exception of *mulato*) those of common usage, nor for that matter are they generally found in contemporary or period literature."[9] Colloquial speech, he points out, makes a series of fine socioracial distinctions much like those of the colonial *sistema de castas* in its terminologically most complex form. This point of view is misleading, however, for the absence of socioracial terminology in the colonial documentation frequently means only that members of the lower classes were not involved in the events being discussed. As to the racial distinctions employed in everyday speech, it is likely that the terms in use in Antequera were more varied than the broader categories distinguished by the priests and census takers. This does not invalidate the present analysis, however, but only indicates another level of "reality" that must remain inaccessible given the kinds of data available.*

In any case, a model of socioracially defined estates with subdivisions based on other criteria clearly oversimplifies the complex stratification system of Antequera. In order to gain a fuller understanding of the system, it is necessary to concentrate on the principles or criteria of rank rather than on the definition of more or less discrete strata. As Gerhard Lenski observes, categorical or taxonomic concepts are inadequate to the task because they force the analysis into an either-or mold that compels one to choose between what are often two (or more) faulty views. This problem can be avoided by

---

*I feel that these lacunae can only be filled by means of ethnography, but even here the possibilities seem limited. Most of the terms employed in the *sistema de castas* are no longer in common usage in highland Mexico today, though the most basic ones would hold some meaning for many people. Only in the coastal areas with plantation agriculture and the presence of Negroes and people of black mixture is one likely to find a terminological system that approaches the complexity of the one reported by Faron for the coastal Chancay Valley of Peru.

employing variable concepts that allow one to ask *to what degree* a given phenomenon is present.[10] The significant question is not whether an estate system or something else existed in Antequera, but what were the criteria of rank, what was the relative importance attached to each of them, and how did they change through time?

Social stratification arises in societies with productive capacities above the subsistence level as a mechanism for the distribution of scarce values. In its most fundamental sense, stratification may be equated with the distribution of power within a community, and one may speak of socioeconomic strata whenever certain social segments gain privileged access to basic resources and the tools and techniques of production.[11] In many ways, colonial societies represent systems of stratification par excellence with their emphasis on domination, subordination, and exclusive rights to political control. However, the political features of colonialism should not lead us to overlook the other basic criteria of rank that operate in all stratified state systems. In Weber's terms, these are the "class situation" and the "status situation."

Weber defines class in economic terms: "We may speak of a 'class' when 1) a number of people have in common a specific causal component of their life chances, insofar as 2) this component is represented exclusively by economic interests in the possession of goods and opportunities for income, and 3) is represented under the conditions of the commodity or labor markets."[12] Thus an individual's place in a class hierarchy, strictly speaking, is determined by his power, or lack of it, to market goods, or skills for income in a given economic order. Related to the "class situation" but analytically and often empirically distinct from it is the concept of the "status situation," or status honor:

In contrast to the purely economically determined "class situation" we wish to designate as "status situation" every typical component of the life fate of men that is determined by a specific, positive or negative, social estimation of *honor*. This honor may be connected with any quality shared by a plurality, and, of course, it can be knit to a class situation: class distinctions are linked in the most varied ways with status distinctions. [But] both propertied and propertyless people can belong to the same status group, and frequently they do with very tangible consequences.[13]

The distinction between occupational stratification and socioracial stratification found in Antequera can be analyzed in terms of these contrasting notions of economic class and social status. Access to political power (or in Weber's terms, "party") provides a third dimension to the analysis. This multidimensional approach to stratification presupposes the existence of not one social hierarchy, but a series of social hierarchies, each based on a single criterion. Each of these systems incorporates all members of society, though each may differ internally with respect to complexity, the range of variation, the patterning of the distribution of cases (i.e., individuals or families), the degree of mobility permitted, and the degree of institutionalization or legitimation.[14] Furthermore, there may be a struggle between the different principles of rank: at any one point in time they are apt to differ in importance in a given society and are constantly subject to realignment as sociocultural change proceeds.[15] This dynamic model of stratification leads us away from the often fruitless either-or mode and is useful in determining the nature of the processes of change in Antequera.

The social system in the Valley of Oaxaca during the first half of the sixteenth century was one in which class, status, and power divisions were closely aligned with distinct ethnic and cultural groupings. There was of course a degree of heterogeneity within both the Spanish and Indian segments; Spanish encomenderos and clergy enjoyed more power and prestige than the white artisans, and the line separating Indian nobles from commoners was rigidly drawn. But the status differences among the Indians were less rigid in Antequera than in the indigenous communities, and we have seen that there was little social differentiation among the Spaniards before 1550. The distribution of power was principally a political function of the Spanish conquest, and Indians and Negroes were treated as slaves, with the caciques forming the only intermediate group. Antequera had few Spanish women, but though this soon resulted in a miscegenated population, its members were customarily absorbed into the group of one of their parents. Thus racial and economic factors were of minimal importance to rank, which in this period depended heavily on one's ability to curry favors from the Crown and the colonial administration in the form of encomiendas, slaving licenses, and noble titles.

During the latter half of the sixteenth century this system of stratification began to erode as the city became firmly entrenched and established stronger economic ties with the hinterland. Mining was of some importance between 1570 and 1650, and the increased Spanish interest in land, coupled with the growth in number and kinds of urban occupations (particularly those associated with the silk textile industry), induced a greater range of socioeconomic variation among the whites. The frequency of interracial sexual unions kept pace with the growth of the city, and the miscegenated population emerged as identifiable pariah groups. Though these groups as yet occupied no definable place in the social system, the words mestizo and mulatto, and the generic term casta, came into general use to identify them by what was thought to be their inherently inferior moral and biological nature. The emerging racial and economic criteria of rank thus began to compete with the principle of political power that had been the primary basis of social differentiation in earlier times. The end of the sixteenth century marked the crystallization of colonial urban society in the sense that the determinants of class, status, and power became empirically distinct as the society matured. The nascent group of independent white landowners and merchants and the growing miscegenated population threatened the political power base of the encomenderos, setting in train a series of social tensions and a struggle between different principles of power distribution that remained unresolved at the time of independence.

The decades after 1630 witnessed the rise of small Spanish haciendas in the Valley, a decline in trade (except for the cochineal traffic), the virtual extinction of mining activity, and a retardation in the rate of urban growth. Race became institutionalized as a mark of status as the sistema de castas attained its classic form. By the end of the seventeenth century the category castizo had been added to the hierarchy of basic socioracial positions to help preserve the social and somatic distance between the white power elite and the remainder of society. By now too numerous to ignore and too necessary to the economy to be excluded, the castas were accorded a place in urban society, conceptually ranked between the whites and the Indian proletariat. This partial accommodation of the miscegenated, coupled with the economic instability of the elite and the professional class, acted to strengthen the criterion of wealth as a determinant of rank.

The occupational and marriage patterns of the late seventeenth century suggest that a nascent system of economic classes developed simultaneously with the institutionalization of the sistema de castas. Marriages between whites (creoles) downwardly mobile in the class system and castas desirous of improving their socioracial status cemented the intersection of the race and class hierarchies. Many of the miscegenated (particularly the mestizos) were able to pass as whites, thereby swelling the ranks of the españoles at the expense of the castas. The upward mobility in status, if not also in wealth, of persons of mixed parentage appears to have been greater than previously supposed, and the consequent darkening of the "somatic norm image" of the españoles made mobility within the sistema de castas increasingly easier.

If it was often true that "money whitened" in late-seventeenth-century Antequera, it was all the more true of the eighteenth century, and the process even found some legitimation in law. Parish records and the 1792 census indicate that by the end of the colonial period the complexity and range of variation within the economic class structure were as great as those of the status hierarchy embodied in the sistema de castas, if indeed the latter had not been overtaken in this respect. The city's dramatic growth and the increased opportunities for trade after the Bourbon reforms rendered the sistema de castas all but obsolete as a mechanism of status definition. More than ever, social honor came to be dependent on economic considerations as the number of claimants to white status multiplied. However, the sistema de castas still served important ideological functions for the Spanish elite, and the new categories pardo and morisco were added to the lexicon even though the number of people available to fill them was constantly dwindling.

In terms of influence in local affairs, wealth and power coincided to a great extent in 1792; wealthy peninsular merchants and the ecclesiastical corporations seem to have had a strong hold on both. This had not always been the case, however, and there is good reason for keeping wealth and power analytically distinct. In the seventeenth century, though peninsular merchants were by far the wealthiest members of the community, they took little part in the affairs of local government. At that time a small group of landowning families exercised political power in Antequera. This was especially true of the holders of entailed estates, who were prominently represented in the cabildo and the Church administration, and succeeded in maintaining their influence even when their resources were declining.[16] Access to power in the late eighteenth century, on the other hand, was generally restricted to the wealthy members of the elite, most of whom were peninsular merchants.

How are we to conceive of the relations between the diametrically opposed groups of peninsular Spaniards and urban Indians?* As we have seen, these two segments of the population remained largely homogeneous during the entire colonial period. With the possible exception of the more agrarian-oriented period of 1650–1740, peninsulars always constituted the bulk of the local elite, just as the Indians were almost uniformly relegated to the urban proletariat (caciques excepted). Miscegenation between these two groups almost always occurred in an extra-marital context, since few peninsular males deigned to marry women who were not regarded as españoles americanas. Given the nature of the colonial situation, these observations are not surprising. Of far greater interest, however, is the degree to which race relations in Antequera approximated the general pattern found today in Latin America, particularly in the coastal areas of Brazil and Colombia, which have large black and mulatto populations.

Oracy Nogueira, Florestan Fernandes, and other modern Brazilian sociologists have made great strides in exploding the myth of the Brazilian "racial paradise," fostered in large part by the earlier interpretations of Gilberto Freyre, Frank Tannenbaum, and Don-

---

*Negroes, of course, constituted a third ethnic group, but as I have said, there is little concrete information about them. The size of the black population appears to have steadily declined during the eighteenth century.

ald Pierson. Racial prejudice and discrimination are a fact of life in
Brazil, though they operate in a more subtle and complex manner
than they do in the more extreme case of the United States. The
nature of Brazilian racial identity has also attracted the attention of
several American investigators, and their findings are worth noting.[17] Marvin Harris and Conrad Kottak have noted the referential
and definitional ambiguity built into the complex Brazilian racial
terminology for various black and white mixtures. They point out
that not only is a person's racial identity influenced by his educational and economic status, but there is no common agreement on
the meaning of specific racial terms.[18] In the absence of a clear-cut
descent rule to identify blacks or mulattoes (as in the United States),
racial identity among the miscegenated in Brazil is frequently
achieved and subject to change rather than ascribed at birth. Thus
the ability of some persons of color to overcome the prejudice of the
whites and penetrate into the upper ranks of society militates
against the formation of ethnic consciousness among the blacks and
mulattoes. That race relations in colonial Antequera were in many
respects similar to the modern Brazilian situation should be readily
apparent. The notion that "money whitens," the ambiguity surrounding racial identity, and the achieved component of racial status were all built into the sistema de castas in some degree virtually from its inception in the seventeenth century. Endogamy and
hierarchy rigidly separated the polar types of Spaniard, Indian, and
Negro; but their miscegenated offspring were frequently able to rise
within the sistema de castas and the class system, thereby becoming
partially or wholly white. This is not to say that the structure of society in colonial Mexico was identical in all respects to that of modern
Brazil, but only to point out that the racial dimension of stratification operated in a similar manner. The case of Antequera clearly
shows the historical depth of the generalized pattern of race relations in Latin America today.

The roots of this phenomenon are to be sought not in the late colonial period or in the political upheavals of the nineteenth century,
but rather in formative colonial times. Though it would be wrong to
say that the culture and values of the conquering Spaniards played

no part in the development of the system of race and class described for Antequera, the central importance of demographic and economic factors as determinants of social change in the long run cannot be denied.[19] Among these was the early development of a capitalist socioeconomic system in central Mexico.* From the perspective of Antequera, the problem with the estate model of stratification is that it rests, implicitly or explicitly, on a feudal conception of society and the values of the white colonial elite. Particularly for the seventeenth and eighteenth centuries, the feudal-estate model appears to misrepresent the main trends of economic activity, which had far-reaching consequences for the stratification system. In a word, the present case study can best be understood within the context of a developing system of commercial capitalism.†

Many observers have referred to the pitfalls of viewing the economy, institutions, and structure of colonial Mexican society as basically feudal in nature.[20] Though the wholesale definition of Spanish colonial institutions qua institutions as capitalist is to be

---

*The argument for the presence of an economic class system merits an explanation if only because many writers have expressed reservations about the applicability of the concept of class to colonial Spanish American society. Magnus Mörner, for example, writes: "It is true that during the colonial period, an emerging system of economic classes can be discerned, in the rural sector rather than in the urban. But, as I hope to be able to show, it was the Régimen de Castas that continued to supply the social values, and it was sanctioned in law until the end of the period. There is no reason to believe that, as Marxist interpreters argue, it was only a thin veil cast over a reality of economic classes and class conflict. Such an approach does in fact seem to be insufficient and even anachronistic for analyzing any Western society prior to the French Revolution. In addition, Spanish America obviously was retarded in its social evolution." (*Race Mixture*, p. 54.) Lyle McAlister is somewhat more open to the possibilities of class analysis for the eighteenth century, but is troubled by the lack of adequate data on occupations and the distribution of wealth. In the final analysis, he concludes that "economic classes can probably best be regarded as an incipient situation and as a concept which can best be used for studying social development over a period extending beyond the colonial era rather than for the colonial period itself." ("Social Structure," p. 363.)

† The capitalist mode of production, however, should not be confused with industrialization: some kind of distinction has to be made between commercial capitalism and industrial capitalism. Despite the attention that has been given to these concepts by economists and historians—Marxist and non-Marxist alike—it is surprising how few attempts have been made to analyze the *social* significance of capitalism in different times and locales. The study of capitalism as a socioeconomic system is just beginning to emerge (e.g., Immanuel Wallerstein, *The Modern World-System*), and

avoided,[21] it is nevertheless significant that by the eighteenth century the urban economy of New Spain no longer rested directly on the shoulders of the Indians, but was instead a cash system of free wage labor operating within a fairly free network of international trade and communication.[22]

There was a crucial change in the socioeconomic structure of central Mexico in which profits based on forced labor and head taxes (the prerogatives of political command) gradually gave way to a system of commercial capitalism operating through an open market place and cash economy. The first system was based primarily on the exploitation of forced labor, and depended on a rigid division between colonizers and colonized in which the "profit motive" was limited to the rulers (mainly political officials and encomenderos). Under commercial capitalism, however, profits were based on the exchange of goods and services and were made at various levels of society, not merely among the colonial elite. It was this crucial transition, evident in New Spain as early as the late sixteenth century, that made possible the achievement of social (and racial) status and material wealth, thus creating the preconditions for class stratification. In Antequera this process had clearly passed the "incipient" stage by the end of the eighteenth century and had for some time exerted a significant influence on the social structure. Once the nature of this socioeconomic system is understood, the contradictions between the feudally derived *sistema de castas* and the capitalist-oriented economic class system cease to be paradoxical. They were both integral parts of the Spanish colonial experience in Mesoamerica.

All this brings us to the question of the urban environment in which these developments occurred. In seeking to place Antequera and the colonial Spanish American city into an interpretive, cross-

definitions of it that are meaningful for social analysis are hard to come by. Marvin Harris defines capitalism as "the proliferation of independent associations dedicated to making maximum profits from the marketing of manufactured or traded items" (*Culture, Man, and Nature*, p. 460). The associated economic forms that are most important for the present analysis are private ownership of land and the technological means of production, an inexpensive supply of mobile labor, and price-making markets based on money exchange.

cultural frame of reference, Gideon Sjoberg's model of the preindustrial city comes immediately to mind. By this "constructed
type", which Sjoberg would apply to most of the world's cities prior
to the Industrial Revolution, the preindustrial city is embedded
within an essentially feudal state characterized by complex gov-
ernmental, educational, and economic institutions, an extensive division of labor, and a rigid class or caste-like system in which a small
urban-based ruling elite exploits a large, subservient peasant population.[23] The city serves as a political, religious, and trading center,
and though its residents constitute only a small proportion of the
population, their influence extends far beyond the city's boundaries.

In the case of Antequera, however, the patterns of race relations,
social mobility, and economic class stratification all cast doubt on
the validity of Sjoberg's formulation and the more general prein-
dustrial-industrial dichotomy for understanding urban life.* Consider, for example, Sjoberg's description of the preindustrial urban
society as a rigid hierarchy of power and authority divided into
an upper class, or elite, composed of 5–10 percent of the urban
population; a vast lower class; and various outcaste groups such as
slaves and prostitutes.[24] Vertical social mobility does occur in this
type of society, though infrequently, and the downward movement
of members of the elite is limited to situations where a kingdom or
empire experiences military defeat. All told, "the basic form of the
class structure remains largely unchanged through time."[25] The
data from Antequera clearly show the inadequacy of this formulation for colonial Spanish America. The preindustrial model fits only
if one emphasizes the distribution of political power and ignores the
complex relationship between economic stratification and the socioracial status hierarchy. Furthermore, Antequera's elite was no-

---

* Sjoberg in fact explicitly excludes the European-derived Latin American cities
from his general type, arguing that they do not conform to the general pattern because soon after their founding in the sixteenth century they began to be affected by a
"degree" of industrialization (*Preindustrial City*, p. 63). But unless "soon" is taken to
mean a few hundred years, this qualification is really unacceptable. Colonial Latin
American cities surely were preindustrial. In colonial Oaxaca, for example, water
power was the only known inanimate source of energy, and it would be presumptu-
ous to designate Antequera as "industrial" on this basis. So if the model is found lacking for the Latin American case, it must be for other reasons.

where near as enduring and stable as Sjoberg's account would have it. Indeed, it has been argued that in all agrarian state systems there are generally more offspring among the elite than there are positions to be filled, and consequently downward mobility is more frequent than upward.[26]

Beyond all this, Sjoberg has failed to take the phenomenon of colonialism into account, with the result that he misrepresents the role of merchants and the merchant class in many "preindustrial" cities. He writes: "A few merchants, though ideally excluded from membership in the elite, manage to achieve high status. Most are unequivocally in the lower class or outcaste groups, however."[27] The case of Antequera and other cities of New Spain turns this assertion on its head. During most of the colonial period the wealthiest residents of Antequera were merchants, and most of them were peninsular Spaniards who were clearly members of the elite.

Capitalism as a socioeconomic system is all too often associated with the rise of industrial production in Europe during the late eighteenth and early nineteenth centuries. This has led to an overemphasis on technological factors in the study of long-term social change and in the formulation of typologies and evolutionary schemes. A case in point is the frequently voiced view that the modern phenomenon of class stratification, as opposed to a more rigid caste or estate system, is essentially a product of industrialization and the spread of the factory system.[28] We must not forget, however, that the industrial "revolution" was not merely the result of technical innovation. The readiness of entrepreneurs to adopt new technologies and put them to work was contingent on an evolving socioeconomic system that favored the accumulation of capital, the establishment of new markets, the expansion of channels of trade and communication, and the development of a plentiful and cheap supply of mobile labor.

Several features of the colonial social structure of Antequera described in this book have a decidedly modern look: a developing competitive capitalist economy, an unstable elite, achieved statuses of various kinds, and a significant degree of social mobility. If the present case study has any value for an understanding of Latin

American cities in the twentieth century, it is to caution against making too much of the differences between colonial times and the present. Differences there surely are, but the likenesses are perhaps more striking. The roots of modern urban social systems in Latin America lie not in the adoption of industrial technology, but rather in the spread of a world economy based on the capitalist mode of production. This process began in the sixteenth century, providing the broad economic context of the Iberian conquest of America and giving rise to colonial urban institutions and class systems. Colonial Latin America was soon involved in an international network of commercial capitalism that cut across national boundaries and was not controlled by any one state power. The social consequences of this involvement were initially most visible in the cities and ultimately spread to all sectors of society.

Reference Matter

Glossary of Spanish Terms

Alcalde. Judge and *cabildo* member

Alcalde mayor. Spanish official in charge of a district

Alcalde ordinario. Judge and *cabildo* member

Alférez real. Standard bearer and *cabildo* member

Alguacil. Constable

Alguacil mayor. Chief constable

Alhóndiga. Municipal storehouse and grain market

Arroba. Unit of measure; about 25 pounds

Audiencia. Court and governing body under the viceroy, or the area of its jurisdiction

Barrio. Neighborhood in a community

Cabecera. Head town

Cabildo. Municipal council

Cacica. Female *cacique*

Cacicazgo. Estate of a *cacique*

Cacique. Hereditary Indian chieftain or local ruler

Calpulli. Ward or territorial unit in Aztec society, or the group of families occupying it

Cajero. Apprentice merchant

Carga. Unit of measure; generally one-half of a *fanega*, or about three-quarters of a bushel

Casta. Any kind of animal or human group, but especially those of mixed racial ancestry

Castellano. Monetary unit; the Spanish language as spoken in Castile

Castizo. Offspring of an *español* and a *mestizo*

Cédula. Royal order

Chino. Offspring of an Indian and a Negro

Ciudad. City

Cofradía. Sodality; a lay brotherhood responsible for financing religious services and maintaining the church

Comerciante. Merchant

Corregidor. Spanish officer in charge of a local Indian district

Corregimiento. Jurisdiction or office of a *corregidor*

Coyote. Coyote; light mestizo or offspring of a mestizo and a mulatto

Creole; criollo. Español americano; person born in the New World of putative Spanish ancestry

Doctrina. Parochial jurisdiction or its head town

Ducado. Unit of gold currency, worth 375 *maravedís*

Ejido. Type of community land

Encomendero. Possessor of an *encomienda*

Encomienda. Grant of an Indian town or towns, carrying the right to assess tribute

Escribano; escribano público. Secretary or scribe

Español. Spaniard, either peninsular or creole

Español americano. Creole

Español europeo. Peninsular Spaniard

Estancia. Subordinate Indian community; ranch

Estancia de ganado mayor. Cattle ranch

Estancia de ganado menor. Sheep or goat ranch

Fanega. Unit of dry measure; about 1.5 bushels

Fianza. Bond

Fiscal. Treasurer; prosecutor

Grana. Cochineal

Granero. Cultivator of cochineal

Gremio. Guild

Hacendado. Owner of a hacienda

Hacienda. Landed estate used for both ranching and agriculture

Huerta. Small farm

Indio. Indian

Labrador. Farmer

Limpieza de sangre. Legal proceeding to establish one's descent and freedom from race mixture

Lobo. Wolf; offspring of an Indian and a mulatto

Macehual. Indian commoner

Maestro. Master craftsman

Maravedí. Monetary unit; 300 maravedís commonly equaled 1 *peso de oro común*

Marqués. Marquis

Marquesado. Marquisate

Mayeque. Indian of a subordinate class, below a macehual and usually dependent on an Indian noble; roughly equivalent to a serf; in Spanish colonial terms, a *terrasguerro*

Mayorazgo. Entailed estate

Mayordomo. Majordomo; custodian

Mestindio. Offspring of a mestizo and an Indian

Mestizaje. Race mixture or mestization

Mestizo. Person of mixed white and Indian ancestry

Moreno. Euphemistic term for a Negro

Morisco. Light-skinned mulatto; offspring of an *español* and a mulatto

Mulato. Anyone with some degree of recognized African ancestry

Naboría. Indian of intermediate status between slave and free man who was forced to work for a particular Spaniard or Spanish town

Obraje. Workshop, especially for textiles

Oficial. Journeyman; skilled worker

Oidor. Judge for an Audiencia

Pardo. Euphemistic term for a mulatto; lighter than a mulatto, but darker than a *morisco*

Parroquia. Parish

Peso de oro común. Monetary unit of 300 *maravedís* or 8 *reales*

Plaza mayor. Main plaza or town square

Principal. Hereditary member of the Indian upper class

Propios; propios del consejo. Public land or property

Procurador. City attorney

Procurador mayor. Attorney general of a district

Pueblo. Town or village; usually refers to small and medium-sized Indian communities

Real. Monetary unit; one-eighth of a peso

Regidor. Councilman in a *cabildo*

Regimiento. Jurisdiction or office of a *regidor*

Repartimiento. Labor draft

Repartimiento de efectos. Forced distribution of money or sale of goods to Indians by a Spanish official

Residencia. Inquiry taken concerning the conduct of an official who had completed his term of office or had been removed from it

Sistema de castas. System of social ranking based on race created by Spanish law and the colonial elite; the racial dimension of stratification in Antequera

Sobrenombre. Indian name that followed a Spanish surname

Sujeto. Subject town

Tequio. Indigenous communal labor service involving the cooperation of all commoner households

Tequitlato. Tax collector and law-enforcement officer in Indian communities

Terrasguerro. A Spanish colonial term for a *mayeque*, an Indian of roughly the status of a serf

Tianguis. Indian market

Tlaxilacalli. Ward, *barrio*, or *calpulli*

Tratante. Trader; peddler

Traza. The central, predominantly Hispanic portion of Spanish colonial towns

Vagamundo. Homeless person, vagrant

Vara. Unit of measure; roughly 33 inches

Vecino. Permanently residing Spanish household head in Spanish colonial towns

Villa. Municipal corporation one level below the city

Visita. Tour of inspection; community or church ministered by nonresident clergy

Zambo. Offspring of an Indian and a Negro; *chino*

Race Mixture as Seen by an 18th-Century Peninsular Spaniard

The following account is taken from "Ydea Compendiosa del Reyno de Nueva España en que se comprehenden las Cuidades y Puertos princi-pales, Cabezeras de Jurisdiccion, su latitud, Rumbo, y distancia a la Capi-tal, Mexico," a manuscript written in 1774 by Don Pedro Alonso O'Crovley and now located in the Biblioteca Nacional, Madrid (Vol. 4532).

The races from which the Castas originate are the Spanish, Indian, and Negro. No one would dispute that the Spaniard has more dignity and es-teem than the others, nor would anyone yield to the Negro who is the low-est and most contemptible of the three. Therefore, of all the compounds of these three stocks, it is the Mulatto who is accorded the least esteem. This runs against his natural arrogance of spirit, for he normally conducts his af-fairs with bravery. The Mulattoes believe themselves to be socially superior to the other Castas, and in many places their efforts have proved successful, especially in contrast to the Indians whom they treat as their inferior serv-ants.

If the compound is born of Spanish and Indian parents, he is stained to the third degree. The rule is that Spaniard and Indian produce a Mestizo; Mestizo and Spaniard produce a Castizo; Castizo and Spaniard produce a Spaniard. In reality, however, Indian blood should not be regarded as tainted, for it is just as thick as anyone could desire. His Majesty Philip II gave the Mestizos access to the profession of the priesthood, and this has given some consideration to the mixtures of Indians and European Span-iards who are called Criollos.

Descendants of mixed Spanish and Negro parentage remain tainted for innumerable generations and are unable to escape their heritage or lose their primitive Mulatto quality. Spaniard and Negro produce a Mulatto; Mulatto and Spaniard produce a Morisco; Morisco and Spaniard produce a Torna-Atrás; Torna-Atrás and Spaniard produce a Tente en el Ayre, which is the same thing as Mulatto. This is why they say, and with good reason, that the Mulatto cannot escape from the mixture. He can only lose his Spanish portion, which leaves his character reduced to that of the Negro.

The same happens with the concoction of Negro and Indian: Negro and Indian produce a Lobo; Lobo and Indian produce a Chino; Chino and Indian produce an Albarazado. All of them resemble the Mulatto.

With the continued mixture of Spaniard and Indian there is retrogression back toward the Indian. Spaniard and Indian produce a Mestizo; Mestizo and Indian produce a Coyote; Coyote and Indian produce an Indian. But the pure Indian is just as pure blooded as the Spaniard, and the two are not in conflict with each other as they are with the Negro. Although the Spanish and Indian mixtures cannot escape their condition, they remain uncontaminated regardless of how many degrees they are removed from purity. It would be superfluous to discuss the remaining mixtures, which in the end come down to Spaniard or Indian. Only a final word is necessary about the contaminated Negro compounds.

For those contaminated with Negro blood more than once in their ancestry, the name Mulatto leaves such a taint that their descendants will always be Mulattoes; chemistry cannot help them. The result is the same regardless of the distance from the Negro trunk, whether it be direct or indirect. Whether it concerns the union of a Negro with an Indian or with a Spaniard, or with any compound of them, the result is always a Mulatto.

Many Mulattoes pass for Spaniards, and those known as such are euphemistically called Pardos, in the same way that some Negroes are called Morenos.

Notes

In the Notes I have cited archival sources in condensed form. The major volume (usually *legajo*, but sometimes *tomo*) appears first; the *expediente*, when given, is in large italic figures; and the folios, when given, always follow a colon. Thus, AGN, Hospital de Jesús 285, *98*: 128v, stands for Archivo General de la Nación, Mexico City, Ramo de Hospital de Jesús, legajo 285, expediente 98, folio 128 versa. For those citations that do not fit into this format, I use key abbreviations or even full Spanish terms for clarity. All published works are cited in short form. Further information on the archives and complete authors' names, titles, and publishing data are given in the Bibliography. Other abbreviations used in these Notes are:

AEO	Archivo del Estado de Oaxaca
AGI	Archivo General de Indias, Seville
AGN	Archivo General de la Nación, Mexico City
AMO	Archivo Municipal de Oaxaca
BEO	Biblioteca del Estado de Oaxaca
BN	Biblioteca Nacional, Madrid
CCG	Colección Castañeda Guzmán, Oaxaca
CDII	*Colección de documentos inéditos relativos al descubrimiento, conquista, y organización de las antiguas posesiones españolas de América y Oceanía . . .* 42 vols., Madrid, 1864–84
ENE	*Epistolario de Nueva España, 1505–1818.* Francisco del Paso y Troncoso, ed., 16 vols., Mexico City, 1939–42
Jalatlaco	Archivo Parroquial de Jalatlaco, Oaxaca
Marquesado	Archivo Parroquial de Santa María del Marquesado, Oaxaca
PNE	*Papeles de Nueva España.* Francisco del Paso y Troncoso, ed., 9 vols., Madrid, 1905–48
RAHM	Real Academia de la Historia, Madrid, Colección Muñoz
Sagrario	Archivo Parroquial del Sagrario, Oaxaca

Chapter One

1. Morse, "Some Characteristics," p. 320.
2. Kubler, 1: 68, 73; Smith, p. 5.
3. Kubler, 1: 84.
4. Morse, "Some Characteristics," p. 322.
5. Gibson, "Spanish-Indian Institutions," p. 234.
6. Burgoa, *Geográfica descripción*, 1: 147; Lemoine, p. 195.
7. Castillo Tejero, p. 211; Flores Ruiz, p. 235.
8. Kubler, 1: 74.
9. Bayle, pp. 55–67.
10. *Ibid.*, pp. 56, 125.
11. Moore, p. 61.
12. Gibson, *Tlaxcala*, p. 124.
13. Morse, "Some Characteristics," p. 322; Morse, "Latin American Cities," p. 480.
14. Morse, "Latin American Cities," p. 480.
15. Aguirre Beltrán, pp. 153–89; Mörner, *Race Mixture*, pp. 35–74.
16. Weber, pp. 180–95.

Chapter Two

1. Taylor, *Landlord*, pp. 9–12.
2. Palerm and Wolf, p. 30.
3. Flannery et al., pp. 453–54.
4. *Ibid.*, p. 454; Flannery, "Olmec," p. 99.
5. Flannery et al., p. 452.
6. *Ibid.*, p. 454; Bernal, "Archeological Synthesis," pp. 788, 797; Paddock, "Oaxaca," p. 111.
7. Paddock, "Oaxaca," p. 151.
8. Whitecotton, p. 290.
9. Paddock, "Oaxaca," pp. 126–27.
10. *Ibid.*, pp. 149, 151.
11. *Ibid.*, p. 174.
12. Ronald Spores, personal communication.
13. Paddock, "Oaxaca," p. 226.
14. Spores, "Zapotec," p. 964; Taylor, *Landlord*, p. 17.
15. Burgoa, *Geográfica descripción*, 1: 395.
16. AGN, Hospital de Jesús 119, 7: 1v; AGN, Tierras 2963, *14*; AGN, Mercedes 57: 70v–82r.
17. AGN, Indios 48, *155*: 176v, and 36. *226*: 203r; AGN, Hospital de Jesús 119, *28*; AGN, Civil 1539, *2*.
18. PNE, 4: 191.
19. Puga, fol. 27; AGI, Justicia 231: 63r.
20. AGI, Justicia 231: 71.

21. Burgoa, *Geográfica descripción*, 1: 397.
22. Taylor, *Landlord*, p. 23; Butterworth, p. 40.
23. Paddock, "Mixtec Ethnohistory," p. 373.
24. Seler, "Wall Paintings," p. 259. Archeologists have yet to turn up conclusive evidence of the Aztecs' occupation of the Valley, though a comprehensive survey of Monte Albán conducted by Richard Blanton has produced a quantity of potsherds that may be of Aztec style. As of this writing, the Centro Regional de Oaxaca of the Instituto Nacional de Antropología e Historia is planning some test excavations in the market square of the city of Oaxaca, which overlies the site of the Aztec garrison.
25. *Ibid.*, p. 259.
26. Gay, 1: 281.
27. AGN, Hospital de Jesús 398, 5; Gay, 1: 275; Martínez Gracida, *El rey Cosijoeza*, p. 36. Whitecotton (*Zapotecs*, p. 125) locates this garrison on the nearby Cerro del Fortín, but there is little documentary and no archeological evidence to support this view.
28. Durán, 1: 243–44.
29. Cervantes de Salazar, p. 806.
30. AGN, Hospital de Jesús 398, 5: 268v, 287v, 290.
31. *Instrucciones*, p. 238.
32. AGI, Audiencia de México 1088, lib. 2: 69–69v, and lib. 3: 24v; *ibid.* 355: 306; AGI, Escribanía de Cámara 1045A, num. 52.
33. AGI, Escribanía de Cámara 1045A, num. 52.
34. Barlow, *Extent of the Empire*, pp. 118–19.
35. See *ibid.*, pp. 123–25, for additional information.
36. Schmieder, p. 19.
37. AGI, Justicia 231.
38. Burgoa, *Geográfica descripción*, 1: 42–43.
39. Taylor, *Landlord*, p. 22.
40. Butterworth, pp. 38–39.
41. Spores, "Zapotec," p. 967.
42. AGN, Hospital de Jesús 398, 5: 287v.
43. AGN, Indios 19, 7, and 41, *159*; AGN, Civil 822: 269r.
44. Spores, "Zapotec," pp. 467–68.
45. Whitecotton, p. 136.
46. AGN, Hospital de Jesús 102 (atado 2), *24*.
47. AGN, Hospital de Jesús 285, *98*.
48. Schmeider, p. 23; Whitecotton, p. 138.
49. Spores, *Mixtec Kings* and "Marital Alliance."
50. Whitecotton, pp. 139–41.   51. Taylor, *Landlord*, p. 56.
52. *Ibid.*, p. 33.   53. Spores, "Zapotec," p. 966.
54. *Ibid.*, pp. 968–70.

55. Spores, "Zapotec," pp. 969–70; Whitecotton, p. 143.
56. Whitecotton, pp. 144–45; Spores, "Zapotec," pp. 969–70.
57. Whitecotton, p. 149.
58. Spores, "Zapotec," p. 969.
59. AGN, Hospital de Jesús 102. 52.
60. AGI, Audiencia de México 96; Taylor, *Landlord*, p. 42.
61. AGI, Audiencia de México 2584.
62. Whitecotton, p. 152. See also PNE, 4: 127, for the pre-Hispanic situation in Miahuatlán.
63. The reader desiring more complete information on the pre-Hispanic Zapotecs, particularly their kinship system and religious beliefs, which are not treated here, is referred to Spores, "The Zapotec and Mixtec at Spanish Contact," and Whitecotton, *The Zapotecs*.
64. Fried, p. 235.
65. Córdova, *Vocabulario*.
66. Taylor, *Landlord*, p. 107.
67. Konetzke, *Colección de documentos*, 1: 309.

Chapter Three

1. Cortés, p. 192.
2. *Ibid.*, p. 192; Cervantes de Salazar, p. 805; Martínez Gracida, "Conquista," pp. 622–24; Gay, 1: 369; AGN, Tierras 236, 6: 8r.
3. Cervantes de Salazar, p. 806.
4. Cortés, p. 194; Gay, 1: 349.
5. Martínez Gracida, "Conquista," p. 626; Cortés, p. 192.
6. Cortés, pp. 198, 205; AGI, Justicia 117.
7. Cortés, p. 205; Cervantes de Salazar, p. 808; Martínez Gracida, "Conquista," p. 627; Gay, 1: 390. Jalatlaco later came to occupy this site.
8. Martínez Gracida, "Conquista," p. 628; Gay, 1: 412,
9. Gay, 1: 390; Cortés, p. 227. 10. AGN, Tierras 236, 6: 8v, 67r.
11. *Ibid.*, fol. 67r. 12. AGI, Justicia 231: 516r.
13. AGI, Justicia 231.
14. *Ibid.*, fol. 38r; AGI, Audiencia de México 94, num. 10.
15. AGI, Justicia 231.
16. *Instrucciones*, p. 238; AGI, Justicia 231; AGN, Hospital de Jesús 398, 5: 191r.
17. AGI, Justicia 231: 397v.
18. Burgoa, *Palestra historial*, pp. 30–31.
19. AGI, Justicia 231: 463r–463v.
20. AGI, Audiencia de México 94, num. 10; ENE, 4: 141.
21. *Instrucciones*, p. 238.

22. AGN, Hospital de Jesús 265, *15*; AGN, Tierras 997, *1*: 35r; AGI, Audiencia de México 355; BN, 2450: 315v.
23. García Martínez, p. 53; Gerhard, *Historical Geography*, p. 10.
24. See p. 33, above, for a list of the towns.
25. Arteaga Garza and Pérez San Vicente, pp. 238–40.
26. Gerhard, *Historical Geography*, p. 89.
27. AGI, Indiferente General 107, tomo 2: 386v–392.
28. Taylor, *Landlord*, pp. 17, 31.   29. PNE, 4: 117.
30. Taylor, *Landlord*, p. 36.   31. AGI, Justicia 231.
32. AGN, Hospital de Jesús 293, *140*.
33. Taylor, *Landlord*, pp. 113–14.
34. AGN, Hospital de Jesús 146, *430*, and 446, *1*.
35. Taylor, *Landlord*, pp. 113–14.
36. Gerhard, *Historical Geography*. See especially p. 21 for a detailed map of overlapping civil and ecclesiastic jurisdictions in the Valley of Oaxaca and surrounding territory.
37. AGI, Justicia 231: 462v–463r.
38. "Carta de Don Fray Juan de Zumárraga al Emperador-Valladolid, 1533," in Cuevas, p. 41.
39. AGI, Justicia 231: 23r–23v, 24v, 70r, 71r.
40. *Ibid.*, fols. 23r–23v; Díaz del Castillo, p. 496.
41. *Colección de documentos para la historia de Oaxaca*, p. 14; AGI, Audiencia de México 1841, ramo 1.
42. AGI, Audiencia de México 1088, lib. 2: 97r, 98r.
43. AGN, Mercedes 2, *260*.
44. Gerhard, *Historical Geography*, p. 14.
45. AGI, Audiencia de México 91, ramo 1.
46. Gerhard, *Historical Geography*, p. 50. Also see this source for further changes in the 17th and 18th centuries.
47. CDII, 7: 548–49.
48. AGN, Reales Cédulas Duplicadas 3, *140*: 92r.
49. AGI, Audiencia de México 355; Konetzke, *Colección de documentos*, 1: 309.
50. AGI, Audiencia de México 355; CDII, 7: 547.
51. AGI, Audiencia de México 355.
52. Muriel, p. 25.
53. Burgoa, *Palestra historial*, pp. 30–31; CCG, *Documentos relacionados con el litigio seguido por la Parroquia de Santa María Oaxaca . . . contra la provincia de San Hipólito Martir*.
54. CDII, 7: 543.
55. Ricard, *Spiritual Conquest*, pp. 62–63, 71.

56. Taylor, *Landlord*, p. 165.
57. Ricard, *Spiritual Conquest*, p. 70.
58. Taylor, *Landlord*, pp. 165–66.
59. AGI, Audiencia de México 879; CCG, *Documentos* (cited in note 53, above).
60. AGI, Audiencia de México 1841, ramo 1.
61. Antequera's cabildo and vecinos lodged protests about the matter in 1531, 1532, 1544, 1551, and 1561 (ENE, 2: 100; AGI, Audiencia de México 1088, lib. 2: 78v–79r; *ibid*. 355, and 94, num. 10; CDII, 7: 547).
62. Gerhard, *Historical Geography*, p. 49.
63. *Ibid*., p. 72; Taylor, *Landlord*, pp. 36–37.
64. AGI, Justicia 231: 104r, 173v, 207v, 483r; AGI, Audiencia de México 1088, lib. 2: 78v–79r; AGI, Patronato 54, num. 7, ramo 2.
65. These incorporated the villages of Patlaquistlauaca (now Yodocono or Chindua); Teguastepec and Nanacaltepec; Yolotepec; Tamasola, Suchitepec, Axomulco, Amatlán, and Cacatepeque; Sosola; Malinaltepec; Etlatongo and Huautla; Chachoapan; Apoala; Ixcatlán and Nopala; Tamazulapan; Azuntepec, Epustepec, Necatepec, Olintepec, Tepexistepec, and Zoquitlán; Sola and Istayula; Coatlán, Miahuatlán, Ejutla, Elmolongas, Cuixtla, and Suchitepec (different from the above); Totolapa; Ocotepec; Ozolotepec; Calpulalpan; and Chicomezuchil (ENE, 9: 2–43). This list differs considerably from the one given by Taylor (*Landlord and Peasant*, p. 37), which applies only for the early decades of the 16th century.
66. AGI, Patronato 54, num. 7, ramo 2.
67. PNE, 1: 140.
68. AGI, Audiencia de México 102, ramo 3.
69. PNE, 1: 49–50, 74–75, 104, 107, 128–30, 149, 244–45, 250, 284, 295.
70. Gibson, *Aztecs*, pp. 62–63; Taylor, *Landlord*, p. 143.
71. Taylor, *Landlord*, p. 143.
72. ENE, 9: 2–43.
73. ENE, 13: 34–46.
74. AMO, *Actas de Sesiones*, 1564–1642.
75. Taylor, *Landlord*, p. 37; AGN, Indios 10 (primera parte), 20; AGN, Mercedes 59; 309; AGI, Audiencia de México 355.
76. PNE, 1: 49–50, 74–75, 104, 107, 128–30, 149, 244–45, 250, 284, 295; ENE 13: 34–36.
77. ENE, 9: 2–43.
78. Taylor, *Landlord*, p. 17; AGI, Justicia 231.
79. AGI, Justicia 231.
80. AGI, Audiencia de México 1088, lib. 2: 77r–77v, and lib. 3: 13r–14r.
81. AGI, Justicia 231: 24r, 476v.

82. *Ibid.*, fols. 479r–484r.

83. *Ibid.*, fol. 207v; AGI, Audiencia de México 1088, lib. 2: 97v–98r.

84. AGI, Justicia 231: 72v, 483.

85. AGN, Hospital de Jesús 293, *135*: 23r, 25r.

86. AGI, Justicia 231.

87. Gibson, *Aztecs*, p. 221.

88. AGN, Hospital de Jesús 147, *430*: 336r–341r. The places of origin of the 12 were Chietla, Texcoco, Tepeaca, Chalco, Quechula, Tenisquiapan, Guatemala, and the Huaxteca.

89. ENE, 2: 96.

90. Taylor, *Landlord*, p. 21.

91. AGI, Indiferente General 1529, num 229: 3v.

92. García Pimentel, p. 61.

93. AGI, Justicia 231: 240r, 441v.

94. *Ibid.*, fol. 240r; ENE, 2: 100; AGI, Audiencia de México 1088, lib. 2: 73v–74v.

95. Fernando Cortés was granted a license in 1542 to take 25 or 30 tamemes from Mexico City to Antequera and Tehuantepec (AGN, Mercedes 1, *234*: 111v).

96. AGI, Justicia 231: 240r; AGN, Mercedes 2, *758*; Borah, *Early Colonial Trade*, p. 28.

97. See map in Borah, *Early Colonial Trade*, p. 28.

98. *Ibid.*, p. 27.

99. *Ibid.*, p. 28.

100. AGN, Mercedes 1, *439*.

101. CDII, 7: 550.

102. *Instrucciones*, p. 240.

103. AGI, Casa de Contratación 197, num. 21, ramos 14, 15, 16.

104. Borah, *Early Colonial Trade*, pp. 94–95.

105. AGI, Justicia 231: 94v.

106. Borah, *Silk Raising*, pp. 14, 18, 24, 15; PNE, 1.

107. AGN, Mercedes 1, *169*; Borah, *Early Colonial Trade*, p. 14.

108. Borah, *Early Colonial Trade*, pp. 33–35; AGI, Audiencia de México 1841.

109. Lee, p. 457; Borah, *Early Colonial Trade*, p. 30.

110. Gibson, *Aztecs*, p. 272; Taylor, *Landlord*, pp. 116–17.

111. Taylor, *Landlord*, p. 117.

112. Haring, p. 158.

113. AGI, Audiencia de México 355: 306v; CCG, loose papers.

114. AGI, Justicia 231: 65v, 439v.

115. AGI, Audiencia de México 1088, lib. 2: 78r–78v; CCG, loose papers.

116. AGI, Audiencia de México 355: 306r.

117. Taylor, *Landlord*, p. 79.

118. Taylor, *Landlord*, pp. 116–17; Cuevas, p. 181.
119. ENE, 4: 142–43.
120. Gay, 1: 546.
121. Taylor, *Landlord*, pp. 117, 121.
122. *Ibid.*, pp. 15, 119, 213.
123. *Ibid.*, p. 116.
124. AGI, Audiencia de México 355: 306r.
125. AGI, Audiencia de México 1088, lib. 3: 25v–26r.
126. Taylor, *Landlord*, p. 116.   127. *Ibid.*, p. 120.
128. AGN, Mercedes 3, *670.*   129. Taylor, *Landlord*, p. 113.
130. Haring, p. 158.
131. AGN, Hospital de Jesús 398, 5: 70v.
132. AGI, Audiencia de México 1088, lib. 2: 67r.
133. ENE, 2: 93; AGI, Audiencia de México 1841.
134. AGI, Justicia 231.
135. ENE, 5: 36–37.
136. AGN, Hospital de Jesús 398, 5: 83v.
137. ENE, 3: 190.
138. AGI, Justicia 231; AGN Mercedes 3, *112*; Borah, *Early Colonial Trade*, p. 9.
139. Borah, *Early Colonial Trade*, pp. 8–9.
140. CDII, 7: 546–48.
141. Cook and Borah ("Quelle fut la stratification sociale") provide an interesting discussion on the effect of the Spanish tribute system on Indian society.
142. CDII, 7: 550–51.
143. Konetzke, *Colección de documentos*, 1: 309.
144. AGI, Audiencia de México 1088, lib. 2: 64v–65r, 79r–79v.
145. AGI, Justicia 231: 603v.
146. AGI, Casa de Contratación 197, num. 21, ramos 14, 15, 16; *ibid.* 475.
147. Konetzke, *Colección de documentos*, 1: 147.
148. AGI, Justicia 231.

Chapter Four

1. Borah, *Silk Raising*, pp. 35, 37.
2. *Ibid.*, pp. 30, 31, 87, 119.
3. Lee, pp. 457, 462.
4. Lee, p. 462.
5. AGN, General de Parte 3, *146*: 68v–70r.
6. Lee, pp. 453, 457.   7. Taylor, *Landlord*, p. 213.
8. *Ibid.*, p. 121.   9. See *ibid.*, p. 137.

10. *Ibid.*, p. 138.
11. AGN, Hospital de Jesús 285, *98.*
12. Taylor, *Landlord*, pp. 116–17; Cuevas, p. 181.
13. Taylor, *Landlord*, pp. 29, 34, 121.
14. *Ibid.*, pp. 17–18.
15. AGN, Tierras 2782, *6.*
16. Zavala and Castelo, 4: 505–6.
17. BEO, *Litigio promovido por padres dominicos contra clerigos por asunto de administración en el pueblo de Santa Catarina Minas.*
18. AGI, Casa de Contratación 294.
19. Zavala and Castelo, 4: 506.
20. AGN, Tierras 2952, *53.* The communities were Ejutla, Ocotlán, Coyotepec, Teozapotlan, Cuilapan, Zimatlán, Santa María Magdalena [Teitipac?], Tepezimatlán, Santa Cruz Mixtepec, Santa Ana Tlapacoya, Ayoquesco, Sola, Teitipac, Tlacolula, Mitla, Chichicapan, Totolapa, Zoquitlán, Miahuatlán, Suchitepec, Amatlán, and Coatlán. Each town was required to send 4% of its population to the mines each week.
21. AGI, Escribanía de Cámara 179B: 10–130v.
22. Zavala and Castelo, 2: 214–15.
23. AGN, Reales Cédulas Duplicadas 16, *319:* 158v.
24. Zavala and Castelo, 4: 504–6, and 5: 112; AGN, Tierras 2782, *6;* AGN, Indios 12 (primera parte), *202.*
25. AGN, Indios 14, *94, 95.*
26. AGN, Hospital de Jesús 398, *5.*
27. Butterworth, p. 45.
28. Taylor, *Landlord*, p. 195.
29. *Ibid.*, p. 200.
30. Ricard, "Plaza Mayor," p. 325.
31. Gay, 1: 547–48.
32. ENE, 4: 142–43.
33. AGI, Indiferente General 1529: 3v.
34. AGI, Audiencia de México 355; AGI, Indiferente General 1529: 3v.
35. AGI, Audiencia de México 357.
36. AGI, Audiencia de México 357.
37. Vásquez de Espinosa, p. 147.
38. CCG, *Traslado del Inventario de los Documentos Relativos a la Fundación del Convento de Santo Domingo.*
39. Kubler, 2: 285.
40. AGI, Audiencia de México 357.
41. CCG, *Libro de la Fundación del Convento y Monasterio de Monjas intitulado Sancta Catharina de Sena.*
42. Borah, *New Spain's Century*, p. 19.
43. AGN, Mercedes 1, *119, 126, 127, 132.*
44. *Ibid.*, 3, *30, 626*; AGI, Audiencia de México 1841.
45. AGN, Indios 5, *66* (on Cuilapan); AGN, General de Parte 2, *408, 624* (on Mitla and Etla, respectively).

46. Zavala and Castelo, 3: vi–viii, and 4: 82.

47. *Ibid.*, 3: 155.

48. *Ibid.*, 6: 394; AGN, Indios 7, *365*.

49. Zavala and Castelo 3: 164, 173.

50. *Ibid.*, 4: 504–6. In 1601, 32 laborers were taken from Antequera's repartimiento and reassigned to the Chichicapan mines.

51. The breakdown of the repartimiento laborers in Antequera in 1609 is as follows. *Valley towns*: Villa de Etla, 46; Huitzo, 26; Villa de Oaxaca, 19; Jalatlaco, 19; Tlacochahuaya, 15; Teotitlán del Valle, 15; Tlalixtac, 12; Macuilxóchitl, 8; Tenexpa, 2. *Mixteca Alta towns*: Teozacualco, 17; Sosola, 12; Nochixtlán, 12; Estela, 5; Iscuintepec, 5; Tamasola, 5; Texotepec, 4; Guaxolotipac, 2; Tiltepec (number unknown). *Mountain Zapotec towns*: Ixtepeji, 8; Chicomesuchil, 7; Atepec, 5; Xaltianguis, 5; Teococuilco, 4; Calpulalpa, 2; Zoquiapan, 1; Ixtlán (number unknown). *Cuicatec towns*: Atlatlauca, 15; Cotahuixtla, 6; Nacaltepec, 4. *Peñoles Zapotec towns*: Elotepec, 7; Totomachapa, 2. *Chontal town*: Xilotepec, 8. This breakdown only totals 298, but both Tiltepec and Ixtlán were almost certainly required to send workers, too. (AGN, Tierras 2952, *53*.)

52. AGN, Indios 3, *428*.

53. Taylor, *Landlord*, p. 146.

54. AGN, Mercedes 3, *691*.

55. AGN, Hospital de Jesús 398, 5: 174v.

56. Cook and Borah, *Indian Population*, pp. 16, 25.

57. PNE, 4: 107, 108, 181, 202; AGN, General de Parte 2, *147*: 52r, and *618*: 146r.

58. AGN, Reales Cédulas Duplicadas 3, *140*: 92r.

59. AGN, General de Parte 1, *815–18*: 151r–151v.

60. AGN, Hospital de Jesús 54: 8v; Jalatlaco, *Libro de Casamientos*, 1611–31; Marquesado, *Libros de Casamientos*, 1664, 1665.

61. AGN, Tierras 236, *6*: 65r–66r.

62. AGN, Hospital de Jesús 54: 10r; AGN, Tierras 236, *6*: 65r–66r.

63. AGN, Tierras 645 (primera parte), *3*: 1r–1v.

64. One check is available for testing the reliability of this census. A similar count made 4 years later, in 1569, showed roughly the same number of tributaries—only 26 fewer than in 1565. More problematic, however, is the apparent exclusion of household servants from these censuses and the obvious underrepresentation of unmarried adults, widows, and widowers. In correcting for this deficiency, I have used the multiplier 3.3. This is a figure Borah and Cook apply in estimating population size from counts of household heads prior to 1557, but I think it is probably closer to the mark than the 2.8 figure they use to estimate population size from post-1557 tributary counts. See their *The Population of Central Mexico*, p. 38.

65. AGN Indios 3, *187*; AGN Tierras 2952, *53*; AGN Mercedes 6: 567v.
66. AGN, Hospital de Jesús 289, *98*: AGI, Audiencia de México 1684, ramo 1.
67. AGN, Hospital de Jesús 285, *98*: 63v.
68. AGN, Mercedes 3, *692*.
69. Puga, fol. 139r.
70. AGN, Hospital de Jesús 285, *98*: 55v.
71. AGN, Indios 36, *318*: 286v.
72. *Ibid.* 1, *216*, and 3, *187*; AGI, Audiencia de México 355.
73. AGN, Indios 52, *89*.
74. AGN, Hospital de Jesús 398, *4*: 19v.
75. Miranda, *Tributo indígena*, p. 22.
76. Jalatlaco, *Libro de los Ornamentos y Bienes de Iglesia de este Partido*, 1611–20.
77. Jalatlaco, *Libro de Casamientos*, 1611–31.
78. AGN, Hospital de Jesús 285, *98*. I have already cited many of the urban occupations of the Antequera Indians. The Nahuas also worked as button-makers, tanners, chair-makers, cart-makers, painters, farriers, and bakers.
79. Butterworth, p. 45.
80. AGN, Indios 3, *196*.
81. AGI, Audiencia de México 355.
82. *Ibid.*
83. AGI, Audiencia de México 98. 100, 102, 107 (ramo 3).
84. *Ibid.* 102, ramo 2.
85. AGN, Hosp. de Jesús 146, *430*: 180r–192v; Taylor, *Landlord*, p. 154.
86. Taylor, *Landlord*, pp. 153, 156.
87. AMO, *Actas de Sesiones*, 1564–1642.
88. AGN, Reales Cédulas Duplicadas 3, *129*: 86r (1590).
89. AGI, Patronato 54, num. 7, ramo 2; Aud. de México 102, ramo 2.
90. McAlister, "Social Structure," pp. 357–58.
91. AGI, Audiencia de México 208.
92. Aguirre Beltrán, p. 245.
93. McAlister, "Social Structure," p. 353.
94. García Pimentel, p. 69; AGI, Indiferente General 1529: 3v.
95. Konetzke, *Colección de documentos*, 1: 256.
96. *Ibid.*, p. 427.
97. Mörner, *Race Mixture*, p. 43.
98. See Carrera Stampa.
99. AGI, Audiencia de México 99, ramo 5.
100. AGN, Mercedes 7: 189r; AGN, Indios 2, *989*: 226v.
101. AGN, General de Parte 3, *338*: 156v.

102. Mörner, *Race Mixture*, pp. 43–44.
103. Konetzke, *Colección de documentos*, 1: 543.
104. AGI, Audiencia de México 1844, ramo 2.
105. Mörner, *Race Mixture*, p. 44.
106. AGN, Reales Cédulas Duplicadas 16, *600*: 316r, and *103*: 113; Konetzke, *Colección de documentos*, 2: 182–83.
107. AGI, Indiferente General 1529: 3v.
108. AGN, Reales Cédulas Duplicadas 16, *362*: 187v; AGN, General de Parte 7, *379*: 267r–267v.
109. AGN, General de Parte 4, *1227*: 231v; AGN, Indios 5, *441*: Hospital de Jesús 102 (atado 2), *19* and *24*. The towns were Teotitlán del Valle (1576), Huitzo (1591), Cuilapan (1638), and Azompa (1638).
110. Gage, pp. 121–23.

Chapter Five

1. Taylor, *Landlord*, pp. 111–63.   2. *Ibid.*, pp. 121–28.
3. *Ibid.*, pp. 133, 152–63.   4. *Ibid.*, pp. 140–42, 160.
5. AGN, General de Parte 7, *114*: 77r–77v.
6. AGN, Reales Cédulas Duplicadas 62, *122*: 79v.
7. AGI, Audiencia de México 355: 109v, 120v–129r, 217r.
8. AGN, Reales Cédulas 23, 9: 43–44r; AGN, Reales Cédulas Duplicadas 36, *381*: 311v.
9. Hamnett provides a detailed study of the administrative aspects of this institution in the Bishopric of Oaxaca during the period 1750–1821.
10. *Ibid.*, p. 6.
11. AGN, Reales Cédulas 2, *189*: 400r.
12. BN, 6743: 277r–290r.
13. AGN, Indios: 13, *235*; 17, *111*; and 27, *199*.
14. AGN, Civil 1539, *2*: 13v–33r.
15. Burgoa, *Geográfica descripción*, 1: 272.
16. AGN, Indios 41, *159*: 190v; 19, 7; AGN, Civil 822: 269r.
17. Burgoa, *Geográfica descripción*, 2: 119–20, 416; AGN, Indios 26, cuad. 2, exp. *86*.
18. Taylor, *Landlord*, p. 103.
19. *Ibid.*, p. 3.
20. Burgoa, *Geográfica descripción*, 1: 272.
21. Sagrario, *Libros de Casamientos*, 1693–1700.
22. Sagrario, *Libro de la Cofradía del Oficio Obrajero, Xochimilco*.
23. CCG, *Protocolo de Diego Benaías*, 1682; AGN, Reales Cédulas 25, *34*: 160r.
24. Burgoa, *Geográfica descripción*, 1: 272.
25. *Ibid.*, pp. 30, 272.

26. Borah, *New Spain's Century*.
27. Bakewell, pp. 224–25.
28. Taylor, *Landlord*, pp. 130, 142.
29. *Ibid.*, p. 16.
30. AGI, Escribanía de Cámara 179B: 12r; AGN, General de Parte 18, *151*: 150r; CCG, loose papers.
31. CCG, *Libro de Despachos*: 25r, 225r–232v.
32. AGN, Hospital de Jesús 69, libro 1: 341r; AGN, Indios 33, *328*; AGI, Audiencia de México 355: 303v.
33. AGN, Indios 36, *318*: 286v.
34. *Ibid.* 43, *21*: 34r.
35. *Ibid.* 52, *89*: 93v.
36. See Gibson, *Aztecs*, pp. 181–82.
37. AGN, Hospital de Jesús 118, *49*: 43r.
38. See *ibid.* 347, *10*: 6–10r.
39. See Gibson, *Aztecs*, p. 182.
40. CCG, *Libro de Despachos*: 68r–71r.
41. AGI, Patronato 230B: 254v; Jalatlaco, *Padrón de 1729*.
42. Taylor, *Landlord*, p. 101.
43. Jalatlaco, *Libros de Casamientos*, 1692–1701; Burgoa, *Geográfica descripción*, 1: 271.
44. AGN, Indios 26, cuad. 1, exp. *33*.
45. Jalatlaco, *Padrón de 1729*; Villaseñor y Sánchez, 2: 114–15.
46. AGI, Patronato 230B, ramo 10.
47. Sagrario, *Libro de la Cofradía del Oficio Obrajero, Xochimilco*; Jalatlaco, *Libro de la Cofradía de Nuestra Señora del Rosario de las Maestras Camiseras*, 1713; AGN, Tributos 43, *7*.
48. Carrera Stampa, *Los gremios mexicanos*, offers a detailed study of craft guilds in New Spain. Unfortunately, little documentation exists for Antequera, but guild organization probably differed little from that found in other major cities in New Spain.
49. Taylor, *Landlord*, pp. 35, 36.
50. *Ibid.*, p. 38.
51. *Ibid.*, pp. 48–49, 65.
52. AGN, Civil 34, *1*.
53. AGN, Indios 49, *159*: 193r.
54. The best sources for discriminatory legislation are the *Recopilación de leyes de los reynos de las Indias*, first published in 1680, and Konetzke's *Colección de documentos para la historia de la formación social de Hispanoamérica*. The *Ramo de Reales Cédulas Duplicadas* of the AGN contains a number of decrees pertaining to New Spain.
55. Roncal, p. 533.
56. AEO, Juzgados, bundles for 1751–55, 1761–70.
57. Aguirre Beltrán, p. 246.

58. Roncal, p. 532.
59. Konetzke, "Documentos para la historia," pp. 585–86.
60. Sagrario, *Libros de Bautismos*.
61. AGN, Padrones 13; AGI, Audiencia de México 2591.
62. Aguirre Beltrán, p. 268.
63. Sagrario, *Libro del Hospital*.
64. AGI, Audiencia de México 2589, 2590, 2591.
65. AGN, Hospital de Jesús 163, *48* (segunda parte): 46r–50r. For other references to non-Indians residing among the Indians, see AGN, Indios 18, *63* (Zaachila), and *110* (Macuilxóchitl); 41, *38* (Santa Ana Zegache); and 54, *31* (Tlalixtac); and AGN, Tierras 2596, *192* (Coyotepec), and 2943, *34* (Sola).
66. See AGN, Indios 23, *287*, and 37, *157*; AGN, Tierras 236, *6*; and CCG, *Registro de Varios Despachos* . . . , fol. 68v.
67. AGN, Tierras 112, *3*.
68. Borah and Cook, "Marriage," p. 961.
69. *Ibid.*, pp. 962–63.
70. Archivo de Notarías, Oaxaca. *Protocolos* for 1700, 1710, 1720, 1736, 1747, 1756, 1762, 1775, 1781, 1795.
71. AGI, Patronato 230B, ramo 10.
72. Sagrario, *Cofradía las Nieves*, 1; AGN, Reales Cédulas 20, *155*: 347r.
73. Burgoa, *Geográfica descripción*, 1: 270–71.
74. Taylor, *Landlord*, p. 160.
75. AEO, Juzgados, bundle for 1641–99, *17*. For hacienda values, see Taylor, *Landlord*, pp. 214–20.

Chapter Six

1. Iturribarría, p. 91.
2. Gerhard, *México*; and Alexander de Humboldt, cited in Brading, *Miners*, p. 14.
3. Taylor, *Landlord*, p. 18.
4. The manuscript total of the 1777 census (AGI, Audiencia de México 2591) is 19,653. Cook and Borah, in their analysis of the data, list the total in one place as 19,610 and in another as 18,558 (*Essays in Population History*, 1: 206, 238). The lower figure is probably more accurate, since in our analysis of the 1792 census (AGN, Padrones 13) we found a similar but smaller discrepancy between the manuscript total of 18,241 and an actual count of 18,008.
5. Gibson, *Spain in America*, pp. 169, 171; Hamnett, pp. 149, 153.
6. Hamnett, p. 148.   7. Dahlgren de Jordán, p. 10.
8. Hamnett, pp. 9, 32.   9. Dahlgren de Jordán, p. 39.
10. AEO, Juzgados, bundle for 1781–86.
11. AGN, Padrones 13.

12. Hamnett, pp. 3, 187.
13. *Legislación del trabajo*, pp. 151–55.
14. Hamnett, p. 187.
15. AGN, Padrones 13.
16. AGI, Audiencia de México 1872.
17. *Ibid.*
18. AGI, Planos de México 556 bis.
19. BN, 2450: 315v.
20. Marquesado, *Libro corriente de Cordilleras comenzado en el año de 1759*: 182v.
21. BN, 2450: 314r–320v.
22. AGI, Audiencia de México 2589.
23. AEO, Juzgados, bundle for 1761–70.
24. AGI, Audiencia de México 2589.
25. BN, 2450: 316r–316v.
26. AGI, Audiencia de México 2589.
27. Taylor, *Landlord*, p. 20; AGI, Audiencia de México 2589, 2590, 2591.
28. AGI, Audiencia de México 2589. The 8 sujeto towns were San Agustín de las Juntas, San Antonio de la Cal, Santa Cruz Amilpas, San Sebastián Tutla, San Francisco Tutla, Santa Lucía del Camino, San Felipe del Agua, and Santa María Ixcotel.
29. Marquesado, *Padrón* 1, 1776–85. The towns were the Villa de Oaxaca, San Martín Mexicapan, San Juan Chapultepec, San Jacinto Amilpas, Santa María Azompa, San Andrés Ixtlahuaca, and San Pedro Ixtlahuaca.
30. The census itself is in AGN, Padrones 13; the summary is in AGN Tributos 34, 7: 51r. Censuses of other cities in New Spain were taken at the same time and are all housed in the AGN. Of these, only the Guanajuato census has been studied intensively (see Brading, *Miners*, pp. 247–60). A previous house-to-house census of Antequera was undertaken by Church officials in 1777 in conjunction with many others in all parts of the Bishopric of Oaxaca. Though this source is more reliable for the ages of adult females and a general demographic profile of the urban Indian and slave populations, we have not used it because it gives no data on occupations. Cook and Borah have made extensive use of the 1777 censuses in their work on the historical demography of New Spain (see their *Essays in Population History*, 2 vols.). The 1777 census for Antequera is located in AGI, Audiencia de México 2591.
31. Aguirre Beltrán, pp. 167, 173.
32. AGN, Tributos 34, 7. This analysis was worked out by William B. Taylor.
33. Our use of the concept of socioeconomic group follows the lead of

Michael Anderson, *Family Structure in Nineteenth-Century Lancashire*, pp. 25–26.
34. Taylor, *Landlord*, pp. 111–63.
35. AGN, Tierras 273, 2: 1–3.
36. AGN, Criminal 101: 86.
37. AEO, Juzgados, bundle for 1812. The information used here and in the donor list later in this chapter was furnished by William B. Taylor.
38. AGN, Bienes Nacionales 553, 8.
39. AEO, Justicia, bundle for 1767–70.
40. Brading, *Miners*, pp. 253–57.
41. Brading, "Government," p. 390.
42. AEO, Justicia, bundle for 1808. The analysis of these data was done by William B. Taylor.
43. Carrera Stampa, pp. 223–46.
44. AEO, Juzgados, bundle for 1751–55 and 1787–90; AGN, Criminal 137, 4.
45. AGN, Civil 1560, 1, 5.
46. Konetzke, *Colección de Documentos*, 3: 821–29.
47. *Ibid.*, p. 828.
48. Archivo Parroquial de Cuilapan (Oaxaca), *Libro de Providencias*, 1771–91.
49. AEO, Juzgados, bundle for 1761–70 and 1788.
50. McAlister, *Fuero Militar*, Chap. 4; Archer, p. 233.
51. Brading, *Miners*, pp. 248–49.   52. Aguirre Beltrán, pp. 268–69.
53. Hoetink, p. 120.   54. Aguirre Beltrán, p. 270.
55. Further research in other localities is needed in order to determine if Antequera was an exception in this regard.
56. AEO, Juzgados, bundle for 1791–94.
57. *Ibid.*, bundle for 1798–99.   58. *Ibid.*, bundle for 1791–94.
59. Aguirre Beltrán, p. 270.   60. *Ibid.*, p. 271.
61. AEO, Juzgados, bundle for 1791–94.
62. AGI, Audiencia de México 2584.
63. AEO, Juzgados, bundle for 1812. This information on the donations was kindly provided by William B. Taylor.
64. AEO, Juzgados, bundle for 1811.
65. See Aguirre Beltrán, pp. 153–54.
66. See, notably, Mörner, *Race Mixture*, p. 54; and McAlister, "Social Structure," p. 362.

Chapter Seven

1. Beals, p. 343; Bagú, pp. 51–53, 103–9; Chávez Orozco, pp. 28, 57.
2. Lockhart, p. 35.

3. Weber, pp. 180–95.

4. Cox, p. 140.

5. Lenski, p. 77.

6. Mörner, *Race Mixture*, p. 54.

7. Fieldhouse, p. 6.

8. Aguirre Beltrán, p. 292; McAlister, "Social Structure," pp. 357–58; Wolf, p. 238.

9. Faron, p. 251.

10. Lenski, p. 20.

11. Weber, p. 181; Harris, *Culture*, p. 414.

12. Weber, p. 181.

13. *Ibid.*, pp. 186–87.

14. Lenski, pp. 79–82.

15. *Ibid.*, p. 81.

16. Taylor, *Landlord*, pp. 159–60.

17. See Wagley, *Race*; Wagley, "On the Concept"; Harris and Kottak; Harris, "Racial Identity"; Harris, "Referential Ambiguity"; and Degler.

18. Harris and Kottak, pp. 204–5.

19. Harris, *Patterns of Race*; Degler.

20. Aguirre Beltrán, p. 290; Bagú, pp. 69–70; Bakewell, pp. 225–26; Chávez Orozco, pp. 23–24; Miranda, *Función Económica*, pp. 9–15; Wolf, pp. 176–201.

21. See Taylor's discussion of economic and noneconomic factors in the operation of the hacienda, in "Landed Society," p. 395.

22. Bakewell (*Silver Mining*, p. 226) sees the transition to an overtly capitalist economy in New Spain as occurring in the latter half of the 16th century.

23. Sjoberg, "Folk and 'Feudal' Societies," pp. 232–33. See also Sjoberg, *Preindustrial City*.

24. Sjoberg, *Preindustrial City*, pp. 108–42.

25. *Ibid.*, pp. 139, 141.

26. Lenski, p. 290.

27. Sjoberg, *Preindustrial City*, p. 120. Southall (pp. 95–98) gives numerous examples to the contrary.

28. Gould.

Bibliography

The bulk of the sources for this book are unpublished. The most important archives I used are the Archivo General de la Nación (AGN) in Mexico City, the Archivo General de Indias (AGI) in Seville, and the archives of the Sagrario, San Matías Jalatlaco, and Santa María del Marquesado parishes in Oaxaca. William B. Taylor has given a comprehensive overview of the archival holdings for Oaxaca in *Landlord and Peasant in Colonial Oaxaca*. Rather than repeat what can be found there, I shall confine my comments to the important sources for social history and the study of urban social structure.

Documentary sources for the pre-conquest period in the Valley of Oaxaca are few, and all of them date from the post-conquest era. There are no surviving manuscripts comparable to the valuable indigenous chronicles and codices that have been so important in reconstructing the cultural histories of the Mixtecs, Nahuas, and Mayas. Nor are there any post-conquest chronicles for the Zapotecs bearing directly on social organization. Most of the Spanish chroniclers of New Spain concerned themselves with the Náhuatl-speaking area of central Mexico and all but totally ignored Oaxaca; the seventeenth-century works of Francisco de Burgoa are the only chronicles that deal extensively with the pre-Hispanic Valley of Oaxaca. The most important sources for the study of Zapotec society at Spanish contact are the *Relaciones geográficas*, compiled in 1579–81 in response to a questionnaire from Philip II. All the surviving *Relaciones* for Valley towns are published and have been used extensively by Ronald Spores and Joseph Whitecotton.

Supplementing the *Relaciones* are the Spanish-Zapotec dictionary and grammar compiled by Fray Juan de Córdova in the mid-sixteenth century.

An inferior and less detailed dictionary, apparently compiled in the seventeenth century, has been published by the Junta Colombina de México. More detailed information on the pre-Hispanic sources can be found in volumes 12–15 of the *Handbook of Middle American Indians*, edited by Robert Wauchope.

For the colonial period, most of the information on Antequera is located in the AGN and AGI, though a number of important early documents from the AGI have been published in various collections, especially *Colección de documentos inéditos relativos al descubrimiento, conquista y organización de las antiguas posesiones españolas* . . . (CDII), published in 1864–84, and *Epistolario de Nueva España, 1505–1818* (ENE), published in 1939–42. Documentation in Oaxaca itself for the sixteenth and seventeenth centuries is rare, most of it having been destroyed in political upheavals or lost for a variety of other reasons. The best sixteenth-century sources in the AGN include records of numerous lawsuits over land and jurisdiction between Antequera and the Marquesado del Valle in the Ramo *Hospital de Jesús*. Also important are a number of viceregal decrees and decisions affecting both Spaniards and Indians in the Ramos of *Indios* and *Mercedes*. Many royal cédulas bearing on the castas of New Spain are located in the Ramo of *Reales Cédulas Duplicadas*. *General de Parte* is another section containing valuable data on Indian labor practices in the sixteenth and seventeenth centuries.

The AGI contains much valuable early material on Antequera, most of it in the *Audiencia de México* section, where there are a series of reports and petitions from Antequera's cabildo and Church officials to the Crown. The sections *Casa de Contratación* and *Patronato* include several wills and personal biographical statements by some of Oaxaca's early conquerors and colonists. An especially thick bundle in the *Justicia* section consists of a 2,000-page residencia taken on Antequera's first alcalde mayor, Juan Peláez Berrio, in 1531, one of the most informative of the few early sources.

Other archives that contain small amounts of relevant material include the Biblioteca del Estado de Oaxaca (BEO), and the Biblioteca Nacional (BN) and Real Academia de la Historia (RAHM) in Madrid. The Castañeda Guzmán collection (CCG) in Oaxaca is especially strong on hacienda and Church records; the Archivo del Estado de Oaxaca (AEO) houses many property inventories and records of civil and criminal suits for the eighteenth century and the last decades of the seventeenth. Little colonial documentation remains in the Archivo Municipal de Oaxaca (AMO), though one book of *Actas de Cabildo* for 1564–1642 has survived. The Archivo de Notarías in Oaxaca has little pertinent information for the present study, but its notarial records contain a wealth of information on the genealogy and property of the elite beginning in 1689. In two important articles Woodrow Borah has supplied somewhat dated but still indispensable inventories of the city's civil and cathedral archives.

The study of social structure in colonial Latin America frequently necessitates the use of quantitative sources and techniques; in my own case, I have drawn most heavily on data in parish registers and census materials for my analysis. The marriage records in Oaxaca's Sagrario and Jalatlaco parishes are especially important. Both of these depositories, together with that of the Marquesado parish, also contain valuable censuses conducted by curates in the eighteenth and nineteenth centuries. Several cofradía record books and episcopal decrees are also extant, and are particularly useful for the study of Church history. A surprising discovery was that the baptismal registers in Antequera did not indicate the racial status of most persons. The city seems to be an exception in this regard, though parish records have been so little studied that it is difficult to generalize.

Census data used in this study come mostly from the AGN and AGI. Tributary counts from Jalatlaco in 1565 and 1569 are based on the records of a lawsuit between Antequera and the Marqués del Valle located in the Ramo *Hospital de Jesús* of the AGN. A list of Indian, mulatto, and mestizo tributaries in Antequera was compiled in 1661, in the aftermath of the Tehuantepec Indian rebellion, and is stored in the *Patronato* section of the AGI, along with other papers bearing on the uprising. In the *Audiencia de México* division of the AGI are the 1777 Church censuses for many towns in the Bishopric of Oaxaca, including Antequera. By far the single most valuable source for the social history of Antequera is the 1792 military census, housed with many other such censuses in the Ramo of *Padrones* in the AGN. Though these censuses have the disadvantage of excluding Indians and slaves, they were among the first of their kind conducted in Latin America. The Antequera census provides a wealth of information on race and occupations, but unfortunately tells us little about family and household structure, for the census takers artificially divided up the entire city into nuclear family groupings, frequently ignoring the basic household units. The analysis of this census presented in Chapter 6 may usefully be compared with D. A. Brading's work with a similar census for Guanajuato.

Finally, several anthropological and sociological studies of race relations in the twentieth century were found to be extremely helpful in understanding the past. The works of L. C. Faron, Florestan Fernandes, Marvin Harris, H. Hoetink, Conrad Kottak, Oracy Nogueira, Julian Pitt-Rivers, Mauricio Solaún and Sidney Kronus, Richard Thompson, Charles Wagley, and Norman E. Whitten, Jr., to name but a few scholars who have dealt with the topic, can be profitably read by those interested in earlier periods.

Aguirre Beltrán, Gonzalo. *La población negra de México: estudio etnohistórico*. Mexico City, 1972.

Anderson, Michael. *Family Structure in Nineteenth-Century Lancashire*. Cambridge, Eng., 1971.

Archer, Christon I. "Pardos, Indians, and the Army of New Spain: Inter-Relationships and Conflicts, 1780–1810," *Journal of Latin American Studies*, 6(1974): 231–55.

Arteaga Garza, Beatriz, and Guadalupe Pérez San Vicente, eds. *Cedulario cortesiano*. Mexico City, 1949.

Bagú, Sergio. *Estructura social de la colonia*. Buenos Aires, 1952.

Bakewell, P. J. *Silver Mining and Society in Colonial Mexico: Zacatecas 1546–1700*. London, 1971.

Barlow, Robert H. "Descripción de la ciudad de Antequera," *Tlalocan*, 2, 2 (1946): 134–37.

———. *The Extent of the Empire of the Culhua Mexica*. Ibero-Americana: 28. Berkeley, Calif., 1949.

Barth, Fredrik. "Introduction," in F. Barth, ed., *Ethnic Groups and Boundaries*. Boston, 1969.

Bayle, Constantino. *Los cabildos seculares en la América española*. Madrid, 1952.

Beals, Ralph L. "Social Stratification in Latin America," in Dwight B. Heath and Richard N. Adams, eds., *Contemporary Cultures and Societies of Latin America*. New York, 1965.

Bernal, Ignacio. "Archeological Synthesis of Oaxaca," in R. Wauchope, ed., *Handbook of Middle American Indians*, vol. 3, Austin, Tex., 1965.

———. "The Mixtecs in the Archeology of the Valley of Oaxaca," in John Paddock, ed., *Ancient Oaxaca*. Stanford, Calif., 1966.

Borah, Woodrow. "The Cathedral Archive of Oaxaca," *Hispanic American Historical Review*, 28 (1948): 640–45.

———. *Early Colonial Trade and Navigation Between Mexico and Peru*. Ibero-Americana: 38. Berkeley, Calif., 1954.

———. *New Spain's Century of Depression*. Ibero-Americana: 35. Berkeley, Calif., 1951.

———. "Notes on Civil Archives in the City of Oaxaca," *Hispanic American Historical Review*, 31 (1951): 723–49.

———. *Silk Raising in Colonial Mexico*. Ibero-Americana: 20. Berkeley, Calif., 1943.

Borah, Woodrow, and Sherburne F. Cook. "Marriage and Legitimacy in Mexican Culture: Mexico and California," *California Law Review*, 54 (1966): 946–1008.

———. *The Population of Central Mexico in 1548: An Analysis of the Suma de visitas de pueblos*. Ibero-Americana: 43. Berkeley, Calif., 1960.

Brading, David A. "Government and Elite in Late Colonial Mexico," *Hispanic American Historical Review*, 54 (1973): 389–414.

――――. *Miners and Merchants in Bourbon Mexico, 1763–1810*. London, 1971.

Burgoa, Francisco de. *Geográfica descripción*. 2 vols. Mexico City, 1934.

――――. *Palestra historial*. Mexico City, 1934.

Butterworth, Douglas, ed. "Relaciones of Oaxaca of the 16th and 18th Centuries," *Boletín de Estudios Oaxaqueños*, 23 (1962): 35–55.

Carrasco, Pedro. "Social Organization of Ancient Mexico," in R. Wauchope, ed., *Handbook of Middle American Indians*, vol. 10. Austin, Tex., 1971.

Carrera Stampa, Manuel. *Los gremios mexicanos*. Mexico City, 1954.

Castillo Tejero, Noemí. "Conquista y colonización de Chiapas," *Los Mayas del sur y sus relaciones con los Nahuas meridionales*. Sociedad Mexicana de Antropología. Mexico City, 1961.

Cervantes de Salazar, Francisco. *Crónica de la Nueva España*. Madrid, 1914.

Chance, John K. "The Colonial Latin American City: Preindustrial or Capitalist?," *Urban Anthropology*, 4, 3 (1975): 211–28.

――――. "The Urban Indian in Colonial Oaxaca," *American Ethnologist*, 3, 4 (1976): 603–32.

Chance, John K., and William B. Taylor. "Estate and Class in a Colonial City: Oaxaca in 1792," *Comparative Studies in Society and History*, 19, 4 (1977): 454–87.

Chávez Orozco, Luis. *Historia económica y social de México: ensayo de interpretación*. Mexico City, 1938.

Chevalier, François. *La Formation des grands domaines au Mexique: Terre et société aux XVIe–XVIIe siècles*. Paris, 1952.

Colección de documentos inéditos relativos al descubrimiento, conquista, y organización de las antiguas posesiones españolas de América y Oceania, sacados de los archivos del reino, y muy especialmente del de Indias. 42 vols. Madrid, 1864–84.

Colección de documentos para la historia de Oaxaca. Mexico City, 1933.

Cook, Sherburne F., and Woodrow Borah. *Essays in Population History*, 2 vols. Berkeley, Calif., 1971–74.

――――. *The Indian Population of Central Mexico, 1531–1610*. Ibero-Americana: 44. Berkeley, Calif., 1960.

――――. *The Population of the Mixteca Alta, 1520–1960*. Ibero-Americana: 50. Berkeley, Calif., 1968.

――――. "Quelle fut la stratification sociale au centre du Mexique durant la première moitié du XVIe siècle?," *Annales: Economies, Sociétés, Civilisations*, 18, 2 (1963): 226–58.

Córdova, Juan de. *Arte en lengua zapoteca*. Morelia, Mexico, 1886.

————. *Vocabulario en lengua zapoteca*. Mexico City, 1942.

Cortés Hernán (Fernando). *Cartas y documentos*. Edited by Mario Hernández Sánchez-Barba. Mexico City, 1963.

Cox, Oliver Cromwell. *Caste, Class, and Race*. New York, 1959.

Cuevas, Mariano, ed. *Documentos inéditos del siglo XVI para la historia de México*. Mexico City, 1914.

Dahlgren de Jordán, Barbro. *La grana cochinilla*. Mexico City, 1963.

Degler, Carl N. *Neither Black Nor White: Slavery and Race Relations in Brazil and the United States*. New York, 1971.

Díaz del Castillo, Bernal. *Historia de la conquista de la Nueva España*. Mexico City, 1966.

Díez de la Calle, Juan. *Memorial y noticias sacras y reales de las Indias occidentales*. 2d ed. Mexico City, 1932.

Durán, Fray Diego. *Historia de las Indias de Nueva España y Islas de tierra firme*. Edited by José F. Ramirez. 2 vols. Mexico City, 1951.

Esteva, Constantino, "Copias de documentos originales en la Biblioteca del Lic. Constantino Esteva." Oaxaca, 1937. Typewritten manuscript, Zimmerman Library, University of New Mexico.

Faron, L. C. "Ethnicity and Social Mobility in Chancay Valley, Peru," in Walter Goldschmidt and Harry Hoijer, eds., *The Social Anthropology of Latin America: Essays in Honor of Ralph Leon Beals*. Los Angeles, 1970.

Fernandes, Florestan, *The Negro in Brazilian Society*. New York, 1969.

Fieldhouse, D. K. "Colonialism: Economic Aspects," in *International Encyclopedia of the Social Sciences*, vol. 3. New York, 1968.

Flannery, Kent V. "The Olmec and the Valley of Oaxaca: A Model for Inter-Regional Interaction in Formative Times," in Elizabeth P. Benson, ed., *Dumbarton Oaks Conference on the Olmec*. Washington, D.C., 1967.

Flannery, Kent V., Anne V. T. Kirkby, Michael J. Kirkby, and Aubrey W. Williams, Jr. "Farming Systems and Political Growth in Ancient Oaxaca," *Science*, 158 (1967): 445–54.

Flores Ruiz, Eduardo. "Sociología histórica de Ciudad Real," *Los Mayas del sur y sus relaciones con los Nahuas meridionales*. Sociedad Mexicana de Antropología. Mexico City, 1961.

Freyre, Gilberto. *The Masters and the Slaves*. New York, 1964.

Fried, Morton. *The Evolution of Political Society: An Essay in Political Anthropology*. New York, 1967.

Gage, Thomas. *The English-American: A New Survey of the West Indies, 1648*. Edited by A. P. Newton. London, 1928.

García Martínez, Bernardo. *El Marquesado del Valle*. Mexico City, 1969.

García Pimentel, Luis, ed. *Relación de los obispados de Tlaxcala, Michoacán, Oaxaca y otros lugares en el siglo XVI*. Mexico City, 1904.

Gay, José Antonio. *Historia de Oaxaca*. 2 vols. Mexico City, 1950.

Gerhard, Peter. *The Historical Geography of New Spain*. London, 1972.

——. *México en 1742*. Mexico City, 1962.

Gibson, Charles. *The Aztecs Under Spanish Rule*. Stanford, Calif., 1964.

——. *Spain in America*. New York, 1966.

——. "Spanish-Indian Institutions and Colonial Urbanism in New Spain," in J. E. Hardoy and R. P. Schaedel, eds., *El proceso de urbanización en América desde sus orígenes hasta nuestra días*. Buenos Aires, 1969.

——. *Tlaxcala in the Sixteenth Century*. New Haven, Conn., 1952.

Gould, Harold A. *Caste and Class: A Comparative View*. McCaleb Module, Addison-Wesley Modular Publications, 1971.

Hamnett, Brian R. *Politics and Trade in Southern Mexico, 1750–1821*. London, 1971.

Haring, C. H. *The Spanish Empire in America*. New York, 1963.

Harris, Marvin. *Culture, Man, and Nature*. New York, 1971.

——. *Patterns of Race in the Americas*. New York, 1964.

——. "Racial Identity in Brazil," *Luso-Brazilian Review*, 1, 2 (1964): 21–28.

——. "Referential Ambiguity in the Calculus of Brazilian Racial Identity," in Norman E. Whitten, Jr. and John F. Szwed, eds., *Afro-American Anthropology: Contemporary Perspectives*. New York, 1970.

Harris, Marvin, and Conrad Kottak. "The Structural Significance of Brazilian Racial Categories," *Sociologia*, 25 (1963): 203–9.

Hoetink, H. *Caribbean Race Relations: A Study of Two Variants*. London, 1967.

Humboldt, Alexander de. *Political Essay on the Kingdom of New Spain*. Translated by John Black. 4 vols. London, 1822.

Instrucciones que los vireyes de Nueva España dejaron a sus sucesores. Mexico City, 1867.

Iturribarría, Jorge Fernando. "Alonso García Bravo, trazador y alarife de la villa de Antequera," *Historia Mexicana*, 7 (1957): 80–91.

Junta Colombina de México, pubs. *Vocabulario castellano-zapoteco*. Mexico City, 1893.

Konetzke, Richard, ed. *Colección de documentos para la historia de la formación social de Hispanoamérica, 1493–1810*. 3 vols. Madrid, 1953–62.

——. "Documentos para la historia y critica de los registros parroquiales en las Indias," *Revista de Indias*, 25 (1946): 581–86.

Kubler, George. *Mexican Architecture of the Sixteenth Century*. 2 vols. New Haven, Conn., 1948.

Lee, Raymond L. "Cochineal Production and Trade in New Spain to 1600," *The Americas*, 4, 4 (1948): 449–73.

Legislación del trabajo en los siglos XVI, XVII y XVIII: relación entre la economía, las artes y los oficios en la Nueva España. Mexico City, 1936.

Lemoine V., Ernesto. "Algunos datos histórico-geográficos acerca de Villa Alta y su comarca," *Summa anthropológica en homenaje a Roberto J. Weitlaner.* Instituto Nacional de Antropología e Historia. Mexico City, 1966.

Lenski, Gerhard. *Power and Privilege: A Theory of Social Stratification.* New York, 1966.

Lockhart, James. "The Social History of Colonial Spanish America: Evolution and Potential," *Latin American Research Review*, 7, 1 (1972): 6–45.

Martínez Gracida, Manuel. *El rey Cosijoeza y su familia.* Oaxaca, 1972.

———. "La Conquista de Oaxaca," in Ernesto de la Torre, ed., *Lecturas Históricas Mexicanas*, vol. 2. Mexico City, 1966.

McAlister, Lyle N. *The Fuero Militar in New Spain, 1764–1800.* Gainesville, Fla., 1957.

———. "Social Structure and Social Change in New Spain," *Hispanic American Historical Review*, 43, 3 (1963): 349–70.

Miranda, José. *El tributo indígena en la Nueva España durante el siglo XVI.* Mexico City, 1952.

———. *La Función económica del encomendero en los orígenes del régimen colonial (Nueva España, 1525–1531).* Instituto de Investigaciones Históricas. Universidad Nacional Autónoma de México. Serie Histórica 12. Mexico City, 1965.

Molina, Fray Alonso de. *Vocabulario en lengua castellana y mexicana.* Colección de Incunables Americanos Siglo XVI, vol. 4. Madrid, 1944.

Moore, John Preston. *The Cabildo in Peru under the Hapsburgs.* Durham, N.C., 1954.

Mörner, Magnus. "La infiltración mestiza en los cacicazgos y cabildos de indios (siglos XVI–XVIII)," *Actas y Memorias, 36th Congreso Internacional de Americanistas*, vol. 2. Seville, 1966.

———. *Race Mixture in the History of Latin America.* Boston, 1967.

Morse, Richard M. "Latin American Cities: Aspects of Structure and Function," *Comparative Studies in Society and History*, 4, 4 (1962): 473–93.

———. "Some Characteristics of Latin American Urban History," *American Historical Review*, 67, 2 (1962): 317–38.

Mota y Escobar, Alonso de. "Guadalajara a principios del siglo XVII," in José Cornejo Franco, ed., *Testimonio de Guadalajara.* Mexico City, 1941.

Murguía y Galardi, José María. "Extracto general que abraza la estadística toda en su primera y segunda parte del estado de Guaxaca y ha reunido de orden del Supremo Gobierno y yntendente de provincia en clase de los cesantes José María Murguía y Galardi." 1827. Unpublished manuscript, University of Texas Manuscript Collection.

Muriel, Josefina. "Notas para la historia de la educación de la mujer durante el virreynato: Colegio de Niñas de Oaxaca, Oaxaca," *Estudios de historia novohispana*, vol. 2. Instituto de Investigaciones Históricas, Universidad Nacional Autónoma de México. Mexico City, 1967.

Nicholson, H. B. "The Use of the Term 'Mixtec' in Mesoamerican Archeology," *American Antiquity*, 26, 3 (1961): 431–33.

Nogueira, Oracy. "Skin Color and Social Class." Pan-American Union. Social Science Monographs 7. Washington, D.C., 1959.

Noveno censo general de población, 28 de enero de 1970. Mexico City, 1971.

Paddock, John. "Mixtec Ethnohistory and Monte Albán V.," in J. Paddock, ed., *Ancient Oaxaca*. Stanford, Calif., 1966.

———. "Oaxaca in Ancient Mesoamerica," in J. Paddock, ed., *Ancient Oaxaca*. Stanford, Calif., 1966.

Palerm, Angel, and E. R. Wolf. "Ecological Potential and Cultural Development in Mesoamerica." Pan-American Union. Social Science Monographs 3. Washington, D.C., 1957.

Paso y Troncoso, Francisco del, ed. *Epistolario de Nueva España, 1505–1818.* 16 vols. Mexico City, 1939–42.

———. *Papeles de Nueva España.* 9 vols. Madrid, 1905–48.

Pierson, Donald. *Negroes in Brazil: A Study of Race Contact at Bahia.* Chicago, 1942.

Pitt-Rivers, Julian. "Mestizo or Ladino?," *Race*, 10, 4 (1969): 463–77.

———. "Race, Color, and Class in Central America and the Andes," *Daedalus*, 96, 2 (1967): 542–59.

———. "Sobre la palabra casta," *América Indígena*, 36, 3 (1976): 559–86.

Portillo, Andrés. *Oaxaca en el centenario de la independencia nacional.* Oaxaca, 1910.

Puga, Vasco de. *Provisiones, cédulas, instrucciones para el gobierno de la Nueva España.* Colección de Incunables Americanos, vol. 3. Madrid, 1945.

Recopilación de leyes de los reynos de las Indias. Edición facsimilar de la cuarta impresión hecha el año 1791. 3 vols. Madrid, 1943.

Ricard, Robert. "La plaza mayor en España y en América Española," *Estudios Geográficos*, 11, 39 (1950): 321–27.

———. *The Spiritual Conquest of Mexico.* Translated by Lesley Byrd Simpson. Berkeley, Calif., 1966.

Rojas, Basilio. *La rebelión de Tehuantepec*. Mexico City, 1964.

Roncal, Joaquín. "The Negro Race in Mexico," *Hispanic American Historical Review*, 24, 3 (1944): 530–40.

Schmieder, Oscar. *The Settlements of the Tzapotec and Mije Indians*. University of California Publications in Geography, vol. 4. Berkeley, 1930.

Seler, Eduard. "Wall Paintings of Mitla," Bureau of American Ethnology *Bulletin* 28. Washington, D.C., 1904.

Sjoberg, Gideon. "Folk and 'Feudal' Societies," *American Journal of Sociology*, 58 (1952): 231–39.

———. *The Preindustrial City: Past and Present*. New York, 1960.

Smith, Robert C. "Colonial Towns of Spanish and Portuguese America," *Journal of the Society of Architectural Historians*, 14, 4 (1955): 3–12.

Solaún, Mauricio, and Sidney Kronus. *Discrimination Without Violence: Miscegenation and Racial Conflict in Latin America*. New York, 1973.

Southall, Aidan. "The Density of Role-Relationships as a Universal Index of Urbanization," in A. Southall, ed., *Urban Anthropology: Cross-Cultural Studies of Urbanization*. New York, 1973.

Spores, Ronald. "Marital Alliance in the Political Integration of Mixtec Kingdoms," *American Anthropologist*, 76 (1974): 297–311.

———. *The Mixtec Kings and Their People*. Norman, Okla., 1967.

———. "Review of *El Tesoro de Monte Albán*, by Alfonso Caso," *American Journal of Archaeology*, 75 (1971): 239–41.

———. "The Zapotec and Mixtec at Spanish Contact," in R. Wauchope, ed., *Handbook of Middle American Indians*, vol. 3. Austin, Tex., 1965.

Tannenbaum, Frank. *Slave and Citizen: The Negro in the Americas*. New York, 1947.

Taylor, William B. "Landed Society in New Spain: A View from the South," *Hispanic American Historical Review*, 54 (1974): 387–413.

———. *Landlord and Peasant in Colonial Oaxaca*. Stanford, Calif., 1972.

Thompson, Richard A. *The Winds of Tomorrow: Social Change in a Maya Town*. Chicago, 1974.

Vázquez de Espinosa, Antonio. *Descripción de la Nueva España en el siglo XVII*. Mexico City, 1944.

Villaseñor y Sánchez, José Antonio de. *Theatro americano, descripción general de los reynos, y provincias de la Nueva España y sus jurisdicciones*. 2 vols. Mexico City, 1746–48.

Wagley, Charles. "On the Concept of Social Race in the Americas," in Dwight B. Heath and Richard N. Adams, eds., *Contemporary Cultures and Societies of Latin America*. New York, 1965.

———, ed. *Race and Class in Rural Brazil*. United Nations Educational, Social and Cultural Organization. Paris, 1952.

Wallerstein, Immanuel. *The Modern World-System: Capitalist Agriculture and the Origins of the European World Economy in the Sixteenth Century*. New York, 1974.

Weber, Max. "Class, Status, Party," in H. H. Gerth and C. W. Mills, eds., *From Max Weber: Essays in Sociology*. New York, 1958.

Whitecotton, Joseph W. *The Zapotecs: Princes, Priests, and Peasants*. Norman, Okla., 1977.

Whitten, Norman E., Jr. *Black Frontiersmen: A South American Case*. Cambridge, Mass., 1974.

———. *Class, Kinship, and Power in an Ecuadorian Town: The Negroes of San Lorenzo*. Stanford, Calif., 1965.

Wolf, Eric. *Sons of the Shaking Earth*. Chicago, 1959.

Zavala, Silvio. *Los esclavos indios en Nueva España*. Mexico City, 1968.

Zavala, Silvio, and Maria Castelo, eds. *Fuentes para la historia del trabajo en Nueva España*. 8 vols. Mexico City, 1939–46.

Index

Index